# Intrapsychic and Interpersonal Dimensions of Treatment

# Intrapsychic and Interpersonal Dimensions of Treatment

*A Clinical Dialogue*

Robert Langs, M.D.
and
Harold F. Searles, M.D.

NEW YORK • JASON ARONSON • LONDON

ISBN: 0-87668-404-5

Library of Congress Catalog Number: 80-7480

Manufactured in the United States of America

To my dear friends,
Joyce and Jason
              RL

To my grandchildren,
Ian and Noet
                        HFS

# CLASSICAL PSYCHOANALYSIS AND ITS APPLICATIONS

A Series of Books
Edited by Robert Langs, M.D.

# CONTENTS

# PREFACE
## by Robert Langs

I have long admired and respected Harold Searles as one of the most gifted and innovative clinicians in the history of psychoanalysis. I therefore anticipated each of the four clinical dialogues with him as a special opportunity for myself personally, as well as for a wide readership, to discover new vistas and to find stimulation and insight in interacting with him close at hand. These expectations were fulfilled for me far beyond anything I could have imagined.

For some time now I have experienced the paucity of stimuli to true creativity that today exists in the field of psychoanalysis and psychoanalytic psychotherapy. The dialogue series of which the present volume is a part was undertaken in the hope that it would provide a format through which direct contact with a number of major writers on psychoanalytic and psychotherapeutic technique could help broaden our thinking. It is to the enduring credit of Harold Searles that he responded in a manner that generated a highly personal and professionally pertinent interchange, suffused not only with his well-known clinical sensitivity but also with a deep sense of himself as a person and as a psychoanalyst. Always adventurous, Searles has a warm, frank, and articulate manner that makes these dialogues a deeply moving experience extending far beyond the intellectual and clinical interest inherent in the issues we discussed.

The dialogue develops as the story of a psychoanalyst, his personal and professional development, the struggles, the hurts, the rewards. It soon became an experience which swept me up and evoked a powerful reexperiencing of my own professional career, my analysis, and my clinical work and writings to a point where new feelings and memories, and new understanding, became inevitable. I very much anticipate a similar response, highly personal and yet broadly meaningful, in all of those who join us in this adventure. In revealing and extending himself, Searles has contributed uniquely to our understanding of both our patients and ourselves.

Participation in an open and candid dialogue of this kind entails many risks. As a participant I experienced great concern regarding my criticisms of the field at large, knowing full well that generalizations are always dangerous and that comments which cannot be documented in specific detail are open to immediate dispute. And yet it is my sincere belief that all too few analysts have questioned and challenged present-day thinking or spoken out in regard to many evident prejudices in the field. I therefore ask the reader to bear with the comments made in the course of these exchanges, to experience fully their sincerity and the important motives which prompt them, and to recognize the necessity to disturb our bias and inappropriate sense of complacency in a way that can occasion a reexamination of our clinical theory and practice. As the reader may know, both Searles and I have carefully and extensively documented the clinical ideas to which we refer in these dialogues. Both of us have written as well of the positive and negative responses to our creative thrusts. I can only add that my experience subsequent to these dialogues has all too sadly borne out the unpleasant and disturbing impression that I offer here regarding the intensely irrational and hostile responses with which psychoanalytic creativity is met in some quarters, especially when it encroaches upon currently accepted therapeutic attitudes and techniques. There is too little truly serious consideration of new ideas, too little willingness to debate them at the level of clinical findings, a situation that must someday yield to more rational scrutiny.

Searles and I met to exchange ideas, to examine our clinical efforts, and to speak on topics of importance to ourselves and other clinicians. We have spoken freely, though within limits, and always in the hope of stimulating thought and growth. And if the reader does indeed have such a response to these transactions, that will more than justify the anxiety and effort involved.

# Chapter 1
# THE DEVELOPMENT OF A PSYCHOANALYST

*Langs:* Perhaps I can begin by telling you something of how I came to call you and how I got to be here. As you know, I did *The Therapeutic Interaction* (Langs, 1976b), and attempted to survey the literature on the analytic relationship as comprehensively as possible. And when I finished—it's actually a story—I had been at a dinner party where I brought up some of the work of Leo Stone, and one of the analysts there felt that I was not representing his position accurately, and he got very upset about it. He angrily said to me, "Why don't you go and talk to him; you'll see, this isn't where he stands." Anyhow, I was rather annoyed at this particular person, but then I realized that his suggestion was a good one. This is something you're familiar with: the curative or creative core to an angry response. And I contacted Stone, and I did meet with him and we recorded a series of dialogues which are now being edited for publication (Langs and Stone, 1980).

*Searles:* The person who had been angered was a third person, is that right, who thought you hadn't been getting the essence of Stone's views?

*Langs:* Right, it was a student of his. And then it struck me that this was really a superb vehicle for communication, for clarification.

The Stone meetings went very, very well and we got into a lot of issues. In looking over the literature, as you must know, there are very few analysts who have written more than a paper or two on anything related to technique and the analytic interaction. To me it's the heart of the matter and analysts really seem to have what Margaret Little (1951) called a phobic attitude toward knowing themselves and their countertransferences.

I met also with Phyllis Greenacre, and I went to London and met with several representative analysts: Hanna Segal, John Klauber, Marion Milner, and Margaret Little. I missed Sandler, but I then did a dialogue with him by telephone. And now yourself.

That's sort of the background. The goal now is just to let our interaction unfold. I would like to discuss some of your contributions to this literature. I'm in a different position in meeting you from when I met with Stone, in that I had a number of issues that I wanted to take up and debate with him. As far as my meeting with you is concerned, I consider you to have been really by far the most sensitive analyst to many aspects of the analytic interaction that have been neglected by let's say, the mainstream of classical analysts. I therefore share much of your thinking. In fact, as I told you some time ago, I even specifically avoided reading some of your papers so that it wouldn't contaminate my own observations and conclusions—so they could be made independently and be validated in a way by your work.

*Searles:* I do an awful lot of such avoidance myself.

*Langs:* But I did get around to it afterwards, to see the extent to which our observations supplement and complement each other, and where we may disagree. I found it absolutely remarkable that, going back into the 1950s, you'd written some very, very important papers that I found, in reviewing the literature, simply have not been given the attention that they deserve, for whatever reason. So, basically, there are many areas that I want to discuss with you, to clarify, to get your present thinking. There are also some areas where I have some very specific questions.

Initially, I'd like to start with some sort of historical perspective on your own development. That's become more and more an interesting part of these interviews and it will come up as we go along; I'm hoping too that this will give you a chance to get your own work into fresh perspective. I know that you're now doing another volume of your collected papers, so I would expect that you've been thinking a lot about your work. I think the preface to your first book of papers (Searles, 1965) is a superb synthesis of your work, a marvelous overview. But I don't know much about your background—how you got into medicine and into psychiatry, things of that sort. Can we begin there?

*Searles:* I'll try to be brief. I've given a lot of fairly schmaltzy accounts of my background in speaking to audiences; I'm used to doing that. I'll try to keep it brief.

I'm the younger of two children. I have a sister who is living; she is four years older than I. She and I learned only about ten years or so ago—I'm already confused about dates—on the death of one of my parents, really not many years back, that there had been a stillborn baby, I think maybe sometime between my sister's birth and mine. That is one measure of the secrets there were in my family life in growing up. It was something that must have had an enormous impact on my mother's care of me, and I had never heard of it until I had long been an adult.

My father was born and lived out his life on the same site in a little village in the Catskills in New York State, a village of 1500 people. I mention that simply because it seems unusual in itself. His father had come over from England at the age of twelve and became an apprentice, at that age, to a tailor in a nearby village in upper Pennsylvania. My father has told me that his father, as an apprentice, received room and board and twenty-five cents a year which he received each Fourth of July. And my father added that, on one Fourth of July, his father had lost his quarter, and all the indications were that he had had to wait until the next Fourth of July to get another quarter. Anyhow, when my father's father grew up he started a men's clothing business in this small town, Hancock, New York, and my father inherited it. Because of an illness on his father's part, my father had to leave high school in the first year to work full-time in the family business, which he continued to do. He married a woman from an even tinier—very tiny—hamlet across the Delaware River in northern Pennsylvania. My mother was one of a larger family. My father had had only a sister about fifteen years older than he, who had served, I think, as a mother to him. My father, in other words, had much of the only child about him—and I sense I'm not interesting you and I hope that I will start to. This morning I got to remembering countless hours I spent sitting in my father's clothing store as a boy with him.

*Langs:* Let me just respond a bit: my thought is that it is a most unusual background for an analyst.

*Searles:* For a psychoanalyst, I think so, yes. My father's paternal grandfather in England was a blacksmith in Cornwall—I don't know where in Cornwall—and my mother had grown up in this very tiny place in northern Pennsylvania, about fifteen miles from Hancock. She was a middle one of maybe six children, I think it was. Her father ran a small store and had a small farm on the side. I was always impressed as a child that my mother knew how to milk a cow. I never saw her do so; but this was a skill she had.

Now my father was a male chauvinist pig to the *n*th degree, absolute *n*th degree. There was much of this Archie Bunker about him. He was a loquacious man, a very warmhearted man, and a raconteur type of person.

I used to spend countless hours sitting in my father's store with him during the financial depression. There was no business. I would look up and down the main street of this village—not a person on the street. There wasn't a chance of a customer coming in.

Twenty-five feet in back of the building, maybe even closer, ran the Erie Railroad which in those days was a major one between New York and Chicago. So it was a tiny village and yet in a sense it had contact with the larger world, the railroad was one thing and the main street of the town which was part of Route 17, which was the major highway artery between New York and the West.

But I would sit in the store with my Dad and listen to him talk and sit almost literally open mouthed in awe. I idealized his mind, as well as other attributes of his, and enjoyed listening to his narratives. One thing he had was an inexhaustible fund of dirty jokes, to which he started subjecting me much too early, really, so that I was very uncomfortable with such things, and his fund of jokes seemed to me as vast as Groucho Marx used to have.

About the male chauvinist pig aspect of him: he was a romanticist. He was working in the store with his father—I don't know at what age, I would think about twenty or so—and he saw my mother walking down the other side of the street and he said to his father, "There is the girl I'm going to marry." I assume there was a lot of split-off homosexual transference to his old man attached to my mother. In any case, he did marry her but it was in no means precipitous; they had an engagement of five years. When my sister came along, she was supposed (I assume) to have been a boy, and was very much a tomboy in her earlier girlhood. I used to sit by, or stand by, while my father and sister ran foot races in which I couldn't participate, just being too small. She was a very athletic, active girl.

My father gave every sign of feeling that he had married beneath him and this was made very explicit. We used to go on Sunday drives, and on occasion he would take the family down to this town called Equinunk, and he would never fail to explain that this name came from the Latin, meaning horse's ass. He said that "Equi" is from "equus," meaning horse and that "nunk," in Latin, means ass. This is a sample of his coarseness. My mother would be in the car, being subjected to this—to such horseshit. Well, I'm going to get bogged down in that.

Now I was always supposed to be a doctor, from my earliest memory. My father put it in a very unsentimental way; he said, "Bud, you go to Johns Hopkins and then you go to Vienna for a while and then you'll have the world by the balls." I thought, as long afterward as when I had started working at Chestnut Lodge, several years out of Harvard Medical School, residency, and all that: "How come I don't have the world by the balls?" This stuff went so deep. My old man's impact on me was absolutely appalling, absolutely indelible, terrible.

But I was always supposed to be a doctor. It wasn't always a materialistic thing. Doctors had a very important part in my father's life. He was basically a physically well man in my early boyhood. Up until about when I was in the fifth grade in school he was a very well man, he was a man in good spirits. He used to go to the hardware store next door where his second cousin owned the store and they used to sell phonograph records and he would come back singing the latest hit and he liked to dance. A very cheerful man, he played a lot of tennis and had close friends, always did, always had close friends

with whom he played tennis or bridge and he played pool on
Saturday night. Drank very moderately, smoked an awful lot but
never any drinking problems.

But then when I was in about the fourth or fifth grade, word came
to the school that my father had to be taken to the hospital; he had an
appendectomy. That marked the first of a series of endless illnesses,
mostly psychosomatic, and he developed asthma somewhere along
in there and had severe bronchial asthma recurrently for the rest of
his life. A very common sight was to see him sitting in the kitchen
smoking this stramonium and lobelia, with a black, dark green, acrid
smoke billowing out and leaning down over it and inhaling it and he
would have to go and vomit it eventually and then his asthma would
subside.

That was very commonplace, and my father was a very—having
been a cheerful man in those earlier years—a very tormented side of
his nature emerged. It seemed to me that all through my growing up
he awoke at least once, and often twice each night bellowing with a
mixture of terror and rage, from a nightmare. It was very frightening,
of course, but part of our lives.

I was saying about doctors playing such an important role in his
life: he went to physicians for his asthma, for severe headaches, for
eczema, for neuralgic pain in his arm, for severe back pain—many,
many different doctors. He had a mastoidectomy a few years after the
appendectomy, and he had a very idolizing kind of relationship to
the little ear, nose, and throat specialist who had operated upon him.
I was just thinking, that doctor made a woman of him: he gave him
this hole behind his ear. But in any case he wasn't only cynical about
doctors, as people who made a lot of money: he genuinely admired
them and, in fact, idealized some of them.

A lot of them, he did not. He was an enormously mistrustful man.
He had a definite paranoid character. My father was prejudiced
against everyone. I grew up in an endemically anti-Semitic area.
Hancock is about twenty miles beyond the borsht belt. There are
none of the hotels around Hancock that one finds a little closer to
New York, but each summer there would be a very large influx of
young people coming there to attend camps, boys' and girls' camps
in the area. There were dozens of them within fifteen miles of my
home town. Beautiful, beautiful country up there. It played a big role
in my childhood.

*Langs:* I know the area a bit.

*Searles:* That's pretty country isn't it? The hills and lakes?

*Langs:* Just gorgeous.

*Searles:* He had more than the endemic prejudice against Jewish people; he had more than that. His paranoid character intensified that; but he was prejudiced as well against people of whatever ethnic background—Irish, Polish, German, or whatever. Ironically, not even England, from which his own ancestors had come, was spared; I often heard him vituperate about the English as not to be trusted.

There was a colony of Italian people in a kind of suburb of our village, people whose parents worked in a wood-acid factory there in earlier years, and people who attended my school and all—very competent, intelligent people; but I grew up with the idea that they were Italians, that they were beneath us.—You see it is hard for me to give you a coherent, brief account.

My mother—I've talked about her semi-farm background and her acceptance of this derogated role; and said that I learned much later of the birth of a stillborn baby somewhere, probably between my sister and myself. My mother was a schizoid-character kind of person. She was a handsome woman. But I remember a real change in her. I remember when I was maybe ten, maybe more like eight, my memory was that my father was cutting her hair. Now, that's not a true memory; but I knew that he was urging her to get a kind of hairdo that was then stylish but looked masculine to me. The back of the hair had a masculine look and she formerly had feminine, long hair.

She acquiesced in that, and that time marked a very fundamental change in her personality, so that she became a broad-shouldered, masculine-looking kind of woman. Within a few years she came home, I remember, with a new hat that she had gotten, and of course hoping that we would like it, and I told her bluntly (she had a tremendous bluntness about her for all of these other qualities that I spoke of, for all of her putting up with the abuse; I developed a bluntness too, like her) and I told her flatly that she looked like Benito Mussolini, which she did with that kind of helmetlike hat. In other words, she had come to show a very masculine kind of side of her nature, and I learned in my analysis that my latent homosexual kind of personality components, such as they are, relate very much to her phallic nature and the many enemas that she subjected me to as a small child. There was an enormous amount of those things.

Now I was always supposed to be a doctor, not only because it was profitable but because doctors were to be greatly admired. I had in many ways a very happy childhood and youth in spite of many, many unhappy aspects. My father's illnesses made for unhappiness. His paranoid nature made for ugliness and unpleasantness and we feared him. He was a man to be frightened of. He had this latent violence in him. He got up one night in his sleep and got his gun from a cupboard where he kept it and went to the door, he thought he heard someone at the door. I never saw the damn gun but I saw his violent nature more than once.

The unhappy sides were the depression, which was a very big factor in my childhood. My family was well-off until the crash which occurred when I was eleven years old—in 1929, you know. We had not been at the top rank of people in our town; the top rank were the really one or two physicians and maybe a banker or two. But we were very close to the top rank in this small town. My parents would go to New York to plays, they never would take my sister and me. But they would go on nice vacations and we went on some of them, too, and we always ate very, very well and I dressed well as my father ran this clothing store and he would use me to put new clothes on when a shipment of them would arrive, and I enjoyed it. I have a very exhibitionistic nature, as is probably obvious to you, and this was fostered in part by him.

My mother had friends; she was not a totally retiring person, except in relation to him. She had women friends with whom she loved to talk and she had her own bridge foursome. She was a better player than my father. They both loved bridge. My mother liked to walk about town, go uptown to the post office and shop and stuff.

Both my parents expected a great deal of me, great deal of me. My mother (it wasn't only that my father decreed that I would become a physician and I did not object at all) actively coached me in spelling and I won the county spelling championship and went with her to the state fair and lost out on the first round—I think it was that I couldn't spell "oppression," which I am sure was a very charged word for me. And I played tennis, my Dad played tennis, as I said; I played football and I was on the football team in high school. I loved to dance, I had a steady girl—a very nice girl—and I was president of my class first year and fourth year and had the lead in the senior play. I was salutatorian all through school. I wasn't the first; the first was a girl, and my mother's competitiveness with me would show. The girl's name was Adrienne, and I would tell my mother I had gotten "96" or something like that and she would say, "What did Adriene get?" And I would say, "98." It was obvious that she was identifying with Adrienne.

By the time the depression came along—it occurred when I was eleven—family money became zilch and we were staving off, really, trying to avoid bankruptcy (which my father did avoid).

They were very, very hard times. I worked in the summers, I worked on the highway some, there wasn't much work around.

When time came for college I went to Cornell. I didn't have any difficulty being admitted there. In those years it wasn't so difficult anyway, of course. My grades had been good. My grades were not unheard of by any means in the town. There were brighter kids than I in the town, but my grades were quite adequate. The money was the big worry, how to get money, and I went to Cornell and lived in a rooming house rather than a dormitory—I think the rooming house was cheaper. I stayed in the same room for four years and started various kinds of work concomitantly with starting college, washing dishes, worked on an N.Y.A. job they used to have that, I think, paid twenty-five cents an hour; worked dusting in the library, the main library. That's how I spent my Saturday evenings—dusting in the goddammed University library. I really got into a monastic life there.

It was a very rude change for me because I was not an introverted study bug. I was a guy who loved to dance. I used to date, not just one steady girl but I had an active dating life and had friends in my home town and my father had set before me, and I had accepted, a course of study—you know—eight, ten, twelve years, and I broke up with my steady girl who was a couple of years older than I and who I knew wanted to be married. I couldn't ask her to wait eight to ten years. I broke up with her because, too, I felt hurt at her lack of interest in my schooling. How could she be interested? She couldn't share it, but that was a painful damned thing.

So I settled into a kind of monklike existence and I found Cornell very inspiring though, very inspiring. There were a lot of very good people there, of course—good student body, young people who were really ambitious and going places, and the beauty of that area different from my own home town area. It was really an exhilarating thing to me.

I got a lot out of Cornell but I was very, very hard driven, tense, studying all I could, not doing well, I remember getting four "D's" in the midterm exams—four "D's"; I had never known such grades. I kept slugging; being able to cope with failure was a very important maturing experience to me. I got into Phi Beta Kappa.

I learned in my fourth year that if my faculty adviser had been at all capable and attentive, he could have had me living in a free honorary fraternity where I would not have had to do all of the outside work to earn my support. But my faculty adviser was a very eminent physicist—I think he later became a Nobel prize winner—who was not interested in giving advice to the undergraduates.

Now in the summertime, at home between my second and third years, I narrowly avoided a schizophrenic break and things happened that I won't go into but it clearly had those aspects. I was never hospitalized. I never lost any time from work. I never stayed in bed. But it was a very close thing. When I returned to Cornell that fall I cut down my outside jobs because of this from three to two. That's an example of the pressures I was under. Shall I go on with this or not?

*Langs:* Yes, go on, that's fine.

*Searles:* I'm getting there. Now I used to think, before I went to college, about what I wanted to do. I was to be a physician; that much was ordained and I didn't rebel against it. But I did think some of what I wanted to do, and I had a feeling that I wanted to help people, and I wondered: Did I want to be a minister?

The church had played an appreciable role in my life, although not a dominant one. My father was basically an atheist, which was one of his unusual qualities, for a small town. I don't think he had been baptized. I remember now, he had never been baptized; that's unusual. My mother was a Methodist Episcopal and she behaved in our family much like a missionary among savages. This was one of the ways where she put us all down, that she was really quite a religious woman and regarded us all as unredeemable rabble. But I used to go to Sunday school each Sunday morning and sometimes, although not always, stayed for the adult church service. I became an usher in the church; that's as deeply involved in it as I got.

I was an usher for a few years and I wondered in the teenage years what I wanted to do with my life. Did I want to become a minister? No, I did not. I never seriously considered becoming a minister. That was as close as my culture gave me for a model of a psychiatrist; that was as close as I got to knowing a psychiatrist. There were no psychiatrists in our town. There were no psychologists, no social workers. It was a limited culture. But I knew I didn't want to be a minister. I didn't know what the hell—

So I went to Cornell and I was concerned all through about money and I applied to, I think, three medical schools in my third year and was turned down by all of them. It was unusual to be accepted after three years and I went on to the fourth year.

And this near-psychotic break thing, the one thing which that had left me was that I used to carry around in my breast pocket some kind of phenobarbital in case I needed it. I don't think I ever took it, but it was an important security thing and I never had any psychotherapy at Cornell. The idea, I think, of going to a psychiatrist at Cornell never entered my mind until now—never entered my head until this very interview. They probably had psychiatrists there, or psychologists, but the idea of—

You see, my family didn't think of any difficulties, including mine, as being psychological. You cannot exaggerate the extent to which we thought concretely and physically.

This thing that I refer to as a near-psychotic episode consisted of strange symptoms that occurred following my walking on the railroad with a friend of mine, a male friend of mine, who was also my sister's steady boyfriend and there was of course obvious intense oedipal stuff going, both positive and negative. And I walked on a rail for a mile without falling off, something I'd never done, and it was in the hot sun and my family, including me, thought that it must have been the sun that did it, and the walk on the rail. We didn't know anything about complicated sexual feelings or murderous feelings such as I'm sure played a role in that episode.

So I went back into my third year and on through carrying this stuff in my pocket, never using it and working and studying, getting good grades as usual. I got through the fourth year, applied and got into three good medical schools. I got into Harvard, Columbia, and Rochester. I picked Harvard because of the prestige; but Columbia, I felt, had a lot of prestige, too—all of them, really. Harvard offered the most help in their catalogue to financially needy students; so I went there.

*Langs:* Let me ask one question. Are you implying then that there was no exposure to anything particularly psychological or analytic at Cornell?

*Searles:* No. At Cornell I had a course in anthropology that I greatly enjoyed, a very good course. In order to get money—this may seem amusing to you—but I equipped myself as a secondary school teacher at Cornell. That is, I took the course that qualified me to be a high school teacher in case I needed to do something to finance medical school. Now, the thought might be amusing because high school teachers have such low pay; but, again, these were still depression times for my family—financial depression times. The high school teacher training curriculum involved courses in psychology at Cornell, all of which, most unfortunately—nearly all of which—were sense organ-physiology type of psychology, not really psychological. I did have one course in psychological testing which was a bit more—well, it was a course in intelligence testing; it wasn't Rorschach. So I didn't get much of the psychology at Cornell.

I went to Harvard in 1940 and it was like entering a new world for me culturally in terms of the Boston Irish accents. It was part of our country but it was real strange to me. I had a very adventurous quality still, something that has been greatly dampened in recent years, but I used to have a lot of forward-lookingness and a lot of adventurousness and I started off and got—I can't remember now where I roomed. Always, money was a concern. I scrambled around and got a lot of help from the medical school employment office—I wasn't the only one in that spot—and got work.

I can't remember now just where the first work was; but I used to go about taking part—I can well realize you yourself may also have done so—taking part as a subject in certain experiments to make money, and I bear a scar on my belly—a very large, unsightly scar—for which I made, I think, fifteen dollars. They put some frozen mustard gas on my belly—this was during the war, you see—and then later some surgical resident at Peter Brigham Hospital who should have known better, when he cut it off he went right across the skin lines and I still have a large scar. Anyone would think it were an appendectomy scar.

I took sodium nitrite one time in an experiment. They strapped me to a table that could be elevated and the thing was that if you did not faint you would receive, I think, five dollars and if you fainted I think you would get fifteen—and I fainted when they brought the table vertical and I got the fifteen dollars. And I gave about, I think, a total of sixteen blood transfusions in my four years. That was incidental, supportive money.

The main work I did, to help support my education, was as a laboratory assistant at the New England Deaconess Hospital, which was one of the hospitals in the Harvard complex of hospitals that specialized in the treatment of diabetic patients. There was the Joslyn Clinic; the New England Deaconess was that clinic's main hospital. They were world famous for treating diabetes. I used to do $CO_2$ exams and blood sugars. I did that one year—I think my first year, maybe my second year—at Harvard, and then I spent a couple of years as a student intern at the same place, very interesting work, very interesting. I lived then in a family residence type of house with about ten such interns, a very, very good place. I had some companionship there.

The last year, the army took over at Harvard and I was one of the three quarters of the student body who went into the army and the other—the elite—went into the navy. The navy were treated like gentlemen and the army guys were treated like dirt.

It has always been a source of shame—as the word comes to mind—to me that I did not get good enough grades at Harvard to qualify for a Boston internship. I did well; but I did not do well enough, and I'll give you a little glimpse at some of the things. Sitting next to me at one laboratory table was the guy next in the alphabet who was the son of a physician, and he said: "You know, Hal, you're not really a bad guy but you're such a meatball" [i.e., greasy-grind]. And I thought, what did this guy know about my life?

Anyhow, I did well enough to get an internship at Cornell which I was very proud of—a straight medical internship, because at this point I was planning on being an internist.

Now I should fill in that while I was at Harvard I started becoming interested in psychiatry and I took an elective in it. Psychiatry at Harvard was very little thought of. Psychiatry was a derogated field. Psychiatry was sneered at at Harvard. Only the occasional oddball became interested in psychiatry. That's not overstating it. But I was enough interested, even in that unfavorable climate, that I took an elective—I think in my third, maybe my fourth year—in psychiatry. I think it was only a one-month elective; whatever it was, I took it. Shortly before this the classic study of the survivors of the Cocoanut Grove—Boston night club—fire had been published, and the man who had done that study, Eric Lindemann—maybe I'm stepping off base to mention—?

*Langs:* Yes, go ahead.

*Searles:* Eric Lindemann was a very effeminate looking man, and I had been trained as a boy to abhor anything that could be thought of as effeminacy; this abhorrence was one of my father's innumerable eccentricities. But Eric Lindemann I admired—and I again want to cry. I am not losing my damned mind if I cry a little.

*Langs:* You're darn right.

*Searles:* But I admired Lindemann very much, he was a psychoanalyst—he was the first psychoanalyst I ever saw. I never met the man. I was a lowly—taking an elective—medical student and he was the visiting psychoanalyst who would do rounds at Mass General [Massachusetts General Hospital]. I admired him a lot and I treated three depressed patients in my month of elective psychotherapy, you see, and my roommate in this student-internship thing at the Deaconess Hospital commented later that he had never seen me smile the whole month. It was really something, how I identified with those people.

But my interest in psychiatry wasn't enough to turn me away from internal medicine. Now, I had settled on internal medicine because surgery—my father had me slated to become a surgeon—I am quite myopic, as is evident to you. My vision is 20/200; I can see at twenty feet what a normal person can see at two hundred feet and I told you that I played high school football, and I did; I was on the varsity and I played end most of the time and I was the only end who was never thrown a pass. I couldn't see that well.

Another incidental thing. At my father's funeral in 1952 I went back to the home town; he had died suddenly of a heart attack after having had angina for some years. At the funeral my father's body was lying there and this funeral director at the funeral home run by a former high school classmate of mine—the small town atmosphere again—and one of the people who came to pay his respects, was the halfback from the football team, a guy I never liked and who never liked me, and he took me to task about why it was that in one particularly crucial game with the team that was our arch-rival from the neighboring town, I had kept letting myself be blocked out, when the opposing team had—no, when our team had the ball, I would let myself be blocked out or suckered out and they would come through and tackle him every time. And what this guy didn't know, he didn't wear glasses, he didn't know what it is for a half-blind person to be trying to play football. I couldn't see the complicated maneuvers.

Anyhow, surgery got ruled out, because I couldn't see worth a damn was one problem, and each of my three experimental dogs died—whether because of my vision or not. But surgery got clearly ruled out and I hadn't had enough exposure to psychiatry.

I am getting more into the nitty-gritty now. In our first year, I think it was, at Harvard we had a course in psychiatry at the Boston Psychopathic Hospital, now called the Massachusetts Mental Health Center, and the head of the department was C. MacFie Campbell, an elderly Scotsman who used to hold this lecture—each Saturday, I think it was—for one hundred and twenty-five people. And he would bring in a patient, interview the patient in a very formal style, and after the patient would leave he would dissertate. He was a very erudite man, and this was the style in those days; the psychiatrists, I think, went to that dissertating—and it was evident that he was a cultured man, an intellectual man, and a dour Scotsman. I again was intrigued enough with psychology in spite of the unstimulating way it was presented that I asked to speak to him after a lecture. I made an appointment, I went to him and told him that I found psychiatry of a lot of interest to me—

Do these bastards you interview weep all the time?—what is there, something about you?

*Langs:* No, but they didn't get into their lives with the intensity that you are experiencing.

*Searles:* You must bring a lot of your therapist's side into these damned things.—Well, I said to him that I found psychiatry a very interesting field but that the thing that concerned me about it was something about—I said it pretty bluntly—how much appreciation does one get from one's patients in the psychiatric field, and he drew back and up and gave me to feel that this was a totally unworthy concern for me to be having. He said tartly something about that one received quite enough and that, anyway, that should not be of any concern to a physician. That was the import of it. So that interview didn't draw me farther into the field, you can be sure.

I liked internal medicine; I liked the idea. I had done well in pharmacology, for example. It turned out, on National Boards I tied for second place in the country in pharmacology. I told you I didn't do well enough to stay in Boston, to my undying shame; but I didn't do badly in all regards and internal medicine, I felt, I had some talent for, and I went to Cornell into straight internal medicine and stayed on for nine months. My last year in medical school had been accelerated because of the war and I graduated in December of 1943 and went to Cornell in January and after the first nine months stayed for an assistant residency, also in internal medicine, which was an honor.

In the course of those eighteen months altogether I encountered, early in it, Harold G. Wolff; you may have heard of him. He is a neurologist who has done a lot of psychosomatic studies including the book called *Human Gastric Function*. He had this laboratory assistant with a gastric fistula, whom he had studied. I experienced Harold Wolff as very forbidding, and I and everyone else I knew experienced him as a very forbidding, perfectionistic man, a frightening man, just like my father, and I was every inch the conscientous intern and assistant resident and I arranged for him to see a patient at the neurological rounds; he made the neurological rounds. I spent four months on the neurology service in that eighteen months— which is a generous hunk of time, getting toward the psychiatric field some—and as the steel door swung shut, after they had gone to bring the patient in and I was alone in that room with Harold Wolff, we were both leaning back against something side by side and I think he was rather casually glancing at me and I felt the blood drain from my face and he said, "Very interesting!" And he wasn't sarcastically needling me; it was much worse than that. I was an experimental object and he was finding this interesting; this is one of the things that I remember. Anyhow, when the assistant residents were appointed, those who didn't make it had to go into the army, and the war was still on; this was life, was real and earnest, you see. So I was fortunate in more ways than one to be allowed to stay for a second nine months.

But as those nine months came toward a close I was faced with a choice. I now had only two choices open to me. I could become a battalion surgeon in the army—I was due to go into the army; there was no avoiding that. The war was on, anyway, and I naturally wouldn't have tried to avoid it—I could either be a battalion surgeon in the army, in the front line, right behind the front lines, or I could become a psychiatrist. I chose to become a psychiatrist primarily to preserve my life, but I had this previous interest anyway, so it wasn't all that bad a fate.

Then I went to the Army School of Military Psychiatry in Brentwood, New York, out near Pilgrim State Hospital, Long Island, for three or four months—I don't remember how many months. It was a very interesting time, very interesting time. I went with my wife and our first child—born actually just a few days after VJ night—and from there I went to basic training up in Carlisle, Pennsylvania, which was a horrible damned experience, horrible. I got through as well as any of them did. I'm not just a cerebral guy who had a close brush with schizophrenia at one time but I've gotten into the rough and tumble of things a lot, too, and I got through that as well as anybody. I applied at the close of basic training to the Ninth Corps Area, which was the Ninth Service Command later, namely, California, the west coast, and I was the only one of maybe one hundred and fifty. I don't know how many were in the basic training, a large number of people. I was the only one who got the Ninth Corps Area. I felt very fortunate.

When I had proposed to my wife back in 1941—she's a nurse, former Massachussetts General Hospital nurse, whom I met when she was graduate nurse working at MGH—I had a number of my courses at MGH in my last year or two and she had not had any psychiatric training. I met her in an orthopedic ward and I told her, when I proposed marriage to her, that she must be prepared to live in California because that was my plan, and I carried through with it enough to apply for that Ninth Corps Area. We went there.

This was in late 1945 or early 1946. The end of the war had occurred while I was in either basic training or the School of Military Neuropsychiatry at Brentwood, and a sudden onset of apathy into the training atmosphere occurred as soon as the war ended, whereas students had been sitting and listening very carefully to the lectures on psychiatry and all sorts of related subjects because, you know, the war was on. As soon as the atom bomb fell and the war ended, there would be several people lying sleeping in the back rows of the lecture hall; it was altogether different.

But I went, with my wife and infant son, out to California, where I was stationed at Dibble General Hospital, a very large general hospital in Menlo Park, California, south of San Francisco, right next door to Palo Alto. Very big hospital which specialized in orthopedic cases—amputees and other people who had suffered major injuries and who needed prolonged orthopedic treatment—and, secondly, specialized in eye injuries—blind patients. The psychiatric service was a minor part of that hospital; but there were a few psychiatrists there and I stayed there, it is hard for me to remember for sure, my total army service was slightly less than two years. I stayed there for maybe six months—yes, six months it was, and we lived in Palo Alto, nearby, for four months; then in South San Francisco for two months.

I enjoyed this psychiatry stuff, I enjoyed it. But it was a very far cry, still, from being a psychoanalyst—very far cry. We had a large number of people coming through there and the chief of our section, a captain, would each day interview patients with a secretary present and other staff, the rest of us, present. A very typical occurrence would be for a catatonic young man to be brought in and the captain would ask him a couple of questions and the patient would say nothing, and not move, and the captain would dictate: "The patient is mute, uncooperative and nothing can be learned from him." And the patient would be dismissed.

One of my tasks was to run a ward of general prisoners. General prisoners were the most severe kind of prisoners in the army. There were some little prisoners—I don't know what they were called—and some medium prisoners; then the worst bastards were the general prisoners and I was still a very naive guy and I was no match for these hardened psychopaths. One or two of them would sit around smoking cigars and just living the kind of life they wanted. I didn't seriously interfere with their doing so but it was a difficult task and I carried it through well and I got reassigned to Fort Belvoir, Virginia.

Fort Belvoir is a very large, is the main Corps of Engineers

headquarters in the U.S. Army. It's a big, permanent military estab-
lishment with a small station hospital. A station hospital, as you
may know, in the army is a small hospital, much smaller than this
Dibble General Hospital was; that was a very big one.

At this small station hospital, this was my first exposure to the
South and this seemed to me very much the South, even though it is
not far south. It was a sleepy area, torpid kind of atmosphere. It was
summer when I arrived there—overgrown fields, lazy, a large wood-
en fan in the ceiling, a large fan slowly turning, didn't really cool the
ward. These temporary buildings—the hospital—like something
out of Tennessee Williams, maybe, I don't know, and I worked there
as a psychiatrist for several months and then I had to do some secret
work for the government that I don't feel free to talk about, but it was
an honor to me to be selected to do it. It involved my staying in
Washington, moving up to Washington.

That was in 1947—I went in the army in July of '45—this was late
'46 or early '47 when I first lived in Washington itself and we had one
child still at this point, a boy. And we moved into a semi-slum area
which has since become a full slum area, all Black now, and when I
moved to Washington I had no anti-Negro prejudice at all. I was very
liberal in my thinking. It has been a sad thing to me to find that
prejudice seeping in, to find that in living in this area, for me it has
been completely impossible to keep that out. I don't think you can
appreciate it, because there is a feeling in this area about racial
relations that is different from that in New York. It has been a
refreshing thing to me when I get to New York to feel the way Black
people respond to you. You don't feel that they necessarily like you a
great deal but there isn't the sullen, passive-aggressive "stupid"
behavior that is really very commonplace in this area.

Anyhow, that semi-slum area was still a white one when we lived
there but we were as poor as church mice and I completed my army
service in this secret government work and I applied meanwhile for a
residency at Winter General Hospital in Topeka, Kansas, run by the
Menninger Clinic people, and was accepted. They had about one
hundred and twenty-five residents then; it was a huge factory of a
place, all these army psychiatrists wanting to get training. I was
pleased to get accepted but I very badly needed personal analysis and
they were able to provde that to only fifteen percent of their residents.
They didn't have enough analysts at Menninger's and I knew that

analysts were relatively plentiful in the Washington area, so I decided to stay in this area.

I never in the world intended to live here, which is the routine story for most people who live in this area: they never in the world thought they would wind up in Washington. Now, remember, I had been a psychiatrist in the army, and this secret work that I refer to was psychological in nature, and I had long since concluded that I wanted to become a psychiatrist. I found psychiatry to tap something in me, much more than internal medicine did. I felt that I could be a competent internist but that I couldn't be anything more than a competent one, whereas psychiatry excited me. I read a lot, I read about seventy books on psychiatry while I was in the army, which I think is somewhat unusual. I started reading Freud then and a whole lot of books, a great many.

*Langs:* That's interesting; I did the same thing when I was in the Public Health Service, read and read and read.

*Searles:* Yes. So I knew by the time the army service was over that I wanted to become a psychiatrist. When I was in Washington—I don't know if I was still in the army or not—I went to a Sullivan seminar one Saturday afternoon. Classes were held—this was in the Washington School of Psychiatry—were held in various public buildings, most of them, or in third-rate law school buildings. This Saturday afternoon I went into this—I think it was the U.S. Public Health Service building down on Constitution Avenue, a very nice, big marble building. I went into a huge room, and way down in a corner of this room was Sullivan. He always had a man sitting by with a kind of recording device no one had ever seen before, it was like a typewriter but with much fewer keys.

*Langs:* Like a court stenographer's instrument?

*Searles:* I guess so, and there was a small coterie of students and it was entirely as though he were Buddha; there was this kind of prayerful awe on the part of the students. This grated on me, obviously, right off the bat. I had previous exposure to him in the Army School of Military Neuropsychiatry because William Porter, Colonel William Porter, who was head of that shcool, had trained in

Washington and knew Sullivan and imported him to give a series of three lectures. And Sullivan turned up there and gave the lectures, and I can't say that I was much impressed with him then nor was I derisive of him; I simply didn't feel that I understood, really at all well, what he was saying. He used, of course, his special language to such an extent.

But I remember this first exposure to that Washington School kind of a contact with Sullivan. I don't remember what he talked about then; but in staying in Washington I saw that analysts were people most of whom had exposure to Sullivan. I went to Dr. Edith Weigert, who was (and still is) one of the doyennes, I guess is the word, of Washington psychiatry and psychoanalysis, the other being Frieda Fromm-Reichmann. Frieda outranked Edith slightly; but Edith was very, very highly thought of, very competent psychoanalyst, had very fine respect and liking in the analytic community. Have you met her?

*Langs:* I never met her. I know something of her writings, which were very effective.

*Searles:* I went to her fully expecting she would make time in her schedule for me, my narcissism was still fairly intact, and I told her my story and she said, "Well, typical obsessive problem," or "typical obsessive-compulsive neurosis"—she used the term obsessive-compulsive, I know that—and recommended that I find an analyst. I never recovered from that, obviously.

*Langs:* I just want to underscore the implications of that incident: I think it is a very important commentary on those analysts who do consultations of this kind, without available time to see the patient in therapy or analysis. I don't know if it cured you of doing it; I don't do it. I feel that you really have nothing meaningful to offer the patient and you traumatize the hell out of him.

*Searles:* No, I don't do it. I might introject something that's been a positively formative experience for me. When I went out to the Menninger Clinic to apply for a residency early in 1946, I had a lot of psychopathology in me. I still have plenty of it, my share, but I had more then, and I was terribly afraid I was homosexual uncon-sciously. I wasn't functioning at all homosexually and was functioning very adequately heterosexually, but I was afraid of the stuff in me I didn't know the nature of, and I read a book on the Rorschach—I was particularly afraid what the Rorschach would reveal—and on the train, on the way out, while reading that book, the hopelessness of trying to manipulate the Rorschach confronted me, so I knew I couldn't. But the thing that pleases me about that visit was that I had an interview with Robert Knight and all he said was, "Tell me about yourself," and, Christ, it just poured out of me, much the way it's doing today, and this was the first time I'd ever told anybody about when—I want to cry again. I haven't told anybody about all this stuff I'm telling you. I said that I used to give a lot of schmaltzy accounts but I hadn't gone into anything like this detail.

*Langs:* No, it's touching you personally. I think it is the nature of the situation, but I hope it's therapeutic too.

*Searles:* Anyhow, I told Knight about myself and I don't know what he said to close, nothing much really, but I respected him a lot. I'd never seen him before. That's why I asked him to do the introduction to my book of collected papers.

So to get back—I looked for an analyst. She said "typical obsessive-compulsive neurosis," and she meant it, I think.

*Langs:* And you were glad to hear it, too.

*Searles:* And she meant, you know, "nothing ominous," and I went and got lined up with an analyst, a guy well thought of and—

*Langs:* You weren't in an institute at the time?

*Searles:* No, wait a minute; I was in the institute. I talk of the Washington School of Psychiatry but I was applying to the Washington-Baltimore Psychoanalytic Institute, it was called then. I actually enrolled in both the Washington School and the analytic institute; I attended classes in both.

*Langs:* And Sullivan was involved as a teacher?

*Searles:* Sullivan was involved only with the Washington School.

He was not in the Washington-Baltimore Psychoanalytic Institute then, if he ever had been.

*Langs:* How was it possible to enroll in two institutes? Do you mean consecutively or simultaneously?

*Searles:* Paralleling. I don't think many classes, if any, were given credit in both institutes, I don't think so. But it was an example of the work load I customarily took on myself.

*Langs:* I can see that to this day. So, there were candidates who were in both Institutes simultaneously?

*Searles:* Yes. The Washington School was not a psychoanalytic institute. It is the Washington School of Psychiatry and was dominated by Sullivan, but the teachers in it—most of them—taught in both the Washington School and the Washington-Baltimore Psychoanalytic Institute.

I went, after the interview with Dr. Weigert, and managed to get time scheduled, by telephone, with the analyst of my choice; but he didn't have time for six months yet to begin with me. Things were tight still; analysts were still scarce, even in Washington. I waited through the six months with a hell of a lot of anxiety going on in me from various sources, a hell of a lot.

I started my first interview with him and at one point I said something about my mother and a few minutes later I said something completely opposite about my mother and he looked perplexed. He said, "I thought you said just a few minutes ago, such and such?" I was sitting, I think, with my feet over the arm of the chair and I just blandly waved aside that paradox and didn't tend to his perplexity at all. In the second interview—these were hour and a half interviews—he said that he didn't seem to be getting it and that he would speak to Dr. Weigert (who was a kind of dean of analysts around here then, as I told you before), and we went ahead with the third interview which had been scheduled. I started with the third interview and in the middle of the third interview he suddenly stood up and in effect said that it was no go. I don't remember what his words were; but I was through.

I was then interviewed by three, as I recall, of the leading lights in

the analytic community including Frieda Fromm-Reichmann, and
it was arranged for me to see Ernest Hadley. Ernest Hadley later on
told me that there had been some concern about me among the
training analysts' body because of the extent to which I was projecting, and he also much later on told me that the former analyst had
told him as his reason why he felt he couldn't work with me was
because I was so anti-Semitic. I was; I'm sure it couldn't have been
anything else, growing up where I did. But I assume that, really, I
was too borderline, I was too sick, I scared him. I treated him with a
kind of fine disdain that I commonly treated my mother. He was a
broad-shouldered, handsome guy, like my mother and I treated him
the way I had been trained to treat my mother and it infuriated him, I
am sure it infuriated him. It could be that he envied the hell out of me
for my WASP background; you see, that's another factor. But mainly,
I think, I was too damned ill. I'd been scared off by people like myself,
I wouldn't work with some of these people who were very much like
me. Anyhow, Hadley took me on, and I said at the end of my first
interview with Hadley—

*Langs:* Before you say that, let me comment briefly because your
story touches upon issues that are very pertinent to psychoanalysis
today. For example, and I will also be quite straightforward, I think
that there is a prevailing attitude among American psychoanalysts
that is intolerant of the more open expressions of borderline or even
schizophrenic difficulties; there is a genuine dread of the psychotic
part of their own and their patient's personalities. For example, did
you read the recent André Green (1975) paper? Do you know much of
his work?

*Searles:* I've heard him talk. I don't know; was it in the book, a
year or so ago, edited by Hartocollis, about borderline personality
disorders?

*Langs:* No, this is now in the *International Journal of Psycho-
Analysis;* it was read at the 1975 Congress; both André Green and Leo
Rangell gave position papers on the subject "Where is psycho-
analysis today?" Rangell's paper (1975), very frankly, was a representation of Freud's position, let's say, after 1923; it was the same stuff
that you get over and over again from classical analysts. Green's
paper was anything but that; it was really a very brilliant paper with

lots of challenges and new ideas in it. In one of his discussions, he made the point that the core of every neurosis is not a perversion—you know, Freud's formulation (1905) that a neurosis is the opposite of perversion—but that the core is a psychosis, in everybody. Very recently, Grotstein (1977a,b) elaborated on the same point. And of course this is a conception that the American analysts did not take very kindly to, at all.

*Searles:* Very neat, very nice; I like that. Of course, *I would* like that.

*Langs:* Green (1975) has written of an interesting syndrome that he calls the blank psychosis. Much of his work is based on Winnicott's ideas.

*Searles:* He hasn't published a book, has he?

*Langs:* Not in English.

*Searles:* I'll read that paper.

*Langs:* Yes, I abstracted it in *The Therapeutic Interaction* (Langs, 1976b).

*Searles:* I'll look it up.

*Langs:* I mention it because long before I read this paper, I had come to believe—and it's not in the least bit surprising—that the core pathology in everyone has psychotic qualities: the psychotic core or psychotic part of the personality. But American analysts are asked to be, in terms of the prevailing trend, someone who has established a very secure obsessive-compulsive defense against that core.

*Searles:* Right. How right you are.

*Langs:* And analysts who deviate from that ideal, from that model, tend to frighten them. It's not a field that welcomes borderline people, and certainly not well-functioning schizophrenic people.

*Searles:* The wealth of creativity is what starts to strike me—

*Langs:* Yes, with their creativity—exactly.

And my experience in England was different. For instance, the Kleinians would take somebody who is psychotic or borderline and help him master his psychosis, or major psychotic sectors of his personality, so that he could be a contributing analyst. Here in this country, this would be absolutely unheard of. One feeling I have about American psychoanalysts, as I look at their diatribe against the Kleinians, for example—which has kernels of truth, of course—is that they're very frightened of primitive mental contents in their patients and in themselves, ans so they try to exclude people who are different, people who get into things that disturb them. They react similarly to new ideas that have the potential to stir up these aspects of their personalities.

So, an analyst who is frightened off by what you are communicating I think represents an unfortunate situation that exists in our field, where we should be open to, and capable of mastering, all types of impingements. The whole literature on the analysis of schizophrenics that you helped to create would never have existed if some courageous candidates hadn't somehow slipped by. American analysts would say, you can't analyze schizophrenics—forget it. This is what Freud said (1911, 1914).

The only reason I go into this is that it is a representative attitude which I think is changing in this country. I think little by little it has to change. But these are some hard facts.

*Searles:* I appreciate hearing a lot of that, though, that I hadn't heard; it is comforting and reassuring.

*Langs:* This is not a specifically unique situation at all, not at all. So you were saying, then, you went to Hadley.

*Searles:* So I went to Hadley and I said at the end of the first interview, in which I had told him a great deal, and, of course, told him in a very confused way, naturally enough, about the first experience—

*Langs:* Oh, let me make one other general comment. It has to do with the framework of the analytic relationship—the ground rules, the way in which the relationship is created; the boundaries and all the rest. I think you are the youngest in the group of analysts that I have interviewed. But if I may be permitted a generalization, they have been terribly traumatized by their analytic experiences. Modifications in confidentiality, in neutrality—rebuffs of this kind—very blatantly traumatic kinds of experiences, are absolutely characteristic. It just struck me as I hear the way the damage was done to you on your way into the field. It's again not at all atypical in terms of how analysts treat candidates; but that's another whole area.

*Searles:* So I asked him if he saw any reason why we couldn't work together and he said, "Hell, no!" and we went ahead working together and I started with him in 1947. I had around seven hundred and seventy-five hours of analysis all together, about six years. It ended with his blessing in 1953, and I graduated from the local analytic institute and became a member of the American [Psychoanalytic Association] in 1953, in the same year.

*Langs:* Does it mean you weren't seen as frequently as five times a week?

*Searles:* That's what it means. I was so low on money that I couldn't afford—I had quite a lot of it at five hours a week but the money ran low and he had to raise his fee and I had to cut down to twice a week for financial reasons. So I was on a two-hour a week basis for part of that time, and he let me run up a bill to him for something like thirty-six hundred dollars, which was a great deal of money in those days, and I paid it off within about one year. After the analysis was over, I received a very appreciative note from him saying that he appreciated the conscientiousness with which I had discharged my obligation to him.

Now in the course of the analysis—did I tell you a little about that? Do you want me to tell you?

*Langs:* Yes, whatever you can share.

*Searles:* I used to go down there five hours a week, most of it seems, in my memory, to have been at five hours a week. I had an early morning hour, about 7:00 AM, and he had one hour even earlier quite a lot of the mornings—six o'clock, he started. He had a farm background, Kansas farm background, and his father told him when he was twelve years of age that he must now go forward, which meant, I think, going out into the world earning his own living, and Ernest worked very hard. His farm background, I had a transference from my mother's, and I used to deride him about being a corn-fed guy from Kansas and he put up with a lot of this kidding in a way that he shouldn't have. But one of the main things that I remember, the first two years, getting up very conscientiously, going to—I was chronically a bit late. That got to him a bit, but not bad for a 7:00 AM hour I drove in from Rockville for. When I started—

I must go back a little bit and say that when I got out of the army and applied to get into analysis, I also arranged to start working at the V. A. Mental Hygiene Clinic, an outpatient clinic in downtown Washington. That's where I got a job as a psychiatrist. They had about fifteen full-time psychiatrists there at the time, all or nearly all of whom were in analysis, most of them young people, and we had an excellent patient clientele of workable cases, fresh cases, veterans recently out of the army, many of them neurotic and very workable neurotic people and it was a very stimulating environment.

I started in analysis with Ernest Hadley a block away—it only happened to be a block away—and I hadn't yet lived out in Rockville. I worked at the V. A. Mental Hygiene Clinic from 1947 to 1949, for two years, and I started in analysis in '47 and I then went out to Chestnut Lodge in June of '49, continuing in analysis, and one of my most frequent memories is how I would get up out in Rockville, drive in for this 7:00 AM hour, free associate as conscientiously as I knew how, and be told once again how hostile I was. And toward the end of two years of hearing this, I remember, as I started out from his office—I started opening the door out into the corridor—it suddenly struck me: "I *do* hate." But it took that long for it to seep in, the realization of my hateful side.

I think he was off the beam in a way, in that what I think he should have been interpreting was my *fear* of my hostility, because I was terrified of my hostility. I was very afraid I would murder someone. I had been afraid for years that I would murder someone. I had thought in obsessive terms of how to arrange things to make sure that I did not kill anyone, stuff that went well beyond a lot of the neurotic psychopathology. I wanted to preserve my good objects from my hatred and he didn't do enough interpreting of my concern to preserve my good objects or good relationships in the face of my murderous feelings.

In any case, another of my most frequent memories is that I would come to express a great deal of hatefulness and hostility in the sessions and find this replaced by feelings of love, feelings of tenderness—the power of my tender feelings. I don't want to go into too much detail about the analysis but this was an important affective experience to me. My grandiosity was something he worked on a great deal. He came to call me, ironically, "God Searles."

*Langs:* That's his sarcasm again.

*Searles:* Yes. One of the men at the V. A. had gotten a position out there at Chestnut Lodge just a few months before I did, and I knew others there in the course of my analytic classes. I went out there to attend a seminar run by Frieda Fromm-Reichmann, who taught in the analytic institute. And remember, this was the Washington-Baltimore Psychoanalytic Institute when I enrolled in it and it split into the two perhaps midway in my training, or somewhat earlier than midway. I should say a little more about the V. A. experience.

*Langs:* As for the split, did you have the choice of which group to stay with?

*Searles:* I don't remember that I had a choice. My memory is that that split had clear geographic meanings—that to have gone with the Baltimore one would have meant getting my training in Baltimore, which was an appreciable drive. People came from Baltimore to attend classes and I don't believe any classes were given in Baltimore; I certainly didn't take any there. It was called Baltimore because it had a lot of candidates from Baltimore, and I guess the training analysts whom these men had they saw in Baltimore; but they came to Washington for the classes. I remember, for example, the seminar at Frieda Fromm-Reichmann's with various Baltimore people present. Her residence was on the grounds of Chestnut Lodge, where she was the director of psychotherapy. Chestnut Lodge was a very important and respected institution—and still is.

*Langs:* Was Sullivan there?

*Searles:* Sullivan never was on the staff at Chestnut Lodge. He gave a series of lectures out there, but was never on the staff. They had a few psychiatrists there who had been analyzed by him and there were a few analysts elsewhere in the area who had been analyzed by Sullivan, or who had had at least some of their personal analysis done by Sullivan; and he did a lot of supervision of people in the area. I was enrolled, as I mentioned, in the Washington School of Psychiatry as well as the Washington-Baltimore Psychoanalytic Institute, as were many people in Washington and Baltimore, and I had two and a half courses from Sullivan. He died midway through what must have been the third course. I never met him personally. I never had supervision from him. I admired him; but it was a far less than slavish admiration of the kind that appeared to imbue these people I've described in the corner of the public health building on that Saturday afternoon. I from the first was put off by his grandiosity, which was enormous. It is easy to talk of the eccentricities of Harry Stack Sullivan, since he's dead; it's not a worthy thing to do. But I admired him. I regarded him as brilliant. I still do regard him as having been brilliant and well worth learning from.

But Ernest Hadley was not Sullivanian. He had had a classical analytic analysis by Philip Graven, who recently died—his death was announced last evening—and Hadley had had further analytic work after his regular training analysis with Graven was over. He had some subsequent analysis from A. A. Brill in New York; he went up there for some analytic sessions—I have no idea how many. He spoke of "Papa Brill" with fondness. Hadley was a classical psychoanalyst and that's been a very important part of a great deal of professional identity-turmoil to me.

*Langs:* Yes, I'm sensitive to that issue. I'm wondering now how you got to what you call an *interpersonal approach*—I call it adaptational-interactional—but you beautifully combine the intrapsychic and interactional or interpersonal realms.

*Searles:* I appreciate hearing that.

*Langs:* Oh yes, which I don't think Sullivan did quite as thoroughly. So I was wondering whether Sullivan's influence contributed to that, or what?

*Searles:* Well, Sullivan's influence contributed, and Chestnut Lodge's was vastly a greater contribution. Now, the classical stuff came from Ernest Hadley and from Edith Weigert. Edith Weigert was my first supervisor. She was not only the one from whom I had the equivalent—what that interview with her had been was the equivalent—of a candidate admission evaluation procedure. That served as my being admitted into the Washington-Baltimore Psychoanalytic Institute; so when she said: "Well, typical obsessive-compulsive problem, eh?" and suggested I find an analyst, this had a meaning that I was accepted into the institute, you see, so I could find a training analyst.

So Hadley was a classical analyst, and he had an important relationship with Harry Stack Sullivan which I didn't know much of, really; but Hadley, at the time I started with him, was editor of the journal, *Psychiatry,* and Hadley had, in terms of the classical—this is somewhat garbled but it will come together as I go on—Hadley had been tied for President of the American Psychoanalytic Association a few years prior to that, I think it was, and in a gentlemanly spirit had yielded to the other person and let him be President. I mention this because Hadley enjoyed a very good footing with the American Psychoanalytic Association and in the course of my training—I don't know what this has to do with Sullivan, if anything; but in the course of my training, I think it was at the time the split occurred, the Washington-Baltimore split. It has started to become more clear to me what must have happened that I didn't realize at the time: evidently when that split occurred, although the Baltimore Institute readily received the blessing of the American as an accredited institute, the Washington Institute was in real jeopardy, and I think that the influence of Sullivan was the thing that gave the American the jaundiced eye toward us, you see, and Hadley, I feel safe to say, was the main influence that enabled us to stay an affiliated institute of the American, because he enjoyed a very secure relationship with the people in the American.

Hadley was editor of *Psychiatry,* and Mabel Blake Cohen, who later on became editor of it for many years, told me one time how the editorship of the journal passed from the hands of Ernest Hadley to those of Harry Stack Sullivan. Hadley got so fed up trying to edit Sullivan's articles—Sullivan had many articles in *Psychiatry,* you know—that one day he just called and had a pickup truck come and put the few files that the journal had into the damned pickup truck and had it driven around to Sullivan's home and turned it over to Sullivan.

Hadley mentioned Sullivan one time only in my analysis. He said how Harry Stack Sullivan can be a very charming, lovable person and can also be a terrible son of a bitch. He indicated his ambivalence for Sullivan. I never got to know Sullivan well enough to see the really endearing side of him.

I should say something more about the time when I worked at the V. A. Mental Hygiene Clinic in Washington, where I worked from 1947 to 1949. I was there when I started in analysis in 1947. I wish I had here in the office a book on group psychotherapy by Florence Powdermaker and Jerome D. Frank (1953)—a big book. I was one of sixteen psychiatrists who, as a small part of our work—most of our work was individual psychotherapy, but I was also doing a small part group therapy as part of our job. Our group therapy was also part of the project that Powdermaker and Frank were studying. Their research concerning the work with out-patients was conducted at the V. A. clinic, and as regards inpatients, at Perry Point V. A. Hospital in Perry Point, Maryland, way up in northern Maryland somewhere. When their book came out I was described (p. 325) as the most passive of the group therapists. To read that description will show you something of how very much I have changed since then. I really changed an enormous lot.

I was early in analysis then, and in the group sessions was really nearly catatonic. I smoked in that era, and in group sessions I used to desperately want a cigarette but did not dare bring my hands up above the table—we sat around the table—for fear the patients might see my hands shaking. I don't know whether they were actually shaking at the time, but I was afraid that they might visibly shake and my thoroughly confident assumption was that, were that to happen, at least two or three of the patients would become hopelessly, permanently psychotic. See how catatonic my dynamics were—my grandiosity implied in that. So I did function, I'm sure, in a maddeningly passive way to the psychologists sitting in the back of the room observing this, and after the group session would be over they would interview me about what I thought of the meeting; that was routine. They were ferociously competitive themselves, very competitive, and they wrote this up. I wish I could show you the book sometime. About how passive I was and how I said little or nothing: that's all very true.[1]

1. [The reader may be interested in these paragraphs from the book cited, by Powdermaker and Frank. The authors are describing the characteristics of individual doctors and I am the "Dr. K"—HFS.]

Then I went out to Chestnut Lodge and by Jesus that place had—I realized just in the last month what a powerful father transference I had to Chestnut Lodge, that the whole place represented my father to me. Because only two things in my life that I know of—apart from my wife, who is so important to me that I don't dare talk about her, really—only two other things or institutions have had such an enormous impact on me. One is my father, and he was such a many-sided man. (And that's something I'm sure I have failed to bring out adequately. A very diverse man, a man with a marvelous sense of humor, an inexhaustible fund of stories; on the other hand a para-noid, bitter, hateful man, a frightening man. A man with many intellectual interests, at least for his cultural climate; he went far beyond what most of the natives of our village were interested in.) And then the second is Chestnut Lodge, a really overwhelming place. Not long back a man who had been a psychiatrist at NIH [National Institutes of Health] and a very capable one—I used to see him when I worked there as a consultant; a very capable guy, worked with psychotic patients at NIH; he knows psychosis—he has really been

---

Dr. K stated that he feared his own need to control and therefore bent over backward in an effort not to do so. For a long time his interventions were halting and timid and he was the most passive of the doctors. He frequently sat hunched up with an impassive expression. Coming from an economically depressed minority group, he was sensitive to discussions of minority problems and tended to divert them.

Although an intellectual himself, he had a mixed feeling toward intellectual patients. He welcomed them as helpers who would see things that he missed but also felt that they were competing with him. He believed that he should facilitate expression of hostility as part of therapy (possibly in line with his masochistic trend) but tended to forestall the development of tension in the group by calling for analysis of what was going on before the patients' feelings had had a chance to develop fully. At one point a patient criticized him severely for impeding spontaneity. In his group there was much discussion of feelings and attitudes but with relatively little analysis or resolution of problems; eventually the members showed considerable rivalry.

This doctor expressed some of his feelings and attitudes and their relation to therapy so clearly that we quote him:

"When I began group therapy, and for at least a few months thereafter, I was in a damned nearly catatonic state during the sessions—unable to move my hands up from my lap onto the table lest they shake uncontrollably, for instance, and too anxious to make *any* comments in some of the meetings. My thoughts, before and during the sessions, dwelt upon the likelihood of there ensuing a maelstrom of hopelessly complicated and uncontrollable hostile and frightened feelings from the patients, or upon showing excessive emotion in the group."

Later he said, "I still feel *much* more anxious in group therapy than in individual therapy. But I have been increasingly and steadily convinced that actually, for a well-analyzed person, group therapy might be even more comfortable than individual therapy. This conviction has arisen from seeing, time after time, how much ego-strength there is in each of the group members, and how they lend very effective support to one another during difficult times."

quite awed at the psychosis one finds at Chestnut Lodge. It is not only that the patients there are very ill, but that one gets involved with them in a way that you don't at all get involved with them hardly anywhere else in the world, on a kind of personal basis and with an intensity and a closeness that is really powerful stuff.

Now at the V. A. Mental Hygiene Clinic, I, like the other psychiatrists, had had a case load of about thirty-five patients, most of them neurotic—not an unusual case load, in other words. I'd see them once a week, twice a week and I'd work like anybody else. And I went out to Chestnut Lodge and in my first week—well, half of my time was devoted to running a ward there; that was routine. Each new person spent half his time that way and half his time treating patients in intensive psychotherapy. In my first week I started on my job as administrator of a ward, and got assigned *one* psychotherapy patient. You see the tremendous shift just in terms of numbers of patients: I had been treating thirty-six patients, now I get a patient and I sort of get some uneasy sense that people are watching me to see if I hold together; and I remember telling somebody that if I hold

---

Continuing his explanation of why he felt less comfortable in group than in individual treatment, he said, "I am especially anxious in the presence of 'social' conversation. . . . One time the members unanimously complained of feeling that they had to work all the time they were at the sessions. I considered their complaint to be well-founded on a real limitation of mine.

"Another thing—I felt threatened at the prospect of closeness between two members of the group. . . . They never seemed to become affectionate toward each other and they seemed very anxious about feeling and expressing affection. But I felt on more than one occasion that the prospect of their doing so was definitely unpleasant to me. It was as though my own security demanded that I be closer to each of the patients than they were to one another. This was something I became aware of only in the latter months of working with my group; heretofore they had been so distant from one another that the problem did not present itself. During one meeting about six months after the group started I became aware of anxiety at a time when the patients were having a lively discussion (about five of them were present), and I had been silent for perhaps fifteen minutes. I experienced the sensation of being farther and farther out of the group, being totally unnecessary and unnoticed. It happened that the anxiety was mild enough to allow me to see what was going on in myself, and I did not feel anxious in any of the later sessions when that situation arose.

"Between meetings I kept having fantasies that a certain psychotic patient would go berserk and beat up the other patients and myself. I had felt this about him in individual sessions too, but in the group I had not been aware of this fear. Even during the meeting during which he said to me, 'To hell with you, Agnes,' and things became very tense, I did not feel afraid of his assaulting me but rather was conscious of the need to control my anger toward him because of the need to handle this situation comfortably since the other patients were looking curiously to see how I took it. The recognition of the unconscious factor underlying my anger allayed my anxiety and when he resumed individual therapy with me after spending six months at a hospital, I felt much more comfortable with him than I had previously, was no longer afraid of his acting out—which he was still doing outside his analytic hours." [pp. 325-326]

together another week I'll get another patient, and that's about the way it happened.

Now it just happened because, in actuality, there weren't a whole lot of new patients being admitted at that particular time. The usual case load for a full-time person, after your first two years when you came off doing ward administration and were devoting full time to therapy, was six. You would see them each four times a week for fifty or fifty-five minute sessions; I always had fifty-five minute sessions with my patients, incidentally—an example of my therapeutic devotion or hyperconscientiousness, or, more likely, both. So that totalled twenty-four hours. That doesn't seem like much, but also there were several hours of conferences each week, and I, like all the other therapists, had a private practice going for a considerable number of hours each week; my private patients would come from Washington to my office at the Lodge. Such part-time private practice was fully sanctioned by Dexter Bullard, the owner and medical director of the Lodge.[2]

2. [My brief remarks on the occasion of my being awarded, on May 2, 1965, the Frieda Fromm-Reichmann Award by the Academy of Psychoanalysis are relevant here, regarding my experiences at Chestnut Lodge—HFS.]

Dr. Salzman [Leon Salzman, M.D., President of the Academy], Ladies and Gentlemen:

Back in 1949, when I first walked onto the ward at Chestnut Lodge to which I had been assigned as administrative psychiatrist, I was of course feeling very awkward, self-conscious, out of place. I had not gone more than a few steps when an attractive, confident, and self-possessed young woman swept up to me and said breezily, "Good morning! *I'm* schizophrenic; how are *you?*" The degree to which I felt tongue-tied on that occasion is much the way I feel here, no matter how different are the circumstances.

But one thing, at least, I'm able to say here—to say how deeply gratified I feel by this honor which you bestow upon me. My working for so many years predominantly with schizophrenic patients would have been impossible but for the emotional support, as well as the illumination, which I have received from my colleagues. It is so inordinately difficult for schizophrenic persons to convey their overwhelmingly intense feelings of dependency and of love and adoration, that one tends to feel confirmed, in working with them over long spans of time, less in one's capacity for love and usefulness and skill, than in one's sense of basic worthlessness, futility, and interpersonal malevolence. One's colleagues who are doing the same sort of work help so much, sometimes in their positive acknowledgments—of which this present one is paramount in my whole professional career—and sometimes, at Chestnut Lodge at least, through their providing a daily fare of jungle-warfare professional competitiveness which makes one return to one's session with the chronically schizophrenic patient in relief and gratitude for this haven. It all helps. Seriously, I have seen many institutions where, so it seemed to me, the staff members provided much less of positive acknowledgment to one another than did those at Chestnut Lodge, and the level of workaday competence among the Lodge staff members, relatively few of whom have written of their accomplishments, was sufficiently high so that anything which one could learn from one's patients, which one's colleagues did not already know and daily use, was bound to represent a contribution to the literature. It has not been an easy thing, however, for patients to get things through my head. My mother used to say, proudly, "You can't tell Harold a thing." Since, then, in my growing

Now, my first Chestnut Lodge patient [i.e., hospitalized there]—
well, I hoped to convey to you the realization from my having
conducted this group therapy in the way that you've heard and from
my having done individual therapy at the V. A. clinic in really a very
obsessive fashion, that my dynamics were predominantly obsessive-
compulsive. I would not consciously say an angry thing to a patient,
hardly at all, that first two years at the V. A. clinic—very obsessive—
and at the end of each interview, typically, after the patient had left, I
would make brief notes about what had occurred and moreover, what
I planned to go into with the patient when we would meet next week.

I remember one borderline young woman came to the V. A. clinic
and got into treatment with me, and after a relatively few sessions she
was doing something that tended to irritate me considerably. But I
couldn't tell her so, and she finally said, "You *are* angry at me, *aren't*
you?" And I couldn't permit myself to confirm that indeed I was. In
fact, I think I even disclaimed it or, at best, tried in a very businesslike
way to ask her where she had obtained that impression, and in so
doing I was identifying, as well as I was able, with my analyst. She

---

up, to be bone-headed has been a highly prized thing; this has caused no little exasperation to
my patients, one of whom said, "What do I have to do? drive a nail through your head?"

Secondly, I want to note the irony of this occasion, considering what has transpired in the
past. Never have I been turned down with more coldness and lack of interest, in a job interview,
than I was the first time I had an interview with Dexter Bullard. It may be because I had had no
personal analysis at that time, and people were, as I later found out, not accepted without
having had at least some. The second time I applied to him, I had had a good deal, and felt
much surer of my ground—so sure, in fact, that I informed him that I did not feel that I wanted
to work with schizophrenic patients, but that I felt particularly at home, and effective, with
what I termed hard-hitting obsessive-compulsive patients. He, inscrutable man, said nothing.
You see, although I was aware that Chestnut Lodge was a psychiatric sanitarium, I really
didn't know to what a degree it specialized in the treatment of schizophrenic patients. To show
you further how ill-informed I was in that era: these were the days when, in my personal
analysis, I kept telling my analyst either that I was so perfectly well that it was absurd for me to
be in analysis, or in such danger of imminent disintegration that: "You'd better get a bed ready
for me at Chestnut Lodge." That is, I had had the illusion, for a long time, that if a bona fide
analytic candidate became psychotic, during his analysis, he would be treated free at Chestnut
Lodge. Much later, after I had been working at the Lodge for several years, my private criterion
as to how I was progressing in the financial world had to do not with how lavish was my home,
or how many cars did I have, but rather that I had accumulated enough money that I could now
afford as long as, say, six months in this fine sanitarium where my patients were living for an
abundance of years.

Certainly one of my most difficult times at the Lodge was my first two weeks there. I had
been working with twenty-eight patients in the V. A. outpatient clinic in Washington; but a
whole week passed, at the Lodge, before my first therapy patient was assigned to me, and at the
end of the second week, so I felt it, the powers that be were sufficiently reassured that I was not
cracking up, under the strain, so that they accorded me a second patient. The first patient was a

showed excellent judgment, thereupon, to leave the session never to return.

I'm sure you would call my identification with my analyst, in that instance, a hostile one; but Hadley was very classical, very classical. He hardly ever expressed anger to me or acknowledged that he felt angry toward me, hardly ever. Ernest Hadley, to the very best of my recollection, never made an interpretation except within the closing minutes of a session. He was very stereotyped. It took me many years to become able to make an interpretation any time when it was timely to do so, even in the opening moments of a session. It took me many years to become free from my identifications with some of his more obsessive qualities.

*Langs:* Yes, it has been said that most analysts get fixated with the level of knowledge at the point at which they graduate from an institute; it's a great struggle to get beyond that. Analysts are also fixated, I think, at the level at which their own analysts were functioning; and it takes a lot of personal self-analysis or another analysis to modify much of that. There is another point there too:

---

man with whom I worked for two years, and I remember that in one staff presentation of my work with him, I became sufficiently bogged down in anxiety so that, in an hour-long presentation, my chronological account never even reached the point where he had been admitted to the Lodge. The second patient was a woman with whom I worked for nearly fifteen years. I remember one hour, in either the thirteenth or fourteenth year of the work when we were sitting in my office, directly across from one another and quite some distance away. She was a very domineering woman, and absolutely required a kind of funeral-parlor distance and stasis about our seating arrangement; why I acquiesced to this, I shall not endeavor to go into. At any rate, I recall breaking a long silence by saying to her, rather balefully, "I was just wondering, Edith, whether you have had more of intensive psychotherapy than anybody else in the world." She, as was her custom, neither twitched nor said anything. I later learned that the answer to this question in my mind was no. At least a few patients at the Lodge have had more than she, although not with the same therapist, and a few months ago, a British analyst mentioned to me that she had been working with a schizophrenic woman for something like twenty, or maybe twenty-five, years.

At times when things have been on the bleak side, I have often recalled, in amusement at my own kind of blind and unthinking persistence, a cartoon which appeared in the *New Yorker* many years ago, and is to be found in their 1950-55 album. It shows a prisoner sitting on his lower bunk at night, writing on a tablet on his lap, "Dear Alice: How are you? I'm fine and getting along O.K. Today was my first day in the rock quarry. I busted up them rocks like nobody's business. You know how strong I am, Alice. The guard said he never saw a guy bust up them rocks so good the first day out. . . . "

During my second year at the Lodge, in 1950, I received from Frieda a complimentary copy of her book, with a penned note, "Thank you so much for your nonpsychotherapeutic treatment." Being rather highly paranoid in those years, I immediately felt that she had formed some adverse conclusion as to my psychotherapeutic capabilities. But then I recalled that, not many days before, as doctor on call one evening I had given her something for, as I recall, a sore throat. But I confess to some lingering uneasiness about that note.

the issue of what the analyst or therapist reveals to the patient. It is too broad an issue to discuss in detail right now, but I think that the acknowledgment of these feelings—

*Searles:* Yes, the acknowledgment of them to oneself, yes.

*Langs:* —is open to discussion. I would seriously question whether the most appropriate response is to directly share such responses with the patient. Implicit acceptance of them is to be preferred; but to deny them modifies the frame. You are are saying that Hadley, as a classical analyst, responded quite directly.

*Searles:* He denied it.

*Langs:* So, he denied it directly.

*Searles:* I said to him one time something about his negative feelings toward me and he said, "I've never had anything but friendly feelings toward you." He once told me how he liked to think of himself, in his doing of analytic work in general, as being in a sense up on a shelf—that was his figure of speech—kind of observing I don't know what. He didn't say "observing," but he did emphasize this vantage point up on the shelf. Schizoid, schizoid kind of stuff.

*Langs:* Yes, but Freud's writings, and the attitude of analysts at the time you were analyzed, played right into that: the idea of the analyst as a mirror, almost a nonparticipant. These are conceptions to which you strongly objected. I was going to ask you when you began to write, but from the beginning, you thought of the analytic situation as a place of interaction, a bipersonal field.

*Searles:* Yes.

*Langs:* But here, Hadley was attempting to remove himself from the interaction, to insist that your reactions are purely transference, purely intrapsychic. You see, that is what I thought you also were leading up to: that the kind of so-called interpretations to which you must have been subjected mostly had to do with what was going on inside of you, exclusive of anything you were actually picking up from him.

*Searles:* Exactly, exactly. Exclusively in me and how hostile a person I was, this is very much of the thing.

*Langs:* That is so typical of so much so-called analytic work. When you first mentioned this business of two years of telling you how angry you are—

*Searles:* Hostility was the word, it wasn't anything as warmly human as anger. It was called hostility; for me it seemed more sinister, really, or far beyond the pale.

*Langs:* Yes, devoid of really human feeling. I began to wonder— and I am being quite speculative—how much he was projecting onto you, and how much he was denying and trying to put into you.

*Searles:* A great deal. I wasn't totally naive throughout all of this. For example, when I took my American Boards in 1951—see, that was midway through my analysis or near the last third of it—and told him I learned that I had passed them, his only response and—he had never taken the Boards—his only response was to tell me of a lawyer patient he had had one time who thought that, just for the hell of it, he would take the American Board of Psychiatry exam and he studied for it for about three weeks and took it and passed it. I had enough sagacity to know that Ernest was very envious. Likewise, when in the course of my analysis my father had to get a herniorrhaphy and went down to New York City to New York Hospital where I had trained— Cornell, there—to have it and I went up to visit him, I was very, very pleased at how the nurses took us to be brothers because we looked so alike. My father had never had a brother nor had I, and this was a very pleasing thing to me and I came back and told Ernest how pleased I was that the nurses had found my father and me to be alike that they had mistaken us for brothers. He snorted, "Well, you are both interested in the same woman." Well, there again I knew he was envious, the poor devil, he couldn't help it. You see, when he was twelve years old he had this separation from his father whereas I had enjoyed something with mine, sitting in the store with him long after that age, and had a kind of companionship with him that most kids really don't have with their father because my father's work was in the store right below the flat where I spent my years growing up.

*Langs:* You know, you are describing a host of self-revelations by Hadley, which, of course, also abound in Freud's case histories, for example. I am listening and I hear how much you knew about his personal life, how he introduced many personal comments. And I would be interested in your thoughts about that and how you experienced it.

*Searles:* Very helpful, very, very helpful. It would have been intolerably impersonal without them. A lot of it was pretty impersonal anyway; but there was enough leaven of a person there to make it reassuring. It was very useful. Now I'm mindful, also, that very important realms went unanalyzed in me because of those responses—very important realms. For example, when I said at the end of the first interview, "Do you see any reason why we can't work together?" and he said, "Hell, no!" I tremendously appreciated that and I needed that assurance, because I had come away from the experience with the first analyst and—I remember now—I had come away with a feeling of profound despair that nothing in me was communicable to another human being. Now, I hadn't *concluded* that that was so, but I had been left greatly *fearing* that that was the case.

And so when Ernest said that—"Hell, no!"—it was an assurance that I really desperately needed. But it meant that the whole depressive, despairing side of me, which had been a very major part of my nature, was largely swept under the rug. It wasn't entirely, because I do remember having enough of despair in my analysis so that Ernest had occasion to make an interpretation to the effect that my despair had to do with my being—well, I don't know how he phrased it; he didn't put it this stiltedly—had to do with the despair about being unable to hold on to a regressive position, that the despair was a kind of clinging-to-illness type of thing, and that it had a positive, constructive side underneath it, and that I was despairing because I couldn't stave off maturity, you see. He didn't say that but that was the essence of his comment. At least I had enough of conscious despair that he found occasion to make an interpretation about it. But by and large, the feelings of depression and despair which I have experienced have been since my analysis, and I have had a tremendous lot of such feelings—tremendous lot. I'll give you another example of how something got swept under the rug.

*Langs:* Something other than the despair?

*Searles:* Yes. It is other than the despair.

*Langs:* I do want to hear about it, but if I may, since what you are describing is so rich in implications, I want to point out that you are dealing with modifications in the frame, a human frame that is not quite as rigid as the image suggests.

*Searles:* Referring to the patient-therapist context? Is that what you mean by "frame"?

*Langs:* The ground rules, implicit and explicit, of the analytic relationship. I'll detail much of this later on, but to say a bit now: Marion Milner (1952) first called these tenets the framework of the analytic situation, the framework of the bipersonal field, as I prefer to put it. It's too rigid a metaphor because it is a human frame: it is a form of unconscious communication by the analyst; and there must be a certain flexibility which is far less than usually conceived. But if we define it ideally in terms of its dimension, we could identify it as a template which would include anonymity, total confidentiality, neutrality, and the rest. We can then talk about modifications in this frame without assuming that they are necessarily helpful or destructive—or that they are necessarily anything. They have many implications and functions, and we can derive them empirically. It's an area—I have to say this to you—it's perhaps the most important area that I think you have most neglected in your writings. In reading your work, I have been struck by your failure to get around to the management of the framework and its functions, even with your sensitivity to the interactional aspects of the analytic interaction. I don't want to go into this point at length today, but I could start you thinking about it.

*Searles:* Well your book, *The Bipersonal Field* (Langs, 1976a), is something I should read, isn't it? I have a number of your earlier books now.

*Langs:* I'll see that you get a copy of it.

*Searles:* I would appreciate that.

*Langs:* Yes, it will clarify some of my present thinking. I think it could evoke many discussions, particularly with your sensitivities. I was thinking of these issues as I read over your material in *The Nonhuman Environment* (Searles, 1960). And I am aware that you modify the frame in certain ways, which I hope to discuss with you. I know that you mention tape recording an analysis (Searles, 1972, 1975), and things of that kind. You seem never to have paused to examine the frame, and bringing that issue to your attention, I hope will be constructive for you in this exchange.

*Searles:* I think it will. I feel sure it will. It is something I'm conscious of now that you talk of the need for this.

*Langs:* Good, it will start you going. You are exceptionally open to new ideas. So, what I wanted to say about the modifications in the frame that you are describing—and again, I am speculating—they could function to create a king of pathological symbiosis, or some type of unconscious fusion experience; it also has manic qualities.

*Searles:* Manic—"Hell, no!"—it's manic; you're right.

*Langs:* Yes, it offers you a manic defense—his behaviors, where he responds to you directly and noninterpretively.

*Searles:* Yes, in support of your idea it could at least be said that Hadley had a kind of well-controlled, hypomanic energy—not blatantly so; it was subtle.

*Langs:* And it needn't be that gross. I have found—and I've done a lot of studies of the frame by now—that as a rule, when the analyst modifies the frame, he tends to generate a misalliance (Langs, 1975b). You would, I think, call it a pathological symbiosis in which separation is denied, as are depressive problems. I have to say that this is the case on both sides, of course—for both the patient and the analyst—and it would deprive you of the opportunity to really experience, analyze, and work through these crucial issues. The fact that he interpreted some of this verbally is relatively insignificant, because there was no rectification along with such efforts. And I think that what you are saying is that the real experience of these issues occurred after your analysis was over.

*Searles:* Was later, oh, yes.

*Langs:* It was a problem that could only be worked over afterwards. You see, inherent to modifications in the frame is some kind of fusion or merger. They have all kinds of unconscious meanings and functions, but fusion and denial are usually involved, including denial of separateness, ultimately, of death. But it is not at all surprising that you are aware that these behaviors on his part deprived you of analyzing certain sectors of your pathology; though I must add that few individuals are capable of being consciously aware of these consequences; almost always, such insights—which are virtually universal—are quite unconscious.

*Searles:* At the time, I wasn't aware of all that. It is only in retrospect that I realized it. At the time they were appreciated.

*Langs:* Well, you are typical and atypical—both. You remind me that consciously patients tend to appreciate deviations in technique from the analyst. But if you listen to the indirect material—and if you say to yourself that this is my context for listening and I will listen to these associations as a commentary with valid and distorted elements, you find that the patient first says: Thank you, I feel so much better. But then, as you listen to the next set of associations, he changes the subject, either to self-references which reflect rather straightforwardly the patient's introjection of the pathological unconscious meanings and functions of the deviation, or to other displaced derivative material with similar implications. You hear indirect angry reactions, and the deviation is seen as destructive, or as reflecting your weakness and incapacity to manage things—within yourself and the patient. You have a countertransference problem, they say in some disguised way. The indirect material is always negative.

*Searles:* It is very interesting.

*Langs:* Even though the conscious material is positive. This is rather consistent, by the way, almost universal. So the fact that you are able to appreciate these implications consciously is quite exceptional. When I got to the bipersonal field notion, which I borrowed

from the Barangers—I don't know if you know them; they are South
American Kleinians.

*Searles:* I've heard of Grinberg; he is one, isn't he?

*Langs:* Yes, Grinberg is in Spain now; he was in Argentina. They
are in Argentina. And I read their paper, "Insight in the Analytic
Situation" (Baranger and Baranger, 1966), and the metaphor was just
there; it was a concept I was hungering for, in terms of creating a
meaningful and serviceable metaphor of the analytic interaction. I
was experiencing what Bion (1962) calls a preconception: a state of
tension and needs in search for a realization that would satisfy it,
generating what he terms a conception which here would serve as a
*selected fact* that could give new meaning and synthesis to previously
disparate observations. The bipersonal field idiom did just that for
me, though in doing so, it separated me from my analytic background, which was so different in maintaining a virtually exclusive
focus on the patient rather than on the analytic interaction—what I
now call the continuous, spiraling communicative interaction.

In talking about the bipersonal field, they found it necessary to
introduce a concept of shared defenses that they call *bastions.* I refer
to these as *sectors of misalliance,* a component of the analytic
interaction that gets sealed off from the analytic work based on an
unconscious collusion between the patient and the analyst—which
interferes, of course, with the openness of the communicative field.
Certain material is then excluded from the analytic work until the
bastion or misalliance is resolved. It is an actuality filled with
unconscious meanings and functions that must be rectified; then it is
brought back into the analytic interaction in a form through which it
can be analyzed. Their concept of bastion is an excellent one: a piece
of the field—unconscious elements in both patient and analyst—that
gets excluded by unconscious mutual agreement, and of course
neither side gets the opportunity to work it through analytically.

Your awareness in retrospect of this dimension is connected to one
other point I wanted to make: your excellent paper, "The Patient as
Therapist to His Analyst" (Searles, 1975), has its roots in your
interactional approach and in your sensitivity to introjective processes in the patient—the critical aspect of the analytic experience
neglected by most classical Freudian and Kleinian analysts. And in
your first published paper, on introjection (Searles, 1951), you allude

to the patient's unconscious curative efforts directed toward the analyst, and in your 1975 paper you explore the topic in detail. There you mention that you were aware of curative efforts toward your own analyst—a truly remarkable realization.

*Searles:* In the "incorporation" paper?

*Langs:* No, in "The Patient as Therapist" paper; and I admired the extent of your insight. I knew the title of that paper, but I did not read it until I had written my own misalliance and deviations papers (Langs, 1975b,c) because I wanted to do my work independently. I had already written a paper on the patients efforts to *correct* the therapist (Langs, 1975a). I had not seen the broader implication in terms of curative efforts.

*Searles:* More affect-laden.

*Langs:* Much more; and much more meaningful, too—and to which you were so sensitive. But many classical analysts object to the whole concept. Some will accept my notion that sometimes patients may try unconsciously to be corrective, but they don't believe patients really try to be curative; you—and I—do. And once I read the title of your paper, I knew that you were right; and I got into many interesting areas just based on the title—it was that meaningful to me. When I read your comment about your own analysis, I was able in retrospect to go over my own analysis, which was not only classical but which had a tighter frame than yours—though with the usual share of generally accepted deviations. And I began to realize that of course I too had been involved in such activities.

*Searles:* You mean your work with your patients?

*Langs:* No, I mean in my own analysis, with my analyst.

*Searles:* Oh, yes, your curative—

*Langs:* Yes, but I never even recognized this dimension. I could now identify some of it—in retrospect. And, of course, I think that everything that I've written has exactly that quality, too. If my analyst read my books, he would know what I was trying to help him

to resolve his countertransference—just as my writings are, on one
level, an attempt to resolve countertransferences shared by most
analysts today. Winnicott said that whenever an analyst writes, it is
an effort to complete his own analysis (1949). Well, the other side of
his own cure is his analyst's cure.

*Searles:* It makes a lot of sense, yes, very interesting.

*Langs:* I wanted to interject some of that in response to what you
were saying. But the fact that you were able to become aware of such
unconscious curative efforts in your patients, and especially in
yourself, reminds me of one aspect of Freud's great accomplishments: he confronted mankind's repression of unconscious processes
and contents, and fractured that barrier and became aware of so
much. I am mindful that I am comparing you with Freud, but I mean
it sincerely: there are certain collective repressions and denials that
you were able uniquely to modify. Do you have any thoughts about
all of this?

*Searles:* Well, I've got plenty of thoughts about that, plenty of
thoughts about that.
    I've said that my mother was schizoid and I think that she basically
was—had a kind of woodeness about her in social relations, some of
them. Had a curious nonsexuality about her in some ways; she had a
lot of sexuality, too, but she was like a little girl in a way. Now one
place where her schizoid and depressive qualities would show would
be at the luncheon table. The four of us would be sitting around the
table, a small table, and she would be staring off into the infinite
distance and I, who sat on her right—it was a square table—would
pass my hand in front of her eyes. It annoyed me that she would do
that, and she wouldn't react with anger to my response but she would
react to it; she would come out of her preoccupation. I took it upon
myself, in other words, to do something about her detachment which
the others didn't; I never saw any of them do so.
    In fact, my father, on occasion, would say at the dinner table in
another room—I remember him saying one time, anyhow: "Bud,
there sits the noblest woman in the world." Parenthetically, I've told
you what a male chauvinist pig he was, but he was also a romanticist,
and he meant this in some kind of hysterical, romantic way. He also
had his hysterical side. My mother, poor thing, didn't know how to

react when he said that. She would look vaguely pleased but very uncomfortable, very self-conscious. So such a thing would only augment her schizoid quality.

So I was trying to do something about my mother and she also gave me to feel awfully guilty about her depressive aspects. She often complained of "feeling sick inside" and typically took a nap after lunch for an hour or so; but this never had a quality of her simply needing a bit of rest. It always had a quality of there being something wrong in mother about which the family lived in fear and guilt, and the something wrong wasn't all that intangible, as years went on, because the doctor in Binghamton, a nearby city—we did a lot of going to Binghamton to doctors—the doctor said that she needed her gall bladder removed. She had recurrent symptoms that were considered due to cholecystitis, and we didn't have enough money to finance my mother's getting a gall bladder operation. This was in an era and in a place where we weren't poor enough to be a charity case, and yet we didn't have enough money to pay a few hundred dollars for an operation. So we had every reason to feel that there was mother, unwell inside, and to our great shame and guilt and humiliation we couldn't do anything about it.

Then my father, I've told you of his many illnesses that caused me a great deal of anguish that I couldn't assuage—anguish and guilt. He showed considerable suicidal proclivities. He never made a suicide attempt to the best of my knowledge. But we lived a hundred yards from a railroad bridge. I told you the railroad was only twenty-five feet in back of the building, and we lived on a curve, the outside of a curve, so that as the train came around the curve it really felt as though it was running right through our kitchen. Perhaps you have seen this Woody Allen movie recently, *Annie Hall,* and he shows Annie his boyhood home under the roller coaster. It was very similar. But the bridge was about a hundred yards down the line and my Dad would carry the garbage in a pail down to the bridge and throw it in the river, and there were many, many times during the depression when I had an uneasy feeling—and I think the others in the family did, too, but we never vocalized to one another—that he might never come back, that he would throw himself into the river.

We had on the back porch a clothesline—an ordinary clothesline, old, though, and joined by a little wrapping twine, much smaller than clothesline—and he used to casually put his elbows on this line and lean out over the railing and watch the trains go by. He knew that goddamned little line could have busted and if it had he would have probably broken his neck; it was quite a fall. But in these ways, these tangential ways, there were intimations that he might kill himself. So I had reason to be concerned about him. Years later, he confided to me, one time, "If I ever get my asthma back, I don't know if I'll go through with it." He was clearly implying that he might, in that event, suicide. I simply replied, "That's up to you." By then, you see, I had had so many years of implicit suicidal threats from him that I quietly declined to go on any longer feeling cowed by these threats. Several years later still, he died of a coronary occlusion, when he was sixty-five and I was thirty-four.

I told you about this concern to help people; it wasn't within the family there. It didn't get felt that way; but I think it was contributing.

In any case, Ernest Hadley helped me to become more aware of my wish to help him. I'll tell you one way how he did. Late in my analysis or perhaps after it—no, I don't think so, I think it was late during it—he had to have a bladder operation, a relatively minor one. I think he had a polyp in his bladder. He didn't have to have his bladder removed, but he had to have a bit of a bladder operation, and I went to see him in the hospital and he wasn't feeling well, and in the course of my being there he threw back the bed covers and showed me that he had a catheter in his penis and some bandages holding it there, and any sexual meaning that may have had—exhibitionistic sexual meaning—was very much submerged in his showing me that he was uncomfortable and in physical distress and I was put in, and felt myself to be in, a comforting kind of position toward him, a maternal position I would say, a maternal position.

I remember once saying to him in the analysis sometime much earlier something about how hard he worked. He once confided to me, in a spirit of bitter resignation, that he was working himself to death; he said that clearly. At another time it wasn't in response to any such cynical bitterness on his part, but it was simply an expression of commendation from me to him about how conscientious he was, and how hard he worked and so on, and it was sincere; I really feel it was sincere. I remember his shifting about uncomfortably. He couldn't stand the—I think it was—real expression of positive appreciation of him, but at least he made it possible for me to say it to him.

He didn't rule out my being aware of such a dimension in him. And when I finished my analysis, toward the end of it I came to notice, or think more about, something at my elbow that had been there all along—a set of little figures, horses. Now, parenthetically, I knew that he liked horses, and he had had occasion, relatively early in the analysis, to tell me how as a young man on his ranch where he had grown up, he used to be so strong that he could take a horse by the throat and control the horse, gripping it, steadying it, and I've since learned that he told a number of other people that. I have to assume that he would tell that story at a particular time when he was feeling particularly threatened. I have to assume that. He was a moderately powerfully built guy, not a real big fellow, but a muscular kind of a man, probably in his fifties. I don't know just how old he was when I started, fifty years old or so. But as for his being able to help me or let me become aware of my therapist-orientation toward him—I was trying to talk a little more about the completion of the analysis.

I became aware of these little horses, and I knew of his love for horses, then I realized that they were gifts from people who had completed their analysis. He didn't say that and I didn't ask him but I just realized that they were and I just knew that and I, as we agreed about my completing—it wasn't precipitous, really—I bought him a bull, a ceramic bull, bigger than most of these damned horses, very different from them, and I gave him that and he put that along these things. That doesn't have to do with this therapist stuff as far as I know, but then he had let me know—

*Langs:* It does of course, yes.

*Searles:* Does it?

*Langs:* Well, sure: your gift to him is related to his need for a gift from you. You know, Freud did that too: he rationalized by saying that termination is very difficult for the patient, and a gift to the analyst makes it easier for the patient to terminate. This came up in the Wolf Man's analysis, where he gave Freud a statue of an Egyptian god and was very proud to see it later on in the photographs of Freud's office. So there is a tradition there, but let me say this much since I've started to talk. I was going to hear you out, but you see, it's not only that he communicated a need for you to serve as therapist to him, there's more to the situation. For instance, Olinick (1969), whom you may know, has written that he found that one major unconscious motive for becoming an analyst is a need to work out a relationship with a drepressed mother. He doesn't quite say to cure her, but he's clearly implying that element. So, we all have such unconscious therapeutic strivings, which, of course, you have described very explicitly. Now, I'm trying to understand how it came so much to the fore in your conscious thinking, and how you were able to recognize it as a general principle.

*Searles:* You're going to get the main share of your answer when I tell you more about my Chestnut Lodge experience.

*Langs:* Let me first respond to this part of the answer. You see, what you described then is an analyst who not only overtly invited such responses, but also never understood their actual basis, I suspect, interpreting them primarily as transference—if he interpreted this aspect at all. He sought out your therapeutic efforts in very active ways, and it included major modifications in the frame. I refer to the whole business of your visit to him in the hospital, and his exposing himself to you—and all the rest. And such breaks in the frame contain within them a tremendous impetus for the patient to work over not only his own disturbance and response to it, but also the disturbance of the analyst that gets expressed as a result. As I said before, deviations are the vehicle for powerful pathological unconscious communications that the patient both exploits and tries to resolve. You have been very sensitive to the ways in which interpretations, valid and erroneous, and failures to interpret, and the analyst's general attitude, place meaningful introjects into the patient. The management of the frame has exactly the same implications. As a result, appropriate management of the framework can lead to positive introjects and adaptive cognitive insights, while mismanagements evoke negative introjects and uninsightful interludes—which nonetheless can be turned into something enormously creative and constructive.

As I said, your own gifts and sensitivities, and your capacity to become consciously aware of this, is striking. After all, you certainly are not the only analysand who has experienced this kind of thing. I am reminded of the paper you refer to (Searles, 1975); I think it was Singer (1970) who shared a personal illness with his patients—

*Searles:* His wife's illness.

*Langs:* His wife's illness; and he described how they responded so therapeutically. Well, there is, as I said, always a mixed response: consciously there will be this kind of seemingly positive reaction, but unconsciously there is a negative reaction to the therapist's or analyst's need to impose this need upon the patient, you see. The unconscious component tends to be split off. And here you are describing really massive inputs from your analyst, asking you directly to be therapeutic toward him in a host of ways.

*Searles:* In saying, "I'm working myself to death."

*Langs:* I'm working myself to death; thank you for coming, but now really look at what I'm suffering with. Help me, do something, give me a gift at the end. Oddly enough, in one sense, the gift is almost a relatively sublimated form of what he was asking of you.

*Searles:* Well, now the bull is what—a sexual symbol? Is that what you mean, the particular gift?

*Langs:* Well no, I was just thinking of his requests to you.

*Searles:* I thought the bull expressed my obstinacy, my going against the grain, the conventional grain, and most obviously stubborness, it seemed to me.

*Langs:* Well, to speculate: I would think it also expresses an introject—an image of him that you had taken in.

*Searles:* Yes, he once said that one of his watchwords—he didn't use that word, but he gave me to understand that his basic philosophy was that everybody is free to go to hell in his own particular fashion, which is a lot like my old man—the cynicism.

*Langs:* Right, which brought it up again—as an actual repetition of the past. I feel, and again this is only a hypothesis and I wouldn't attempt to validate it. But based on many observations of my own— let me put it this way, because it struck me this way—you knew

almost as much about his narrative life history as he knew about
yours. Obviously this was not exactly the case, but you knew so much
about his life history.

*Searles:* I knew a few highlights. I didn't feel that I knew in detail
of his background.

*Langs:* Oh, no. I'm saying that a limited narrative history came
out, almost as if he were saying, "Here is my story, help me come to
terms with what is still unresolved."

*Searles:* I formed the idea while I was in analysis, or certainly soon
after, that I think is worth somebody's doing research in, the idea that
an analyst at the beginning of the analysis could provide to his
analysand a quite detailed personal history and that it would have
little or no effect upon the analysis. I've had this feeling that we are
much too guarded about divulging personal details; but I'm mindful
that for the analyst to give a few sheets of paper to an analysand with
a lot of historical details about the analyst is completely different
from the analyst's saying something in an affective way.

*Langs:* I would think that it would have a tremendous detrimental
influence, as a major modification of the frame. I think that all of this
would constitute the misuse of the patient as therapist to the analyst.
There are significant differences for the patient when requests for
cure come unconsciously from the analyst through his inadvertent
errors, and when they arise in more deliberate form—the latter is far
more pathological on the analyst's part and far more disruptive for
the patient. Do you know Bion's (1977) work?

*Searles:* Not much. I read his "Attacks on Linking" (Bion, 1959) a
couple of times. I have his two books but I haven't yet started reading
them.

*Langs:* A lot of what you're writing about relates to the Kleinian
concept of projective identification, and I want to get into that with
you. Bion (1962, 1970) writes about projective identification in terms
of containing functions—the container and the contained. I trust
you can get a feeling for the metaphor. And I think that one of the

unconscious motives for becoming an analyst is to make pathological, inappropriate use of the patient as a container for our pathology, you see (Langs, 1976a).

*Searles:* It makes a great deal of sense, right.

*Langs:* And it is a question how blatantly this is expressed, and
how well you are able to control it—how much you can resolve.

*Searles:* I wrote something similar to that, without using the word
"container," just recently in a paper—something I'm going to give
up at this Masterson conference (Masterson 1978) in the fall—the
borderline conference.

*Langs:* Oh yes, you've written of similar concepts throughout
your papers. I think that some of your sensitivity came from the
experiences that you had, and that there remains more of an unconscious than conscious appreciation of some of the consequences of
these deviations. I would suggest, in the context of this discussion—
for what it's worth—that the notion of giving the patient these sheets
of paper is a very concrete request to the patient for some help.

*Searles:* Maybe so, maybe so. My thought had been that the power
of the transference is so great that it would override such reality data
as that, without distorting to any significant degree the analysand's
evolving transference, as compared to an analysand who had been
provided no such information. That the evolution of the transference
would be pretty much the same—maybe not, but—

*Langs:* I don't think so. Your attitude for the moment is typical of
those who deny the implications of actuality and interactional
realities. In general, you have been very sensitive to this in terms of
the need to distinguish transference and nontransference. You've
also pointed out that incorporations from the analyst can be inte-
grated into, or contribute to, the patient's symptoms. I don't think at
all of a kind of natural or inevitable evolution of the so-called
"transference neurosis." No, for me that is a denial-based myth. I
think that the patient's pathology and assets unfold entirely in the
interaction with the analyst.

*Searles:* It immediately strikes me as making sense.

*Langs:* I think we are being defensive as soon as we try to divorce ourselves from whatever the patient is experiencing.

*Searles:* It immediately makes sense to me as you say that. Let me— shall I slog a little further?

*Langs:* Yes, I would appreciate that. I just want to remind you of something you said (Searles, 1975) that I would like to hear more about. Your statement, and it was clearly something you thought a good deal about, was that the frustration of curative efforts is the single most important factor in neurosis and psychosis.

*Searles:* I know. It may be an overstatement—

*Langs:* You consider it a very powerful factor.

*Searles:* I do; yes I do. I indeed do.

*Langs:* But please go ahead, respond to some of this.

*Searles:* Ernest had told me at one time with—again, he didn't go at great length, but in a brief few comments he expressed that he felt deficient in his knowledge of art, that he had had little experience with it and was aware of his lack. At the time I came for my last interview with him, I brought a gift to him which was the nicest art book I knew of, called *A Treasury of Art Masterpieces*, edited by Thomas Craven. There have been many more impressive ones and beautiful ones since, but at the time that was a very nice one, and I had inscribed it. "To Ernest, my partner in a job well done," and he was very much less appreciative than I had assumed he would be. He was not visibly offended, but he did not find my gift gratifying. He was quite perfunctory, really, and I wondered many times since why he reacted as he did. Did he feel that I was presumptuous in saying that the job had been well done?

I thought later that I knew that he must have thought me presumptuous, because he had let me know toward the end of our work together that he had—he didn't say how many, but I got a distinct sense of something like two dozen criteria for the completion of an analysis. He didn't say how many of those he evaluated me as having fulfilled. I say "me" because it was me; it wasn't this analysis. It wasn't that mutual. It was *me*, how many did *I* fulfill. He didn't say that, but I had every reason to feel that he had evaluated me in terms of how many of those criteria had I fulfilled, and my distinct sense of it, again, was that I had fulfilled something like half of them. In other words, he was a very perfectionistic man. He had told me what a wonderful feeling it is to know from the top of one's head to the tip of one's toes that one does not have to be omnipotent. He had said that in just approximately so many words, and I'm pretty sure I was sceptical at the time, and certainly soon after. I have cynically thought he must have read that somewhere, because he had so little accomplished that task in his own personality; he was so perfectionistic.

But anyhow, I gave him this book—"my partner in a job well done"—and I think that it alluded to our very first interview (although I didn't have that in mind at the time) when I had said, "Do you see any reason why we can't work together?" and he had said, "Hell, no!" And only as I tell you does some of this sink into me, does it sink into me that we had not worked together.

See, that's not fair to him; he's dead—and it's the same with Sullivan. It is a cheap thing to say negative things about someone who has died. I was enormously grateful to Ernest Hadley for what I had gained from him. I was enormously grateful for many years afterward, and it's only been in the last ten or fifteen years that it's more and more become evident to me how very much was not done, how very much was not done.

*Langs:* These are the realities.

*Searles:* But there was a clear link as I see it now between the first session and the final one in terms of the work together and I think that we did work together, we really did work together. I think that one of the ways I was trying to help him was to acknowledge more that we had worked together. I really felt that I was less schizoid than Ernest Hadley and I think a lot of people would confirm that. That wasn't grandiosity. I had a kind—for all this catatonic stuff in the group therapy—of worldliness about me that he didn't have.

*Langs:* Yes, that you wanted to help him have—your gift. This last point brings up again how the gift serves to undo separation; his acceptance of the gift deprived you of the opportunity to really separate, and to analyze and resolve the related issues.

*Searles:* Well, I could tell you more about this that is evidently of interest to you. He had analyzed Dexter Bullard, Sr., who owned Chestnut Lodge and he took it upon himself to talk me up to Dexter Bullard. I don't know his words; but he said to Dexter that I would be a good person to have on the staff or a resident out there and Ernest reported back to me at one time—I didn't ask him to do that, but he reported to me that Dexter had said, "Not yet." I guess Dexter had asked him some details about how far along in analysis I was—I have to assume that—and that I hadn't accomplished enough to warrant my being taken on the staff there. So that was very, very strange stuff for a classical psychoanalyst to be engaging in, let me tell you, as I don't need to tell you.

*Langs:* Yes, all of this relates to some very real issues and to some vital principles of technique.

*Searles:* I'm trying to get to something that is relevant. He twice tried to get me to set up an office in his suite of offices. There were only three offices there altogether.

*Langs:* How did you react to that?

*Searles:* I reacted instantly with appreciation, but no thank you, that I want to get myself weaned away from you or from this situation. I wasn't discourteous or tactless because I did feel honored and touched; but I knew that I wanted to get the analysis over. He didn't say that it would continue the analysis; but I knew damned well that it would postpone the separation, so I said no thank you. He said that twice; he proposed it not just two days or so apart, but at two different phases late in the analysis.

*Langs:* Here, I think of your sensitivity to the therapeutic symbiosis, and the difficulty that the analyst has in giving it up.

*Searles:* I was well aware of that at the time.

*Langs:* Yes, and you were conscious of it and you were able to not participate at that point.

The other comment I wanted to make about the art book is that it came up as we were talking about your therapeutic efforts on his behalf. Here was something he consciously lacked. He didn't state it in terms of his emotional conflicts and needs, but as some attribute that he didn't have, and that he wished he had.

*Searles:* That I had some of.

*Langs:* And you had some of it, which again he wanted to take in from you. See, I get the feeling—I don't know if this is of any value to you at all—but I get the feeling that he reacted the way he did because something finally struck him about what hadn't been worked through; that he somehow sensed the unconscious meanings of this gift, in terms of your therapeutic strivings toward him. It may just suddenly have confronted him with his massive needs for you and for therapeutic efforts from you. This is sheer speculation, but the whole way in which this discussion has unfolded suggests that idea—you have also written about the guilt of the analyst.

If the analyst asks too much of his patients therapeutically, there are detrimental effects. We are never entirely free of such needs and communications. The analyst's therapeutic benefits should come implicitly or secondarily, through the inevitabilities of the interaction, the inevitabilities of major countertransference-based errors cropping up and of a countertransference-based element which creeps in some small way into every intervention. The analyst's pathology plays a consistent role, but should be kept to a minimum and quickly resolved within himself through self-analysis, without directly burdening the patient.

It is just fascinating to me that, as we have examined this area, you have been able to identify so many ways in which your analyst did communicate, virtually explicitly, such needs from you. And you can see that such requests, on the surface, are very flattering. They are quite gratifying in several ways—on one level—and yet again you could begin to think about some of the residuals. But the creative part was that you recognized what was going on. You were able to write about it, and how few people have been able to do that. When I read the literature, I find that so few writers get around to your papers. But

that's so typical; in this area, as I've said, almost no one wants to
know the bibliography; nobody wants to write papers; so few really
want to know what's going on. It's not a personal issue, as I see it.
And you offer so much to someone who would be open enough to
read your work, but many analysts, without realizing it, are afraid to
acknowledge these aspects of the analytic interation. They confront
them with their unresolved countertransferences and threaten their
pathological defenses. And the fact that you were able to do this I
think is very crucial, very creative.

*Searles:* I have a couple of things that I would like to show you, it
will just take about two or three minutes, okay, just take time out?

*Langs:* Sure.

*Searles:* [Searles tries briefly and unsuccessfully to locate the manuscript of the first paper he had written for intended publication in
1949, which Langs brought to publication in 1978 as a result of the
present dialogue.] The first part of it is that transference attaches
itself to real components of the analyst. That was the first part—and
the second part, I can't remember now what it was. It never got
published, but that was where my interests were—that was while I
was in analysis still, that I submitted that.

*Langs:* Yes, I was going to ask you. When did you begin to write?
And what did you first write?

*Searles:* That 1949 (Searles 1978-1979) paper was my first one. This
one [now referring to the manuscript of Searles 1977b] is going to be
published by Kenneth Frank, up at Columbia, who is going to be the
editor of the book in which it'll appear. This paper contains a couple
more vignettes from the analysis, if I have time to tell you about
them.

*Langs:* Please do.

*Searles:* Should I read it?

*Langs:* Sure, whatever is easier.

*Searles:* In this paper entitled, "The Development of Mature Hope in the Patient-Therapist Relationship," I said:

"I have a vivid memory of an experience of mine as a patient in analysis, more than twenty years ago, when I became conscious of a previously repressed hope entirely at odds with what I had felt to be my singlemindedly hoped for goal—namely, my parting from the analyst. From very early on in the analysis, my feelings about being there had oscillated between a conviction that I was on the verge of such overwhelming insanity that, as I frequently admonished the analyst, 'You'd better get a bed ready for me at Chestnut Lodge' (one measure of my true nuttiness being that I assumed that, for anyone so special as an analytic candidate, the Institute would arrange free treatment at that expensive place, where I had not yet gone to work), and a conviction, on the other hand, that I was so manifestly and totally well that the analysis had now become absurdly superfluous.

"At the time the incident in question occurred, my self-evaluations had pretty much stopped oscillating and I had long since settled into a consistent, unremittent bellyaching that the analyst was refusing to let me have done with this idiotically unnecessary analysis. He indicated the end of the session during which, for the $n$th time, I had been carping thus. I got up from the couch, as usual.

"The next thing I knew, I was walking toward him; he was standing by his chair, no doubt preparatory to my walking out the door as usual. As I walked the couple of steps to him, I did so suffused with romantic love of which I had been entirely unaware, but which had a quality of having been there all along. I embraced him and said, fondly, pleadingly, companionably, and above all romantically, 'Ernest, *when* are we going to get this analysis over with?' I referred to the analysis, here, clearly as being in the nature of some inherently meaningless courtship-ritual which was being imposed from without upon both of us, and which we had to get behind us in order, at long last, to consumate our fully-mutual love for one another. For all my gripingly impatient hope of getting the analysis over with, it was now immediately clear to me that I unconsciously had not had the slightest intention of leaving him; my unconscious hope had been, on the contrary, for us fully to possess one another.

"Incidentally, I give him high marks, indeed, for his reaction to all this. His neither returning my embrace nor saying a word, left me free to make this discovery without his being, on any mature and realistic level, rejecting or scornful of me, or threatened by what I was doing. I assume that he had long been aware of my unconscious romantic attachment to him, for he showed not the slightest trace of surprise.

"Before going on to the next aspect of this paper, I shall present a second bit of relevant patient-data from my own analysis. When I went to Dr. Ernest Hadley for my initial interview, I went with the conscious hope of finding relief from a great deal of severe anxiety and despair and, far less importantly to me, of discharging successfully the training-analysis requirement for graduation from the analytic institute. He was standing outside the door of his office when I walked toward it from the waiting room. I had the distinct sense—not a delusion, but a nonetheless vivid fantasy—that he, standing there, was Cerberus, the three-headed dog which guards the entrance to Hades.

"I have remembered this impression many times during the more than quarter century since, and have never thought much about it, beyond preening myself a bit at this evidence of some familiarity with mythology. Only during the last few years have I found it significant that I was not so afraid, after all, that Dr. Hadley would not let me *escape from* his office (Hell), but rather that he would not *let me into* it. You see, early in our third session, my first training analyst had suddenly stood up and permanently dismissed me. The despair which I brought into the first session with Dr. Hadley was despair lest I would prove hopelessly unable to communicate my innermost feelings to any human being. At the end of that first session, during which I had sat, following his direction, in a chair opposite him, I asked, 'Do you see any reason why we can't work together?' He assured me, briefly but emphatically, 'Hell, no!'

"The point I am trying to make here is that it was only a few years ago that I realized that the Cerberus-Hell imagery indicated that, at the time, I unconsciously *hoped* the analysis would prove to be hell, a sought-for hell which I feared that its guardian, Cerberus, would prevent me from entering. It would take me too far afield, here, to pursue in detail the determinants of my hope that the analysis would be hell" (Searles, 1977b, pp. 10-11).

And then I go on with some details about why my unconscious guilt, where it had come from in childhood, I think.

Do you want me to tell you a little about that Chestnut Lodge stuff?

*Langs:* Yes, do you want to say anything about this as it connects to what we've been talking about?

*Searles:* I mention it as to the termination thing. I had wanted rid of the analysis, at one early juncture in it, for something other than worthy, mature wishes to be free of a symbiosis. There was an awful lot of denial involved in my romantic attachment to him.

*Langs:* What I'm impressed with in this context is the way in which you expressed yourself again through a modification in the frame, through the direct physical contact. In my experience that type of response usually occurs when the analyst has also been modifying the frame. Freud (1912) and Greenacre (1954) said something like this: one modification begets another. Modifications by the analyst stimulate the patient toward those kinds of expressions as well.

You can see how often we come back to the framework. And the particular form of expression that you described is filled with meaning—that it was enacted rather than experienced in some other form. It seems to me, overall, that the many deviations that you experienced personally influenced your subsequent writings. And I think that your experience is more typical than not, but that your adaptive responses over the years have been rather unique and innovative. Frankly, I believe you will find this an interesting area to think about. It was such a pervasive problem. And it was treated as a bastion—it never was analyzed. Perhaps this is one reason why, in light of your unusual sensitivities, the frame was excluded from your writings. I've begun to realize that the pervasiness of deviations in so-called training analyses has led to major countertransferences and blind spots in regard to the frame in a vast majority of analysts.

*Searles:* I shrank back when you said that you were going to tell me frankly.

*Langs:* I'm sorry I put it that way.

*Searles:* Because I had the fantasy that you were going to say, "You have never had any analysis at all."

*Langs:* Yes, but these are the fears that we all entertain on some

level when we get to know the implications of what happened in our
own analyses. But that's what's fascinated me about your insights.
Even with my sensitivity to these realities and their consequences,
and my awareness that I too in my analysis experienced all sorts of
deviations, I could only take my research so far—you extended my
findings. Incidentally, I too am very much aware of many constructive helpful dimensions to my analysis; I wouldn't be here today if it
wasn't for my analysis—and I mean that in the most positive sense. It
seems to have unleashed important elements of creativity in me; I do
not see myself as inherently innovative.

   *Searles:* It certainly unleashed a lot.

   *Langs:* Yes, it's not part of my self-image and it never was. That's
why *The Bipersonal Field* (Langs 1976a) will always be one of my
favorite books. I became creative by getting in touch with the
unconscious creativity of the patients presented to me. It's the only
way I knew; it is the only way I still know. I can't create the things
that patients can unconsciously evolve—in one or two words or
sentences, and so beautifully.

   *Searles:* I have patients I feel that way toward, too.

   *Langs:* So, I say this in terms of trying to maintain a balanced
view. I'm very critical of many of these practices and oversights. I
think they have their destructive dimensions that are unnecessary;
they will be eliminated if we learn more and discover how to better
manage our countertransferences. At the same time, these errors and
deviations need not fully destroy the analytic experience—though
sometimes they do just that. Some very, very positive things may
come out of it nonetheless. It's often a matter of sectors of misalliance; though, as I said, I do think there are deviations and errors
that can basically undermine the entire analytic experience. Still,
patients are very resilient; they can tolerate a great deal and can
handle a lot without going crazy—though that is in no way a licence
for the analyst to be abusive—consciously or unconsciously. I think
that analysts have underestimated, as you very well know, their
patient's intact ego functioning, especially their unconscious capacities. I was so pleased when you spoke of regression, not as some
helpless abandonment to psychosis, but as an adaptive response.

Well, I've said a lot. Perhaps you can now finish up Chestnut Lodge.

*Searles:* I could start Chestnut Lodge. There is so much to it; but I will at least get a start on it.

At the V. A., as I mentioned to you earlier, I had had this borderline patient who said, "You *are* angry at me, *aren't* you?" and I had either disclaimed that I was, or had proved totally unable to confirm that I was. And when I got out to Chestnut Lodge I got this first patient, a man who was in his third admission to Chestnut Lodge, a paranoid schizophrenic man about thirty years of age, and who in his second hospitalization there had cut his throat with a straight razor and would have died had Alfred Stanton, who was a doctor on call that day, not gotten there with unpredictable promptness. In other words he was a very, very ill man—very, very ill—and he, and similarly ill subsequent patients, were patients for whom the classical model wasn't adequate.

It quickly became evident that you had not only to become able to feel anger toward these people, you had to become able to express it— to find ways to express it. They could not make do with a classical analytic thing, and in my opinion that's still true, notwithstanding Boyer's reporting (1961) that a relatively classical model is indicated for these people. I like and respect Bryce Boyer a great deal; but I cannot go along with that particular concept of his.

*Langs:* Yes, let's define that. What do you mean when you say a classical model?

*Searles:* Well, a classical analytic model would involve the analyst's not expressing any feeling toward the patient other than a relatively impersonally friendly interest and attentiveness.

*Langs:* Concern?

*Searles:* Yes. It would not involve—as the simplest prototype—his expressing anger to a patient.

*Langs:* What would he do if he was feeling anger toward the patient? What do you think the model would call for? And what if the patient either consciously or unconsciously perceived it?

*Searles:* What would he do? He would withdraw from the patient. He could not stay with those patients [at Chestnut Lodge]. He couldn't stand it. They were too maddening. He couldn't simply sit and feel furious and think tactically how to use the fury; he couldn't do it. They were too overwhelming for that, these patients. They were too difficult to be with, too difficult.

*Langs:* So the variation in the classical model as you have defined it is that there are times when the analyst must directly express his conscious hatred and tell the patient of it.

*Searles:* I think that he needs to have some opportunity for catharsis, really, in working with people that ill. Now, I say that with some misgivings, because it may not be true. I *can* say it's true that I *think* that that's the case.

*Langs:* Yes, it's a delicate issue. How familiar are you with Winnicott's writings in this area?

*Searles:* Fairly familiar, I've read a moderate amount of his work.

*Langs:* "Hate in the Countertransference" (Winnicott, 1949).

*Searles:* Yes, I read that and Hadley read that. At the time that came out, Hadley made a couple of references to it and was obviously very stimulated by it; it was a new thing, yes.

*Langs:* Well, Winnicott specifically stated that at some time the patient has to explicitly experience your hatred. I think that it's in that particular paper that he said there are some twenty ways that the mother expresses her hatred for her child. The analyst, too, has ways of expressing his hatred of the patient, such as ending sessions, being silent, and creating a necessary but depriving frame—things of that sort. So that there are ways, channels, of expressing inevitable feelings of hatred, but you are saying that at times you feel that an explicit allusion to them is necessary?

*Searles:* Very explicit expression of it, in quite blunt terms.

*Langs:* Verbally?

*Searles:* Yes, verbal, Yes, I worked there fourteen and a half years. I never hit a patient; but one time a man and a woman simultaneously attacked me. They were working in conjunction. They had a relationship together. They were both very paranoid and both attacked me at once. It was not a really dangerous attack, but I was enough put upon—and there were no aides to help me—so that I kind of hit at them. I don't know that I hit either of them at all seriously; but these were very, very ill patients out there.

*Langs:* Unfortunately, we must stop now. This has been a most illuminating beginning. I look forward to our next meeting with great anticipation.

*Chapter 2*
# REACTIONS TO NEW IDEAS
# IN PSYCHOANALYSIS

*Langs:* I thought that perhaps we should begin where we left off. I felt that the narrative that you were developing—and we just started, if you remember the last time, to get into some discussion of technical issues—but the narrative was really very, very interesting, and moving and useful. You had reached the point where you had just gone up to Chestnut Lodge.

*Searles:* I had not actually remembered with any clarity where we had left off last time and I was meaning to ask you. I couldn't remember whether we had gotten beyond the period of work at the Lodge.

*Langs:* No, I would like to hear about it. This is helping to give a different, more personal tracing of your development—as compared to your preface in your 1965 book where you so nicely trace out the formal development of your ideas in various areas. I've been getting a remarkably frank and lucid picture of the development of your career. And we were learning how your interests and ideas developed. So, if you can kind of get back into that mood, and flow. You were just beginning to approach how you came to Chestnut Lodge and what happened there.

*Searles:* I see. Well let me ask this. I am so apt to get bogged down in reminiscences about Chestnut Lodge that I want to ask if you have any thought about how far along you would like for us to get today in any narrative?

*Langs:* I don't want to tax you too much. Let's keep it open. If there is a lot to say about your stay at the Lodge—your reminiscences—then let's hear it. I'm certain that we are going to get into a lot of important issues. Get yourself into it and let's see where it goes.

*Searles:* All right.

I can't recall the spirit in which I went there. It was certainly a prestige thing. The Lodge has high prestige locally as well as farther afield. The people there were very cliquish. During my previous two years at the V. A. Mental Hygiene Clinic, they had rubbed me the wrong way very much—and I can say that just in recent months, incidentally, something occurred that gave me that old feeling of being shut out from the Chestnut Lodge clique or club. I have been in full-time private practice, away from there, for so many years.

Now I wasn't at all long in getting accepted by the club. It never occurred to me that I would have difficulty in that regard, once I had obtained the position—that would be a wrong impression to give. I went there promptly enough, after a couple of years of work as a psychiatrist at the V. A. clinic and while I was still in analysis.

*Langs:* When you touch upon something that evokes a question that I wanted to ask you—or a necessary comment—I would like to interupt if I may. Feeling outside of the club is, I think, a very important experience.

*Searles:* That's how I feel toward the American Psychoanalytic Association, to a very large extent. Now, I am a member of it, and I've developed, through a bit of work I've done in the American, a very solid respect for the people I've worked with; but I've worked there all too little with them. I've to a large extent shunned them.

*Langs:* Yes, and what has their attitude been toward you? One of the subjects that I wanted to discuss further with you has to do with the mainstream of American psychoanalysis, the classical analysts, and your impressions of your relationship with them. Perhaps we can talk about this globally, as well as specifically. There are impressions that I have that I want to share with you and it is something that I am familiar with personally. And I would like to hear your thoughts about why things are the way they are, as you experienced them. Could you say some more about that?

*Searles:* Well, my feelings about Chestnut Lodge are so complex, and in a way so heavy, that it is very difficult for me to get into them with any strong hope of getting back out of them again, you see, at all soon. The word that came to mind is that I adored the place. I never thought of that before—that I adored Chestnut Lodge. I was aware of being enormously attached to it—and by "it" I mean it includes a lot of the nonhuman environment. It is a beautiful place, very beautiful place. The patients I worked with I became very profoundly attached to. The staff members I enjoyed working among, even though I was a relatively reclusive type of person—not as much so as a few of the people there, but definitely on the reclusive side.

The first book I wrote was *The Nonhuman Environment* (Searles, 1960). I talked with Frieda Fromm-Reichmann briefly about it, and I don't remember just what encouragement she gave me; she gave me some encouragement. I showed her a one-page outline of what I had in mind, and she encouraged me to go ahead with it.

*Langs:* What year was that?

*Searles:* Well, I don't remember any more. It was very early in my stay there. I went there in 1949. That first book appeared in 1960; but I started working on it several years before it appeared. I have files that would locate that date [which proved to be in 1955 at the latest—possibly a year earlier]. Once I set to work on it, I did not tell my colleagues what I was working on, and I think that none of my colleagues knew what I was working on, really. It is an example of how privately I worked—even though in other regards there was a lot of rubbing elbows with the colleagues there, and I was very proud of having the most sought-after "small group" as years went on that anyone had there.

*Langs:* This would be a small group?

*Searles:* A small discussion group that met twice a week. The whole staff of about twenty-four psychiatrists were divided into about four groups, each of which met at a regularly scheduled time for an hour on a Tuesday and an hour and a half on a Friday to discuss, particularly, countertransference problems—but, really, whatever people were having the most difficulty with in their psychotherapeutic work. It was a technique of psychotherapy and it was something that the sanitarium set up and paid us for doing. It was part of our work there.

*Langs:* About your working in isolation: How much of that came out of a personal inclination? And how much of it did you experience as your working in an area where you didn't feel that there was an opportunity to share ideas, in terms of some unique ideas that you were working over that others did not seem to grasp?

*Searles:* I felt that our whole staff at the time, early at least in my work there, were permeated with a great deal of omnipotent strivings. Surely I was imbued with a tremendous amount of that. I told you how Hadley joked derisively and referred to me as "God Searles."
I was often amused in the staff presentations that occurred once a week—formal staff presentation where the therapist would present his work with a patient; the whole thing would take an hour and a half. It was the big meeting of the week and they were very, very stimulating—very, very worthwhile activities—and as years went on, I felt that a very excellent book could be written about the psychotherapeutic technique of working with schizophrenic patients based primarily upon those staff presentations, because they showed such a wide variety of psychotherapeutic styles, and that's one of the strongest qualities of Dexter Bullard, Sr.—that he left us room to exercise and develop an individual style to quite a great extent, far more than I think is the case in a number of other institutions that I can think of. He thought of it as "letting people run their own show," I think he put it. This was not to any total extent; he very much ran the sanitarium. But there was still room for considerable autonomous functioning.
I was going to say that, as regards the omnipotent strivings, I was often amused that it seemed to me that the characteristic atmosphere of the discussion period following the presentation involved each

person who talked, talking in isolation from the others. Each of them talking, of being his own audience or talking for posterity or talking to God. I wouldn't want to overemphasize it, but I definitely felt that there was a relative lack of providing warm support to one another. Perhaps there isn't much of that, anyway, in post-doctoral kinds of activities; but surely at the Lodge there was a lot of our being caught up in omnipotent aspirations.

*Langs:* What about the other side of it, in terms of rivalry, jealousy, and the like?

*Searles:* Yes, I was thinking, the obvious professional competitiveness was keen. I was going to mention that I was the only one of six applicants selected to work at the Lodge. At the time that I applied, there were six applicants—at least one of whom, I think more than one, I knew. I knew of at least one other who was highly thought of locally. In other words, there was some pretty intense competition for a position at that time.

Again, how to convey in any brief space what that place meant, and means, to me is very, very difficult. Recently when I was getting together my collected papers—or second book of collected papers (Searles, 1979a)—I realized that the reason that I had tended to postpone doing so is because doing that involves my reliving so much of what I went through at Chestnut Lodge, and the one biggest, heaviest feeling, and the strongest feeling I have is of grief— grief that my patients did not thrive more than they did. That has caused me a great deal of grief.

*Langs:* What about—it is way ahead of your narrative—but isn't there some of that grief in response to the separation experience?

*Searles:* From the Lodge? Oh, yes.

*Langs:* I've noticed in your writings that grief and loss come up in that context.

*Searles:* Oh, yes. Another, close second feeling is a sense of loneliness, of missing the companionship of the colleagues who were there when I wanted to come out of my reclusiveness. They were around, and also the nursing staff and the aides, and to a certain extent the patients, in passing, too. But it was a community, very much a kind of community that had complex relationships going on in it.

*Langs:* What you are saying, too, is in keeping with your symbiosis paper (Searles, 1971). You are describing an aspect of the holding environment for the therapist.

*Searles:* Yes. Your book has had such a great impact upon me— I'm about two-thirds through the reading of it right at present. I've been reading it the past few weeks and, as I say, it has had such a strong impact on me that I've been a bit concerned that it would too much influence what would otherwise be a larger picture of my development. But I *have* thought that the whole Lodge is a kind of holding environment for the therapists there.

*Langs:* This is one of the things I wanted to say to you. I really thought about this, and the way I thought it the first time is really the truth: my first thought in reading your symbiosis paper was that I was able to identify certain experiences in my own work with patients that had troubled me, and that you were helping me understand and that I had begun to conceptualize in my own, but strongly related way. So much of what you and I write about, communicate, are so strikingly parallel. It's really fascinating, especially in light of how few analysts have written in these areas. I really experience you as the one analyst who is closest to working over and writing about subjects that I have worked over and discussed. And this was true the first time that we had contact, in relation to your paper on the patient as therapist to the analyst (Searles, 1975), as you may remember.

*Searles:* Yes.

*Langs:* Let me just go over that. I've been wandering a bit, but I think this review will be of interest to you. At the time that you had written that particular paper, I had written one for the same volume (Giovacchini, 1975), called "The Patient's Unconscious Perceptions of the Therapist's Errors" (Langs, 1975a). I had written there of the patient's efforts to correct the therapist—a concept that reflects some of my early intellectualism and the limitations of my interactional ideas. Giovacchini then sent me your paper, "The Patient as Therapist to His Analyst" (Searles, 1975), because it was so closely related to my contribution. And as I said last time we met, I promptly put it in a drawer for about a year or so. As you are saying, I didn't want to be influenced by it—except for the fact that I knew from the title that your concept was broader than mine, and much more to the heart of it. It wasn't just a matter of correcting, and as I have recently put it, supervising (Langs, 1978b); it really was unconscious efforts to cure. And what was typical of the ties between our work was that I then developed a series of observations, largely through the supervision of psychotherapy, and by working with a different kind of patient population from yours, that very extensively confirmed and extended in some ways the observations that you had made with the patient population that you have worked and written most about, the schizophrenic. And it has been utterly fascinating for me to experience this and to wonder about how to account for it. And I must say that I have only the most sparse thoughts on the subject, such as our respective sensitivities to introjective processes in the patient and the influences of the analyst's countertransferences. I should also mention that prior to my recent careful study of your work, I had read just a couple of your papers. I had your book (Searles, 1965), but I don't think I had really read very much in it.

*Searles:* In the collected papers book?

*Langs:* In the collected papers, yes. I had *The Nonhuman Environment* (Searles, 1960), but I must tell you in all honesty, I still haven't gotten to that, except to skim it.

*Searles:* Oh, really?

*Langs:* I've gotten to references to it in your other papers, but I'm now so damned busy, it was hard to do it justice. But I am now preparing to go back to it, because I want to also trace out some more of the particulars of your work. I've even been referring people to it based on my initial impressions.

*Searles:* I refer people to your *Bipersonal Field* (Langs, 1976a) particularly, and recently—

*Langs:* To me, it is with that book that I really begin to get into the areas of interest that we share. I consider my early technique books (Langs, 1973, 1974) as preliminary to this phase—much of it lies latent there, though I am clearly moving toward it. Something happened to me between the writing of the technique books and *The Bipersonal Field;* it was an important period of transition (see Langs, 1978c). So few American analysts—or British—have gotten into these issues; and I feel that you and I are among the exceptions.

As I said before, your symbiosis paper (Searles, 1971) is a case in point. To cite one example: I had been working over the problem of why some patients do not communicate analyzable derivatives. Few analysts have the perceptiveness to see that as a problem; your conception of the autistic phase of therapy or analysis, in which the patient is doing his own therapeutic work and the analyst does not, for the moment, exist as a meaningful object (person), is an effort to comprehend a basis for that phenomenon. I have some different but related ideas, which I have just begun to write about (Langs, 1978a, 1978-1979).

You are, in my experience, one of the few analysts who provides me with ideas that go beyond the hard core of current psychoanalytic thought, and who stimulates in me definitely creative responses, as well. Bion does that for me in other ways—and quite often; a few others do that occasionally for me, such as Khan and André Green— to name two who occur to me right off. And I refer now to concepts that are immediately relevant to the clinical situation and to unre-solved—and seldom recognized—clinical issues.

This relates to our unfinished discussion, a moment ago, regard-ing the mainstream of American psychoanalysis and those who are not in the mainstream. It is my impression that it is the analysts who are far more creative, and far more into—in terms of technique and the clinical situation—into interaction, who are to the periphery, while those analysts who can restate the old theory in ways that deceptively seem original are the heroes, as I would put it, of the main body of analysts, such as the echelon of the American Psycho-analytic Association (see Langs, 1978c, chapter 16). And our literature reflects this deadness or sterility; there are few papers today which touch in a very meaningful way on unique aspects of the analytic and therapeutic interactions that need yet to be understood and resolved.

I seldom have a reaction of the kind that I have in reading much of your work in response to the writings of most of the analysts on technique, or to most of the papers that I read in general. I will find an occassional paper interesting, fascinating—things of this sort. I read all the papers that come into the Journal, as well as a good deal more, so I do a lot of reading of present-day efforts in the field. But the personal experience and sense of innovation is seldom present. With your writings it's almost like a symbiosis forms between you and me, as I read your papers. It has been said of Winnicott that he communicated in a kind of transitional way.

*Searles:* That's a very interesting idea, yes. As to what you were saying a moment ago, I do feel I am a very symbiotically oriented kind of person—very much so.

*Langs:* Yes, and your papers create a symbiotic response in me. There is no question about it. I must tell you I didn't realize this until we talked together and I experienced it that way. But it opens up certain areas of experiencing and understanding that are not otherwise available—just as with a patient, experiencing the interaction leads to realizations that are otherwise closed off.

*Searles:* See, I think that some of this helps account for why I would be so reclusive, you see?

*Langs:* Yes.

*Searles:* If I am not reclusive I get into being so goddamned symbiotic, and it involves feelings of a kind of surrendering to the other person that I find unacceptable to me; so it's a kind of a chronic conflict, really. This *Nonhuman Environment* book (Searles, 1960), when I was writing that—to give you an example of my self-isolating qualities—I finished one of the chapters midway along in the manuscript, and came home and cackled exultantly to my wife, "They'll have to have an oxyacetylene torch to get through that one!" Not many people bother equipping themselves with oxyacetylene torches, so it's no great surprise that the book hasn't been read as much as I often wish it had been.

*Langs:* There are many analysts, however, that hold your work as a whole, and that book in particular, in high regard—including some child analysts I know.

*Searles:* That was my big wish—that the child analysts would find that a very fundamental contribution. I really thought they would, and it was a source of a great deal of hurt to me, and it very much influenced my feelings about the American Psychoanalytic, that such leading lights in it as Edith Jacobson, for instance, never had a good word to say for my contribution. That really bothered me.

*Langs:* Right, yes.

*Searles:* Nor Mahler. Mahler never knew I existed until a very few years ago.

*Langs:* Yes, isn't that discouraging? How does one deal with it? I have similar feelings about my work. And one then wonders if one is being overly narcissistic, and overvaluing his work—it is so difficult to maintain a clear perspective.

*Searles:* Yes. I hope we can get some clarification on this as we go along, because at the Lodge, not only I but the colleagues there, to a degree created their own rejected position, as I think I told you regarding an experience I had at a meeting of the American Psychoanalytic Association in December of 1953. I was on a panel headed by Frieda Fromm-Reichmann, and there were three others of us. It was a panel on intuition, the use of intuition in psychotherapy, something to that effect [the exact title was, "Intuitive Processes in the Psychotherapy of Schizophrenics" (Fromm-Reichmann, 1955)] and as we were talking and presenting our papers, I was struck by how much we all sounded to be martyrs, these heroic martyrs doing—

*Langs:* I just spent last week working over the question of whether I am trying to be a martyr—the initial negative reactions in some quarters to my efforts make such a consideration necessary—it's one of the "rewards" for creativity.

*Searles:* Yes, so I thought there is something here that is curious— that either we are all terrible masochists or we aren't leveling with this audience about the pleasure one gets out of working with schizophrenic patients. We are presenting it too much in terms of the courage it requires, and the dedication and the anguish one goes through, and the terrible feelings of hopelessness, and so on, and we were trying to set ourselves apart—and, I think, to a degree successfully. We managed to set ourselves apart from and above the general run of the colleagues. So that then we would—I, at least, would get feeling, later on over the years, very wounded that they weren't more accepting of me, see? So I was trying to have it both ways.

*Langs:* Yes, but even your reflection on these issues is unique— and again, I share these concerns with you. I have the impression, too, that many innovators in all sorts of fields have been forced to ask themselves these questions in some form—issues of martyrdom and masochistic gratification. Racker (1958) has a paper on the analyst's masochism, the danger of seeking pathological masochistic gratification within the therapeutic interaction. I think that has to be distinguished from nonpathological masochistic qualities in the analyst's experiences that needn't be countertransference-based. So the whole issue of martyrdom and masochism in the analysts or therapists who work with severely disturbed patients is critical, but then, so is the issue of martyrdom in the analyst who writes creatively and who moves against the mainstream. He is going to have to face the ostracism of his colleagues on some level, you see?

*Searles:* That's right, and I faced an awful lot of that—as I'm sure you, too, have done. I faced an awful lot of that. My feelings toward the American Psychoanalytic are based partly on experiences I had when I was working at Chestnut Lodge. I presented papers at the American about eight times, and I'm very proud of having done so. But without any exception that I can remember offhand, the discussant responded in a patronizing kind of fashion. The audience, I thought, liked my papers. I think that's fair to say; in general, the audiences did. But the discussant—the discussions of them were usually given as by a teacher trying to be patient, instructing a pupil about the fundamentals of psychoanalysis. It really annoyed me greatly.

*Langs:* The trend generally is that you should come back to using more classical concepts, the same language—the same mold.

*Searles:* Yes. For example—this wasn't a time when I presented a paper—I remember a Sunday morning plenary session of the American Psychoanalytic at which Robert Waelder was the speaker, and he spoke with such fine disdain of "those who attempt to psychoanalyze schizophrenic patients," and he spoke with rich, humorous disdain, and it really was very shocking to me, because it seemed to be so callously disregardful of what schizophrenic patients were to do. Because the only other things they were receiving in the way of attempted treatment in that era were lobotomy, electoshock treatment, insulin coma, and then, as years went on, more and more drugs.

*Langs:* Have you thought about why they had that attitude toward such work, and whether it is especially characteristic of American analysts?

*Searles:* I haven't thought about it in terms of American psychoanalysts as compared with French ones, for example, or British ones.

*Langs:* I found that the British—well, certainly the Kleinians—are prepared to analyze schizophrenic patients, whatever criticisms we would have of their techniques. I found the British more tolerant of the severely disturbed analysand, and more creative in response to him than I have seen with my colleagues in New York. I find them to have quite a different attitude, far more characteristic of the one that you are describing.

*Searles:* Did I mention to you the first time we met that I have realized, in the years since I left Chestnut Lodge, that I probably inherited an appreciable amount of animosity that Frieda Fromm-Reichmann had engendered? She was a very much beloved and admired person not only locally but, of course, the world over. But she was a fighter. Our view of it at the Lodge was that she would go off to a meeting of the American Psychoanalytic and fight the good fight, and the impression that I had was that she would fight successfully, very strongly, a very powerful person for all of her diminutive stature. But it was also my impression that she did not trouble herself to be particularly diplomatic as to how she felt about some of the more conservative people she encountered at meetings of the American; so that I can believe that they were left smarting by her bluntness. So that then, as I came along on the scene, to some extent—although I don't like to think to any large degree, but to some extent—following in her footsteps, I think probably I inherited some of the animosity that these people had developed toward her.

Since a number of colleagues were closer to Frieda than I was, and since a number of people have figured as importantly as she in my training, it has been difficult for me to realize that many people assume me to have been a protégé of hers. It actually was only a relatively few years ago that it occurred to me—accustomed to regarding myself as an appreciably abrasive person in my own right—that some of the stress I underwent at meetings of the American was, in the sense I've mentioned, inherited from her earlier presentations there.

As for the years at the Lodge, the one biggest thing I learned was that the work with those patients required a degree of explicit, acknowledged emotional involvement with them in the work, greater than a neurotic patient could make do with. This was not a solo discovery I made, but was one that each of the colleagues made in the course of his work there, and it was a common part of the mores there. I mention that partly because a year ago, in June of '76, I went up to Mt. Sinai Hospital in New York and interviewed a patient, who turned out to be a schizoid patient, in front of an audience—a staff there of one hundred and fifty people, residents and senior staff, too. Ed Joseph had arranged for me to come there, and that kind of interviewing has been, incidentally, my favorite professional activity in the years since I left Chestnut Lodge in 1964, and even starting a couple of years or so before I left there. That is something that I am enormously proud of being able to do, is to interview a patient in front of an audience. I interviewed this young woman at Sinai and it was filmed by Peter Robinson Associates. Peter Robinson is a man who did a film called *Asylum*, which has been seen by a fair number of people. I think it's about Ronald Laing's treatment or hospital over in England, or one he used to have. Robinson had filmed, in Canada several years before, an interview Laing did and one I did of a young woman patient. So Robinson and I arranged to have this interview at Sinai filmed with the idea of marketing the film. And he has never gone ahead with the marketing of it, without even telling me why he has not. His crew failed to get the first few minutes of the interview, which was too bad; but the project still was salvageable. Another thing that may have affected him, may have made him decide not to market it, was that in the approximately forty-five minute discussion period following the interview, also filmed according to plan, not one single favorable comment was made among many that were made by that staff. This is to the best of my recollection and with the exception of a kind comment made by my host, Ed Joseph. Many, many very condemnatory remarks were made. The degree of isolation one tends to feel in that setting is, of course, extreme; but I was supported by the certainty that a number of my Chestnut Lodge colleagues from days of yore, and in all probability a number of those currently working there, would have conducted the interview in the way basically as I had.

*Langs:* Could you say what they objected to?

*Searles:* The Sinai staff, as I heard them comment, had a traditional medical orientation toward patients. They sounded so clinical: a doctor does not speak in such a blunt way and with such a degree of so-called personal feeling to a patient. A patient is someone to treat with a kind of distant care, emotionally distant care.

*Langs:* And your interview had these qualities?

*Searles:* It was much more involving than that, much more locking horns with this young woman and being in a way personally involved with her, in the way that at Chestnut Lodge we found that one simply had to be to get anywhere in working with such people. I have mentioned this Mt. Sinai experience in detail simply because it was among the most stressful of a very great many essentially similar experiences I have had.

*Langs:* So what you are saying is that in order to sustain this kind of work and the clinical investigations that are related to it, you have to have some support from somewhere.

*Searles:* I think some sense of membership in some kind of group or aggregation, some kind of—

*Langs:* That's an interesting point, because I have no sense of membership at all. I'm getting my support through invitations from all over the country, analysts and others—some of the analytic institutes outside of New York have welcomed me. But that isn't really membership; it is just an awareness now that my work is beginning to reach people. I have no group to identify with at all. And while I will spare you the details, I have been quite isolated—professionally and even socially. And while my work is now moving in directions beyond the classical mold, it draws its basic sustenance from classical clinical theory. Still, it is a departure—and I feel one that is soundly documented and validated. But those niceties are ignored, logical disputes or disagreements are eschewed—differences and uniqueness must be destroyed. That brings up another danger: that of seeming paranoid. And yet, I don't see my work as nearly as pioneering as yours.

*Searles:* Oh, I think it is very, very pioneering work, yours is—this bipersonal field. I find a great deal to admire in it. It is very boldly innovative in many regards.

*Langs:* Perhaps—as I say, I find it hard to maintain a perspective. But my efforts to seek out the truth and to question shibboleths when my clinical findings directed me to do so has negatively influenced my local professional standing among analysts—though I have had very positive responses from analysts elsewhere and even occasionally from someone in New York. I feel very much on shakey ground in discussing all of this—I keep thinking that I am over-estimating my importance or exaggerating the envy, hostility, and isolation. I can only assure you that there is a strong basis for what I am saying, and that, in one way, these reactions suggest to me that I am really being creative—they are typical of responses to true originality.

My support comes from these sources: the invitations I spoke of and the positive responses of my audiences; my students who are not analysts but therapists; and the indirect, unconscious communications of my patients—that most importantly of all. There were strong efforts made to have me desist from the work I was doing, the observations I was making, the way in which I was teaching—active efforts at suppression. And this is where martyrdom came up and I had to keep asking myself, Am I trying to be a martyr? Am I inviting all of this condemnation? And I've absolutely decided that this is not martyrdom or masochism, but a love of truth—yes, a dedication to fathom the truth regardless of personal cost; an obligation and responsibility to patients that cannot in good conscience be otherwise. I sense a similar credo in your efforts—enormously. The love of truth in the face of pain, the necessary pain that goes with discovery and apparently, with getting into new areas and ideas. You see, I think this is where a lot of opposition comes from: new ideas frighten many analysts and impinge upon areas and countertransference-based gratifications and defenses that they find too difficult to confront and modify—resolve.

I'm convinced that clinical creativity in analysis touches upon unresolved countertransferences that are shared by the group. Racker (1957) wrote beautifully of how analysts can pass on to their analysands their blind spots, their countertransferences—it is an obvious point, but one whose implications tend to be ignored. There is a kind of massive sharing; it's like the Emperor's new clothes: there is a great need to conform even when one senses that something is awry. And only babes dare speak the truth—no one else dares to do so.

So, my main support came from my patients, where I worked with my principles and got *indirect* confirmation—not a direct thank you or some other form of conscious agreement, but quite derivative, unconscious validation.

*Searles:* I was down to Georgetown [University Hospital, in Washington] on Thursday. I go down there for an hour and a half once a month, and have done so for ten or more years. There are maybe eight residents there regularly, and I was strongly recommending your Bipersonal Field book (Langs, 1976a) to them and telling them how very useful I'm finding it. I am sure they would get a great deal out of it. It's excellent.

*Langs:* Let me bring you back now to where you were in your story. You mentioned the Sinai visit while you were describing your Chestnut Lodge experiences—the fact that you were personally involved, communicated personal things to your patients.

*Searles:* Yes, these people at Sinai were reacting in the spirit of traditional medically trained psychiatrists who are accustomed to treating patients for a few months only, and are accustomed to treating them with the use of drugs. Their treatment orientation permits the therapist to maintain a relatively high degree of emotional distance from the turmoil that is going on in the patient—and, of course, a dry tangible distance from becoming aware of the patient's projection of his pathology upon the therapist. There is absolutely none of this looking seriously at the question of whether the patient unconsciously regards the doctor as, or assumes the doctor to be, crazy. None of that, not a bit of that, and that's the kind of thing that my interviews regularly bring to light: the way the patient feels toward me; and his perceptions of me as crazy are perfectly physiologically normal in relation to his transference to me from his childhood figures. But the doctors who are psychiatrists in the traditional sense aren't really exposed to that.

*Langs:* Nor are the doctors who are analysts in the traditional sense. They will acknowledge now that Freud's mirror metaphor (1912) was a bit extreme and that there is a kind of a live interaction. But it is more lip service than a continuous scrutiny of the unconscious qualities of the interaction—the continuous communicative interaction, as I now term it. It is thought of more as a relationship than as an interaction.

*Searles:* I tell you—I think, as we talk—I feel sure, speaking for myself, that I do some of what I'm going to describe, and I personally assume that you also do, and it is namely this: as we move into being as close to a patient emotionally as we feel the work calls for us to be, I think that we are not able to integrate some of the most hurtful, distancing images which the patient has of us—and of which we have of the patient, also. And I think there is a very powerful tendency for those images to get displaced onto the colleagues, and for us to feel those colleagues don't understand us, and feel alienated from them. I'm trying to say that in our work with patients we have this simultaneous combination of intimacy and that kind of remoteness, remoteness on our own part toward the patient and remoteness on the patient's part toward us, which is extremely difficult not only for the patient, but also for the therapist, to experience in awareness.

The therapist, for example, tends to take unconscious refuge from this enormously conflictual countertransference experience in projecting onto colleagues, and others, the more negatively-toned images of himself, and to displace upon those colleagues and others the more negatively-toned ones among his perceptions of the patient.

*Langs:* This is related in some ways to Stone's (1961) concept of deprivation-in-intimacy. Interestingly enough, he tended to emphasize the deprivational aspects of the analytic situation and experience, rather than the other side: the gratifications of being held analytically, understood, gaining insight, and the like. On the whole, writers have tended to emphasize one or the other, rather than maintain a kind of balanced picture, identifying where the appropriate gratifications are coming from, where the frustrations arise—and the influence of each.

I think that what you are saying, too, is that in any professional activity, when an analyst begins to get involved with an outside group he ultimately has the responsibility to recognize that, at least on one level, displacements from his work with patients may play a role. Is this a fair statement?

*Searles:* That makes sense, right.

*Langs:* In one regard, this is a reminder that, as analysts, our main and first responsibility is to our patients and to our clinical work. And I think there is little doubt—and this has been said, too—that some of the difficulties analysts have in their organizations have to do with their using them as a field or arena to kind of live out expressions of their frustrations, anxieties, and countertransferences in their work with their patients.

You are also saying that while there was isolation while at the Lodge, some working over of ideas on your own and some wish to not share certain aspects of your thinking, there was still a positive setting available to you.

*Searles:* Very much so.

*Langs:* A human and nonhuman setting, which held and nurtured you.

*Searles:* That's right, and which I associate with my home town. Chestnut Lodge is small as hospitals go and my home town certainly is small as communities go. There was a sense of being in some kind of contact with everybody there. It was kind of a group of manageable knowability.

*Langs:* Yes, and from what you are saying it seems that it contributed to the way in which your work unfolded and flourished, your productivity.

*Searles:* Very much so, and the length of stay of patients there, which can be astronomical by any ordinary standards, did a great deal to make for the richness of the community. There would be patients there and staff members who had worked there for many years, and the patients would be known, really, some of them, for decades past.

*Langs:* It became somewhat of a home for both.

*Searles:* That's right, very much so; that's right. What I now get thinking about is one of the paradoxes of working there: one could not afford to be treated there oneself. Very strange. And the whole culture of wealth that these patients represented, wealth far beyond that of all but maybe one staff member I knew over all those years who had come from that same social class, really—upper class. That made for very striking phenomena. I'll give you one example. Frieda Fromm-Reichmann lived in a modest, two-story wooden dwelling that had been built on the hospital grounds for her, close to the main building of the sanitarium. She had a therapy group of several schizophrenic patients going for some time—I don't know for how many years but for some of the time late in her life there—and she described to us one time having her group patients come to a dinner at her home. She described the kind of comments they made upon seeing the interior of her home, and what amused her in their comments was the condescension which showed through their politeness. Although these people were living on wards—and some of them for years—that were very far from palatial, they had come from such homes that they wouldn't be caught dead living in such a modest place as Frieda Fromm-Reichmann was living in, for example.

It was in ways like that, often very subtle ways, and one of the things that was sufficiently subtle that it only dawned on me gradually, over a number of years, was that by these wealthy people's standards, a physician is a servant. When I was a boy, a physician was the most esteemed citizen in our community—the few physicians we had. It is altogether different with upper-class people. A physician is in the same general category as a cook or a butler and altogether different.

*Langs:* What you are touching upon is an area that you are enormously sensitive to: the role of reality in what happens in the therapeutic experience; the role of actualities on both sides, really, and not only in the immediate therapeutic relationship between patient and therapist or analyst, but also in the wider setting which serves as the backdrop for therapy.

*Searles:* And this certainly was a factor contributing to my treatment results being less than I had hoped and striven for, because as one of these patients would become well, she would start manifesting certain upper-class kinds of behavior that were perfectly normal for her to manifest but that, regrettably, caused me to feel feelings of social inferiority that were very painful to me and that clearly had not had sufficient work in my own personal analysis. I could easily produce proof of that, if any were needed, because I had done the same thing with my training analyst—had managed to find areas where I could feel superior to him, and where he wasn't sufficiently sure of his ground to treat them as neurotic character traits.

*Langs:* That's an area of the analyst's vulnerability that seldom is spoken about, and almost never written about.

*Searles:* And that touches on a big realm that I find an awful lot of occasion to mention to people when I go about teaching—namely, the analyst's envy of the patient.

*Langs:* Yes, I've thought of envy a lot in recent years. You've written on jealousy between the patient and analyst (Searles, 1973a, 1979b), the analyst's jealousy of the patient and the patient's introjection of such experiences. I really wondered how much of that was jealousy, and how much of that was envy—and how you would distinguish between the two. As you know, the Kleinians write a good deal about envy. Melanie Klein (1957) identified envy as a basic and primitive emotion which she felt was biological in its roots. It was that crucial, intense, and destructive. And I wondered what thoughts you have had about jealousy and envy, and their functions in the analytic or therapeutic interactions.

*Searles:* Yes, I've written a very long paper (Searles, 1979) about jealousy—jealousy involving an internal object. In that paper, I'm trying to describe jealousy that involves only two actual people and an introject in one or the other of them. And you know, the usual distinction between envy and jealousy is that most writers describe envy as involving two people and jealousy as involving three and perhaps more.

*Langs:* Yes, and jealousy tending to involve the person's whole objects, and envy part objects. I thought of that because you were saying that this distinction needn't be the case. Now in this paper, you didn't distinguish between envy and jealousy. How would you do it now?

*Searles:* How would I? Well, I would follow the traditional distinction that one envies the other person for possessing some thing one wishes one possessed oneself, whereas in jealousy one wishes to have the place in some second person's eyes that this third person enjoys in his or her eyes.

*Langs:* So it would be triangular, but it needn't be just two people.

*Searles:* That's right.

*Langs:* You would always have a triangle, but an introject could be a part of the triangle. The other has to do with wanting to possess some part of the other person.

*Searles:* Yes, but I have a lot of thoughts about envy in analytic work. I have worked—as I am sure you have, too—with quite a number of analysts or therapists, analysts in training, or people in allied professions who do psychotherapy. These people surely show a great deal of competitiveness, as therapists, with their own therapists, as well as that envy of the therapist's function that is general among patients, but particularly so with them. At least it is particularly evident that they have much competitiveness and envy in that dimension.

Now, that certainly has been well known to me for a long, long time. But what I had not realized until the last very few years was how competitive I am with the patient in his analysand-role—how much I envy him for being an analysand, and how much I assume that if I had the freedom to be in his place on the couch, I would do a vastly better job of being an analysand than he is doing. That's been quite a revelation to me. Even as recently as two years ago, I wasn't much aware of this aspect of my competitiveness with, and envy of, my analysands. It did occur to me, you see, it's been so long since I was in analysis that I have forgotten the power of the resistance so that I fantasy myself there on the couch being the analysand free from any resistance.

A few years back some of it started to dawn on me in relation to one male analysand who was very difficult, very slow moving. I was thinking, during one of the sessions with him, that if *I* were on the couch, I'd *really* free associate; *I'd* know how to do this stuff. But then I thought, "Yes—but suppose *he* were the *analyst*? How free would I be if he were sitting in my chair and I were on the couch?" It seems to me that that is very pertinent, because he was projecting onto me, year after year in our analytic work, all kinds of attitudes and feelings that were related to his resistance. You see, his resistance was based on unconscious perceptions of me as being murderously threatening, for example, and in many ways forbidding. So I was thinking that if I were on the couch and he were in my chair, how free would I be to function with this man whom I knew to be in reality very forbidding and with a lot of murderous feelings and so on.

*Langs:* When you would be unconsciously perceptive of these attributes?

*Searles:* Yes, but still I think it gets back to this realm of envy. I think that I must not be the only analyst who envies his patients for their being in analysis, and the fact that I am a training analyst is very limiting to me in many ways. I am less ready to go running to somebody to get some personal help than I would be otherwise. I'm afraid the word would get around that old Searles is having his head examined, better pick one of the other plentiful training analysts in the area.

*Langs:* Yes, the things that leak out. I have a paper (Meissner and Wohlauer, 1978) for our next issue of *The International Journal of Psychoanalytic Psychotherapy* on the hospitalized physician, a subject that you must know a good deal about.

*Searles:* Yes, I do.

*Langs:* And Myerson (1978) wrote a beautiful discussion of that paper on the hospitalized physician as the fallen man, taking Conrad's *Lord Jim* and Camus' *The Fall* as literary illustrations of fallen men. Myerson asks, How did they reconstitute, how did they repair the damage? And he shows the options that such a person has. One of them appears in the paper by Meissner and Wolhauer (1978): a physician took as his means of self-cure making his therapist the fallen physician, making his therapist fail and kind of trying to put it all into the therapist in order to free himself of his sense of failure. So, I think that the analyst who thinks about going back into analysis has to work out something about being the fallen man, and the fallen idol and all of that, plus face some of the realities of the kinds of complications that do come up.

One of the things that I've envied a bit as I've learned so much about the functions of the frame is the analysand who has a secure frame in his therapy or analysis of a kind that I never had.

*Searles:* Secure frame in his work with you, do you mean?

*Langs:* Yes, in terms of what that offers in the way of a basic hold and container, a place of safety, and the rest. I think of you as I say this: I think I will be forever ungrateful and angry about the modifications in the framework of my analysis and its lasting effects on me. And then I have to have a perspective: such deviations have been and still are a reflection of a shared blind spot; it has taken analyses a long time to consider such matters as total confidentiality

and neutrality for training analyses. There is a movement among
candidates of late that is forcing the American analyst to think about
the ramifications of these modifications in the frame. As I've gotten
to understand the frame and its influence, pursuing my studies even
though I was told again and again that I'm too rigid and should back
away, I discovered that it affects the communicative qualities of the
interaction, what the patient will actually tell you consciously and
unconsciously. The analyst's management of the frame is so filled
with meaning and importance, and is so basic, that I have repeatedly
been able to validate my position in this area, and I keep discovering
more reasons why maintaining the frame must be the basic attitude.

So, there are many reasons why the analyst experiences envy of the
analysand, and he has to be in touch with it and to keep it under
control, to not feel unduly guilty. I think of your paper on guilt in
the analyst (Searles, 1966). This too can be a very pertinent issue, and
the patient will unconsciously perceive unresolved conflicts in this
area—and exploit them without being aware of the sector of misalliance; and, of course, he will often be curative as well.

From the beginning, you showed a significant awareness of the
patient's unconscious sensitivity to the analyst, his unconscious
perceptions, his introjections—you have had a remarkable openness
in this respect. I often wonder why analysts are so refractory to
understanding this dimension of the interaction. Why do they retreat
from it? I've commented on this blind spot earlier; I wonder what
thoughts you have about it. Perhaps you can comment further, too,
on the broader issues that have come up.

*Searles:* Yes, let me try to see if I can get a hold of this some more. If
many members—you are in the American Psychoanalytic, aren't
you?

*Langs:* Yes.

*Searles:* If many members in the American Psychoanalytic are
indeed oriented toward excluding people such as you and me, who
are trying to bring something rather radically new into the field, why
are they? Well, I think there is something about narcissism involved.
I think that they are able to maintain a kind of idealized image of
themselves which they don't want threatened. That's a banal enough

way of putting it; but I think the fact of the matter with me is that I was not able to maintain that, and if I had been able to, I'd probably be pushing you away. I could tell you where some of that started being lost to me was really relatively early in my personal analysis, when I was working at the V. A. clinic for two years—before I went out to Chestnut Lodge, even. I used to feel, you see, that I had—as we all had—I'd had considerable success in the competitive professional realm. I'd been accepted for a number of good things and here I was: I had started to get into analysis, and I was working with the patients, and I was at the height of my obsessive-compulsive, smug self-satisfaction, really. I would have an interview with a patient, he'd leave and I would make a few notes about it and make a note of what I planned to go into next time. I was feeling really unexaminedly good about myself.

Then I began to find that, sometime after this or that patient had left, maybe later that day, I would think, "My god! Did I say *that* to him?" Something would come back to me, something very hurtful that I had said to him, very insensitively hurtful. I started being better able to identify with the patient and think about some of these things that I had said that I thought were so superlative, really felt to be on the receiving end of. Right from there on I was no longer able to maintain an image of myself as being so satisfied with myself; I just couldn't.

Then when I got out to Chestnut Lodge I plowed in the depths of despair, spending years with someone who didn't talk, for example. Yesterday I saw a man who is currently on the Lodge staff, and with whom I work in supervision. He mentioned to me, incidentally, that he had worked for a year with a patient there who never spoke to him the whole year, and a couple of years later the patient came back to visit the Lodge and this doctor was coming out the front door and the patient said, "Dr. ———, how are you?" It was the first time Dr. ——— had ever heard the patient's voice. Going through stuff like that, narcissism can't flourish in that kind of setting; it can't.

So these guys in the American Psychoanalytic have been able to maintain some image of themselves that they feel kind of comfortable about and that they don't want disturbed. If I hadn't become disturbed, I'd probably be one of them. But I didn't choose to have things disturb it; things just came along that robbed me of it. I'm sure I have more narcissism than I want to believe, and maybe more even now, than they have; but in any case I think there is this factor of narcissism involved in the exclusion process you spoke of.

*Langs:* Yes. Perhaps you will think more about these questions, because I think you will find there are many levels of answers—yours is a very fascinating one. First of all, I think you are saying that certainly by the time you got to the Lodge and worked with patients of that kind, no matter how massive your narcissistic defenses were—we'll call them that—they were under assault by your patients. You imply that it would take a remarkably dense, overly rigid therapist to not experience the battering down of those defenses—yet many therapists have done just that.

The other point I would like to make is that you remind me of something that I have been struck with in regard to the clinical analytic literature: that most of the presentations relate material about the patient, while virtually never mentioning anything about the analyst—unless the paper deals with countertransference issues. The writer seems to assume that in most instances the analyst has functioned perfectly throughout the period of analysis that is being described, and that a continuous communicative interaction does not exist—or that the patient's associations could have meanings divorced from the therapist's interventions.

*Searles:* Exactly, exactly, and that is just complete rot to me. It's not only an incomplete picture, but the hell of it is that the parts that are left out are the most important parts.

*Langs:* Yes—it is an absurd picture.

*Searles:* The very parts that it omits are the most important parts.

*Langs:* And this prevails in the literature. It is just so striking with case reports, with clinical discussions; I could offer countless examples. I just happened to read the second Kohut book, and it's characteristic of his vignettes in both of his monographs on narcissism (Kohut, 1971, 1977). But the same is true of Kernberg's work (1975; see also Masterson, 1978)—it's there with most analysts. Even when they get into countertransference, they do it as if its expressions were sporadic, occasional, instead of part of a continuous communicative flow. Countertransference is seen as blatantly cropping up from time to time, and as something to be rid of. It is not seen as inevitably present in every silence and intervention, as part of the continuous interaction, and as something to be mastered, minimized, and always recognized, especially in its more subtle or chronic, easily missed expressions. And I very much believe that once analysts revise their view of countertransference and of the analytic interaction, there will be major modifications and corrections in our clinical theory. Much of this has to do with basic analytic methodology, the understanding of unconscious communication, and the essentials of the listening process (Langs, 1978a).

Now, this leads me to an important question related to how the analyst works. You are quite sensitive to your own inner state, your subjective thoughts and feelings—you make considerable use of them in understanding your patient and yourself.

*Searles:* I do try, indeed, to be so and do so to the best of my ability.

*Langs:* Now, the question comes up then. How do you go about safeguarding that the preponderant nucleus is not countertransference-based, and that it is perceptive and valid, and in the interest of the patient? I am saying "preponderant nucleus" because I would agree with you that anything you experience will have some element of truth related to the patient—Racker (1957) made that point, too. But we know that there is always a mixture of truth and distortion in our subjective responses; they are never free of countertransference-based influence and therefore some element of distortion is inevitable. But we are interested then in developing our use of subjective reactions in a manner that is primarily or preponderantly valid vis-à-vis the patient. What measure do we take to insure that this is the case?

For instance, in reading your symbiosis paper (Searles, 1973a), this was a question that I came back to a number of times. You describe apparently meaningful and very interesting subjective experiences that helped you define, for example, the phases of your work with patients—helped you identify that you are in a particular stage of analysis, let's say, the ambivalent symbiosis phase. Now, a lot of that determination comes from what you are experiencing subjectively, especially as you write and describe it. So the question that occurs to me—because I am a real bug on methodology and on validation—is, What efforts do you make to validate your subjective experiences and the inferences you derive from them? How do you go about it? Have you been concerned with that issue? We are talking about the analyst's pathological narcissism; we are being very honest with each other. Do you simply take it at face value? I think you can see the scope of the question; it is a very crucial one.

*Searles:* Yes, I know. I realize it is a very crucial question, and I think that in terms of my work with patients, a case could be made that I tend to get very involved emotionally with my patients and that the termination of the work with them is perhaps more often than not fairly ragged.

*Langs:* You're being honest about it. I think that's true of every analyst, some more than others, of course.

*Searles:* Your question is one which has been raised to me many times in various forms. The question has been raised to me, or the challenge expressed, or the criticism made: How do I know that it is not coming predominantly from me, from some unconscious, unworked-through area of myself, such that this material (these feelings, fantasies, and so forth) which I am assuming to belong primarily to the patient, belongs instead, primarily, to me. Well, there are a number of safeguards. One, a patient who is able to tell me when something is quite off the mark. I find that very reassuring.

*Langs:* You mean consciously?

*Searles:* Yes, consciously able to tell me that that is irrelevant to the best of his knowledge at the moment that, no, that's off the mark. I find that reassuring, I find that reassuring that such a patient is not going to be likely to become compliantly conforming to some unconscious fantasies of mine. That's maybe pretty close to the surface.

*Langs:* Let me just ask you this: How often do you find a patient capable of doing that?

*Searles:* Yes, not uncommonly.

*Langs:* That's interesting; this must have to do again with differences in our styles and ways of working, and in what we identify as confirmatory and nonconfirmatory responses from patients. In my own work, and in my supervision of residents and younger therapists, I find valid conscious disagreement and conscious recognition of errors by the therapist extremely rare—occurring largely under circumstances of blatant errors, and even then quite rarely. It may be that you create a particular kind of atmosphere, or it may be something about the patients that you work with.

*Searles:* I think I do create a particular kind of atmosphere, because I make far more interpretations with various of my patients than most people would—far more, so that my patients are relatively content that some of my comments are useful and others aren't. I don't devote the care and study to the fate of each interpretation which your book strongly recommends—and which is, indeed, eminently sound. But the stance which I have developed has been arrived at over many years, from a starting point of following quite slavishly the model that I had in my mind of my own personal analyst, whose interpretations were limited to the closing minutes of the session, as I've told you. And how long a time it took for me, many years, to become loosened up enough to make an interpretation within the first few seconds of the beginning of a session, for example.

*Langs:* Let me say something, now that you mentioned the capacity to loosen up, to change, to separate oneself from one's analyst and his technique, and from one's colleagues. One of the very positive things about my alienation from my colleagues and Institute is that it helped me to resolve a good piece of—I'll never resolve it entirely—but a good piece of my largely inappropriate need for their approval, for their sanction, for their love, which had been among the conscious motives for my work. Some of that had to do with my needs to belong and with wanting to prove that I had been well worth accepting as a candidate. These needs are reflected in my technique books (Langs, 1973, 1974), which I wrote with my teachers at the Institute in mind. At the time, I believed that what I wrote was true, and I was already establishing my independence by writing in ways regarding which they openly disapproved, but nonetheless their pressures and my needs led to compromises, unexamined biases, and misstatements of which I only became aware later on.

*Searles:* I was wondering how you could have changed so quickly between those books and the bipersonal field book.

*Langs:* I wish that I had made some personal notes or spoke into a tape recorder, because I think now that it was a very interesting period, the beginning of a series of transitions—I had little sense of their broader implications at the time. A lot of the discoveries and changes came out of just dogged observations and a determination to discover the truth and to be rid of restrictive prejudices—a "let the chips fall where they may" sort of approach. And much of it stemmed from the concept of the adaptive context, of an adaptive-interactional approach to everything in the therapeutic interaction. I found that if I just took things like alterations in the frame or any intervention by the therapist as an adaptive context, and listened to everything the patient said as what I call a *commentary* in the intervention (Langs 1978a)—a mixture of valid perceptiveness and distorting fantasies—whole worlds of insights opened up to me. I would first look at it as valid commentary, as the truth, and then I would look at what's distorted—it was always both—a *commentary* and a *transversal communication* which conveyed both truth and distortions, and which had to be seen and treated as such.

*Searles:* Very good, excellent.

*Langs:* And I just had to follow the truth of what the patient said until the point of distortion—the point where self-knowledge and other associations from the patient indicated that distortions, falsifications, pathology were now becoming major factors. Much of the creativity that I put into *The Bipersonal Field* (Langs, 1976a) book came out of being in touch with the unconscious communications from both the therapists and patients—

*Searles:* It is beautiful, yes.

*Langs:* And yet none of my reviewers have commented on this dimension of my work. But, to finish up an earlier topic, there is a positive side to alienation, and to having to validate observations that threaten other analysts and are rejected out of hand by them. You become your own person, freer to observe and follow a given line of thought, no matter where it takes you. And you—at least, I—become a more careful observer. You are forced to validate your findings and to sharpen the validating process and discover its essence psychoanalytically. I am willing to face my errors, and there have been a few, but I have had to insist on a sound methodology—listening and validating.

And those pressures, then, served me well—I didn't give up—I searched even more intensely. Is this anything that you experienced in any kind of a way?

*Searles:* Not as severely as you have—again, I'm sure, because of differences in backgrounds. Where I grew up in this small town, there was an enormous emphasis on being liked by people, and I became a member there of various in-groups, and was well-schooled in the marketing orientation, as Erich Fromm called it (1947), so that, partly as a result of that home-town experience, I've stayed in enough touch with people so that, for example, locally, about ten years ago, my fellow-members of the Washington Psychoanalytic Society elected me to a term (1969-1971) as president, and it meant a great deal to me. It really meant an awful lot to me, that I was that much accepted by the colleagues—it really meant a great deal to me. And I mentioned the small group thing at Chestnut Lodge—how pleased I was that mine was the most sought-out one there. That, too, meant an awful lot to me. I did manage, all along the line, to gain and maintain a good measure of acceptance from one group or another of my colleagues. I did manage, but only by a lot of concerned effort, really. But that concern with group-acceptance has limited me, too, because I am probably never as free as you are from concerns about what people will think of me. That dogs me in my work, whether it's because of my being conscious of being a training analyst—and what will people think of me, a training analyst, doing such and such? Or, as another example, years ago, after I left the Lodge and kept on working with a couple of patients from there, Dexter Bullard, Sr., [the Medical Director of the Lodge] was close to being a third presence in the room, as my externalized superego, in my work with those two Lodge patients; I was troubled for years with the question:

What would he think about the work I was doing with this patient? I'm much too hag-ridden with such concerns. As still another example, I am not free from concern about what classical analysts would think—and there may not be any such persons really, but there is some kind of structure that's in my mind so that I am not as free from it as I think.

*Langs:* Let me clarify: on one level, I really feel that I have freed myself in many ways, but I don't mean to imply that it's not still a great concern. In fact, one of the things that disturbs me the most at this time—in all honesty— is that I am still too preoccupied with just that very area. How much is my work being accepted? when will I have my day? when will they regret it? when and how will it all be resolved? There is something I haven't worked through, I know it, I'm working on it. Still, I think that in terms of what I'm writing and creating now, I have become far more free of these shakles than I had been before, in a very positive sense. I didn't mean to imply, though, that it doesn't remain a kind of hurt and almost a damned obsession.

*Searles:* You had asked, what about this question about whether in my placing as much reliance as I do on subjective factors, how do I know that I'm not getting away from the patient and the patient's needs, how do I validate it?

*Langs:* Yes, let's get back to that question. You said that you were active enough so that you have conscious responses from your patient to turn to.

*Searles:* Yes, so that the patient can be relied on to validate or invalidate my responses; that's one big factor.

*Langs:* Yes, but in that respect you are—so far, and I am sure you will want to elaborate—confining yourself to conscious responses. I was going to ask you, What about the unconscious responses? What about the subsequent indirect communications?

*Searles:* You are much more sophisticated and have developed your concepts much further than I have in that realm—namely, your attentiveness to the patient's subsequent reaction to your interpretation. You have gone much further than I with seeing whether the flow of the associations is toward opening up new areas, or the patient's bringing in references to helpful people elsewhere (who represent the analyst whom he unconsciously is finding helpful), and so on, that you describe in your book. Or whether there tends to be a closing off of associations, or references now to unhelpful people, and so on. I have not elaborated my concepts that far.

As to validation, I do rely heavily on the reactions of colleagues. For all I've said about the American Psychoanalytic Association, when I go around talking, in many places people feel that what I am saying strikes a chord in them and does help to illuminate their work with their patients. It tends to reassure me of the validity of my concepts. Now with any one patient, the question of whether my subjective response is a valid one or not, I always would use a test of seeing where does my response fit in with the patient's developmental history, you see?

*Langs:* Yes, that's a dimension that you have developed far more than myself.

*Searles:* That's one rule of thumb that I would always use.

*Langs:* You keep a great and sensitive eye on the genetic counterpart of whatever is going on between you and the patient. That seems to be one area that you continuously monitor among the many things we have to monitor. Now, how does that help you validate your subjective experiences? Can you elaborate on this?

*Searles:* Well, my response—my so-called subjective response—is one that I can readily identify as presumably having been at work in the patient's mother, for instance, in his childhood, or at work in him toward his mother during those early years. This sense of the identifiability, or locatability (in the patient's developmental history) of my response, tends to assure me that this response is not out in left field.

*Langs:* So, validation is found in the presence of some fit genetically?

*Searles:* Yes.

*Langs:* Now, do you also continue some form of subjective monitoring of yourself—apart from, in conjunction with, the material from the patient?

*Searles:* In reply to your question I want to emphasize, first of all, the role of clinical experience. So often, people regard me as either possessing a remarkably therapeutic intuition, or being, possibly, more than a bit crazy in my seemingly off-the-cuff responses to the patient, or both. But the fact is that the subjective experience I am having with the patient in the immediate situation is being monitored, constantly, by a part of my observing ego, in evaluative comparison with a contrast to the decades of clinical experiences I have had previously, with hundreds of patients I have interviewed in those earlier years. I came to Chestnut Lodge, in 1949, with the conviction that if psychoanalytic therapy had any chance of becoming available to the droves of patients who needed it, it must become something highly teachable, from one generation of therapists to another, rather than being left so largely, as it was then, in the realm of a highly exclusive capability possessed by only a handful of seemingly almost uniquely intuitive persons, such as Frieda Fromm-Reichmann.

I think an aspect of this problem is that the general population, including most psychiatrists, tends to regard the schizophrenic patient not as being essentially like the rest of us, but as being, rather, a unique, set-apart creature, understandable not at all to ordinary mortals, but only to persons who are at least half-crazy themselves. Thus, to grasp more about the timing and dosing of my expressions of affect to a schizophrenic patient requires that one has gotten largely free from the mythological view, which I have just mentioned, of the schizophrenic patient. One can learn reliable psychotherapeutic principles from working with him, principles applicable to patients—psychotic or neurotic—who follow him in one's accumulating clinical experience over the years of one's practice, just as is true of the borderline or neurotic patient.

Secondly, in answer to your question as to whether I continue some form of subjective monitoring of myself (apart from, or in conjunction with, the material from the patient), I want to speak of a typical situation in my work with an erstwhile markedly schizoid patient with whom I have succeeded in developing a therapeutically-symbiotic kind of relatedness. I would identify much with him, through my feeling a sense of oneness with him, not constantly but as a basic kind of feeling, very different from the alienated kind of unrelated state that had prevailed. I would expect to find, in this symbiotic relatedness, a sense of interchangeability, so that I would easily feel in the patient's position and he in mine, as part of the oneness, and with that I would feel a sense of not readily being able to ascertain where the primary locus of a feeling is coming from— whether it is primarily, say, the *patient's* anger or sexual feeling or fond feeling or dependent feeling that's being the primary thing at the moment, or whether it's *mine*—and the better the relationship goes the less it matters.

*Langs:* You have a capacity for preparedness and a tolerance for really softening, opening up, your ego boundaries temporarily. And again, I think that most American analysts maintain their separateness, their identity, their boundaries in a very sharp way, despite what they write about empathy (see Langs, 1976a). Such fluidity and openness is, for them, enormously anxiety provoking.

*Searles:* I think so, too. I realize that; I know that.

*Langs:* And even when it hapens to them, they attempt quickly to reconstitute, rather than pausing, tolerating the state a bit longer, and understanding what they are experiencing.

*Searles:* And I talk of ambivalently symbiotic relatedness because the feelings of love and hate do change so rapidly and unpredictably.

*Langs:* Could you clarify that comment?

*Searles:* I don't think it necessary to repeat here, in any full detail, the concepts I discussed at length in my paper entitled, "Phases of Patient-Therapist Interaction in the Psychotherapy of Schizophrenia" (1961). There I described that the phase of ambivalently symbiotic relatedness gives way, as further resolution of the mutual hatred is accomplished, to the phase of preambivalently symbiotic relatedness, which is a phase of very predominantly loving and contented relatedness, of the same nature as that which prevails in the oneness involving a confidently loving mother and her contented and thriving infant.

*Langs:* The preambivalently symbiotic phase always seemed odd to me, because you're postulating a sequence that includes autism in ambivalent and preambivalent forms, even though you say genetically that the preambivalent phase would probably occur first.

*Searles:* Earliest, yes.

*Langs:* Would you clarify?

*Searles:* As regards the sequence of appearance of the successive phases of patient-therapist relatedness, it seems to me eminently natural that, as the necessary regression occurs on the patient's part—and, to an appreciable degree, on the therapist's part also—over the course of the therapy, it is the developmentally *earliest* phases which come to light *latest* in this sequence.

I must say that, as years have gone on I have come more and more to question whether there *is* any preambivalently symbiotic phase to be found. I fear that I've made a kind of shibboleth of it, and it's a nirvana kind of concept; it may be more wishful thinking than anything else. But, as I just mentioned, I have thought that it has its prototype in the kind of relationship a mother and a well-cared-for infant have with one another, where there is relatively little hate in the relationship, relatively little in the way of pain and discomfort on the infant's side and it's as near a sense of blissful oneness—and contentment, as I feel it with patients, a contented sense of oneness—as life on earth can provide. And it is quite different from the rapidly changing hate and love and turmoil of the ambivalently symbiotic thing.

*Langs:* Would that exist as a factor that helps to resolve the autistic phase? Do you think that something like that would be going on?

*Searles:* Oh, yes. I mention in that one paper I wrote (Searles, 1973a) that the *patient* needs to become the *analyst's* maternally protective shield before the patient can become able (partly by identification with the freely-dependent analyst) to utilize the analyst as his (the patient's) maternally protective shield in the manner which Khan (1963, 1964) has described. The analyst comes to surrender himself to the patient's autistic world as being (in the context of the analytic session) the analyst's world also. And I think that the more you yourself can report that kind of experiences with patients, the more you would move away from any position of being accused of being rigid or anything of that sort.

*Langs:* So you have, then, the phase of therapeutic symbiosis. And you're saying that you are able to do more interpreting in that phase, because the patient acknowledges your existence and the impact of your interventions.

*Searles.* That's right, and also because I am being receptive of what the patient is saying at a deeper level. I haven't thought of that before; but if I feel so able to feel in the patient's position, or he in mine, then he is going to feel more that listening to what I have to say isn't any kind of put down for him.

*Langs:* Yes, and this will be the bulk of the analytic work in this phase, and that leads toward differentiation.

*Searles:* I think it leads toward this, what I call preambivalent kind of relatedness, where there is the diminution of the hateful aspects, see?

*Langs:* Yes.

*Searles:* There gets to be more realistic reasons for contentment in what's happening.

*Langs:* Right, as a movement toward integration then?

*Searles:* Yes.

*Langs:* And then that would be really working toward the goal of—

*Searles:* —of individuation?

*Langs:* —of individuation and the end of the analysis.

*Searles:* That's right.

*Langs:* Much of the active analytic work is done during this therapeutic symbiotic phase then? Much of the active part of intervening?

*Searles:* I think so.

*Langs:* I like your concept of therapeutic symbiosis. I refer to it in a paper I just wrote (Langs, 1978-1979), and I see it is a version of the bipersonal field concept. But you have helped me to see that there are definitive qualities to the way in which the presence of the two people can be experienced. Within the bipersonal field, the relatedness may be autistic—limited, one-dimensional—or symbiotic, leading toward individuation. I view that as an important elaboration of the dyadic therapeutic interaction. I think, too, that your concepts overlap beautifully with what Kohut (1971, 1977) and Kernberg (1975) have been describing in their work with certain kinds of narcissistic—and, I think, schizoid patients. I don't think that they are only narcissistic. But I think that their views lack the inherent interactional qualities of yours—and mine.

I wonder, however, if Kohut or Kernberg would tolerate an autistic phase, or whether they would keep intruding themselves into the interaction, insisting on symbiotic communication with the patient. I wonder if they could be silent, and allow the autism to flourish, to be expressed and then to be modified through the relationship, and eventually through some interpretive work. I think that there are some very crucial principles of technique involved here. Anything else you want to say about the phases of analytic work, while we are on the subject for the moment?

*Searles:* Nothing that I haven't said, really, in the papers that I've written, like "Phases of Patient-Therapist Interaction" (1961). In that paper I did include at least a brief discussion of a phase of individuation. It surely is no coincidence that I've never gotten to write a definitive paper—definitive for me—on individuation. I kept putting that off for one reason or another.

*Langs:* Well, I see that our time is up. It went very quickly for me. There are some issues I hope to get back to next time. Thank you for sharing such a candid exchange.

*Searles:* Before you leave, I have found the paper that I wrote in 1948 that I would like you to read—it has never been published.

*Langs:* Thank you—I'd be glad to read it.

*Chapter 3*
# COMMUNICATION BETWEEN ANALYSTS, AND BETWEEN THERAPISTS AND PATIENTS

*Langs:* There are actually two topics I want to start with, so I'll just choose one. One has to do with going back to where we left off, but I'll get to that secondly. First, I want to ask you about the paper you gave me to read (see Searles, 1978-1979).

*Searles:* The old one? Did you read that?

*Langs:* Oh, I loved it.

*Searles:* Really?

*Langs:* You can't imagine. You may already appreciate what I have to say; or you might not have even thought about the implications of this paper, and it will be my pleasure to tell you about them. You wrote the paper in 1948; I was amazed at several things about it. One is the level of sophistication and the sense of confidence that you had in writing what you did in this paper. I mean, coming as a novice, in the middle of analytic training—it's absolutely breathtaking. And what is the first thing that you tackle? It's so remarkable, because it is almost forbidden territory. It's unheard of even today for a novice to get into issues of the relationship, transference, countertransference, and all of that. Has it ever been published?

*Searles:* No. I was hoping you would be interested in publishing it for historical reasons; that would be a real treat to me.

*Langs:* Oh, not only will I publish it, but I would like to write a brief discussion of it, if I may. The [*International*] *Journal* [*of Psychoanalytic Psychotherapy*] now asks for a discussion paper in response to each original contribution.

*Searles:* I would be very pleased if you did—very pleased.

*Langs:* This will appear sometime in 1978 or early 1979.

*Searles:* I would be enormously pleased. This was written—was it '48?

*Langs:* It was submitted for consideration by the first journal in March 1949.

*Searles:* That is why I enclosed the correspondence. Well, I didn't go to the Lodge until June of '49; so that was before I went to the Lodge, which I thought was kind of interesting, you know.

*Langs:* It is a remarkable paper even today. What I have to tell you is that the *Psychoanalytic Quarterly* (one of the two journals which rejected the manuscript) deprived you of several firsts—and a lasting place in the history of psychoanalysis. Despite that setback, I think you have established your place in analytic history in many ways. I didn't notice the date initially, not until after I read the paper. But there are two reasons for publishing it. The first is its historical interest, both in regard to the changing views on the analytic interaction and in respect to your own personal development. The second is the realization that many of the concepts that you present in this paper are still not incorporated into classical analytic thinking. This paper is as current today as it was then, though then it was actually revolutionary.

*Searles:* I haven't read it in years.

*Langs:* You might want to go back to it and write an addendum yourself.

*Searles:* I might; I don't know. I have so much to do. But I surely would appreciate it if you would publish it and we can make a note here as to whatever you might want to write about it.

*Langs:* In 1952, three years later, Melanie Klein (1952) wrote a paper on the origins of transference. I don't know whether you are familiar with it.

*Searles:* No; I haven't read much of her work. I have read her *Envy and Gratitude* (1957).

*Langs:* Right, I've seen your references to it. But in her 1952 paper, one of the topics she brings up is the role of projection in transference—in addition to displacement. Somehow, this aspect of transference had been lost sight of, though it is something that probably originated with Ferenczi (1909): that the patient may project onto the analyst aspects of his inner self, inner mental world. Much later, in 1934, Strachey picked up this theme, and said something more about both introjection and projection in analysis, largely in the terms of their curative aspects. So, he included a concept of projection in the concept of transference, but it seems to me that it was not until 1952 that Melanie Klein very specifically said that in addition to determinants based on displacements from the past, the patient's transferences derive from projections of part objects, parts of the self, and aspects of his inner mental structures onto the analyst. Now, she published her paper three years after your paper was written, and I've always considered that presentation as reflecting a major revival of interest in that aspect of transference—it is a historical contribution. And here the first half of your paper is on this very subject—which is again incredible, really.

*Searles:* I sent that to the *Psychoanalytic Quarterly*. I also sent it to *Psychiatry*. I don't know if you have the correspondence in there.

*Langs:* No, you didn't include that.

*Searles:* Do you want to see that, or not?

*Langs:* Yes, I'd like to. In fact I would even look at it now. That's interesting that they didn't accept it either.

*Searles:* No, they kept it for nine months. I don't know whether I have a copy of the letter where I sent it to *Psychiatry,* I may have it.

*Langs:* That's interesting. I felt that the rejection from the *Quarterly* through this mimeographed form letter must have been so painful, especially in response to a first paper.

*Searles:* I've had so many such experiences.

*Langs:* Yes, but one of the attitudes that I have made a special effort to develop—

*Searles:* In your editorial work you mean?

*Langs:* Yes. I don't know how it sounds, but just let me say it: I take tremendous pains with first papers and with young authors—

*Searles:* That is a very nice—

*Langs:* To try to accept their papers, to help them revise them, if there is a basic constructive core. And I think that I have been influenced by the attitudes that I experienced in editors and editorial boards toward my new ideas and my early papers, much of it quite insensitive, suspicious, rigid, and the like. It suggests a multiplicity of pathological unconscious fantasies and anxieties.

Your paper relates to a question I wanted to ask you to respond to in a more extended way. Quite early in your career as a therapist and analyst, you became very sensitive to the intricacies of therapeutic interaction and the actualities that have a bearing on the interaction between the patient and the therapist or analyst. For example, the second part of your paper has to do with two aspects of the analyst's subjective experiences: first, his utilizing them to understand the patient even when they contain important countertransference-based inputs—at the time, a revolutionary idea; and second, that they involve attempts by the patient to evoke certain kinds of fantasies and experiences within the therapist, and certain kinds of roles. Now

Freud (1914b, 1920) had touched upon this area, but little attention was paid to many aspects until Sandler, in 1976, wrote a paper on role evocation. So you can see that your paper was quite original in recognizing certain actualities to the therapeutic interaction, a position that became inherent to much of what you have written subsequently. But the question I have is whether you have ever thought about what it is that sensitized you to the actualities of the interaction, to the realities of the analyst's unconscious communications and his subjective experiences, the kernels of truths there, and the kernels of truth in transference reactions?

You see that is a crucial issue. Let me give you just a little more background. Szasz (1963), in an exceptionally original discussion of transference, pointed out that the concept of transference and interpreting something as a transference expression can serve a very powerful defensive function for the analyst, who is saying when he interprets transference: It is not real, it is not me, it is something from within yourself or from your past, you see. Now, you didn't succumb to that defense as most analysts have. To this day I would say that a vast majority of analysts fairly consistently use the concept of transference in a defensive way, in addition to its valid aspects—an attitude that was Freud's, too.

*Searles:* Pardon me—I didn't follow what is true of Freud. Did he succumb to that or did not?

*Langs:* He did. I've been thinking of writing a paper on the subject: "Nontransference and the Discovery of Transference," I might call it. And I feel that I can show from Freud's material that much of what he identified as transference was primarily non-transference—primarily based on valid unconscious perceptions of himself and the underlying implications of his interventions. These were situations in which the realities outweighed the patient's distortions, you see. This is one specific way that I can validate the thesis of both Szasz (1963), and Chertok (1968), who studied the discovery of transference and suggested that there was a defensive component in this, Freud's most ingenious discovery.

And this of course is a heritage he passed on to analysts, which they welcomed in terms of their own needs to deny their actual contributions to the patient's pathological reactions. I would appreciate your commenting on this whole area, as well as any thoughts you have about your personal sensitivity to this area and why you didn't succumb to this defense from the very beginning. You said a little about this last time, but I suspect there is more to it. I went through a transition; I had to learn it along the way. You had a sense of this from the beginning.

*Searles:* As you can see, very little occurs to me right off. I am not sure that I would be able to make any kind of substantive reply to that. I kept thinking about my analysis. I think I told you the crucial things that have to do with that question. I said that I had what I regard as a relatively highly classical analysis, but with these occasional so-called reality responses on the analyst's part, of which I mentioned a number of examples—of which there weren't a great many but there were some, and that I regarded as crucial. For example, when at the end of the first interview I said, "Do you see any reason why we can't work together?" he said, "Hell, no!" very emphatically.

I was trying, of course, mainly to think what there may have been in my developmental years that would bear upon that question. I really am not sure, I could only ruminate on my parents' personalities and so on.

*Langs:* There is a contrast here, in that I am quite aware of certain crucial genetic factors in my sensitivity to the broad influence of countertransference and to the devastating effects of an altered frame. While deviations in my own analysis played a role, these genetic factors loom even larger. With you, at least on the surface, your own analysis seems to have been the major factor. And I think much of it evolved based on major unconscious effects—much of it in response to blatant alterations in the frame which, I strongly suspect, were a powerful means through which his countertransferences were expressed.

I thought, too, of a factor reflected in the paper I read (Searles, 1978-1979): that your appreciation for the kernal of truth in the delusions of a psychotic patient, which you arrived at so early in your career, must have alerted you to the presence of such elements. After that, you would never just think of a fantasy as an intrapsychically isolated mental product, but would think of it as built around current realities. From there it would be relatively easy to soon recognize that the analyst himself generates most of the significant reality stimuli for pathological responses in the patient.

But the other factor is your own analysis. And in that respect, I would stress not only the direct reality confrontations that you experienced, but also other kinds of reality impingements that I think that you worked over more unconsciously than consciously— like your description of the hospital visit, for example.

*Searles:* What is that hospital visit?

*Langs:* When he was in the hospital.

*Searles:* When my father—or when Ernest Hadley was in the hospital, yes. I first thought of a time when my father was in a hospital, and I couldn't recall whether I'd mentioned to you my visiting him there.

*Langs:* With the catheter and so forth, you see. I think there he imposed upon you a reality filled with unconscious implications that you, less consciously and more unconsciously, recognized as very significant. You know, it is always a matter of coalescing factors: contributions from yourself and your analyst, from those residuals from your analysis that intermix reality and fantasy, and from genetic determinants that again mix valid perception and distortion.

I think, too, that virtually every candidate, every analyst-to-be, experiences these kind of reality impingements in his analysis. And then he has a choice: on the one hand, he may join in the defensive denial, the collusion, the misalliance with the analyst and repeat it in some form with his own patients—through misinterventions and erroneous modifications of the frame. On the other hand, he may, for whatever reasons, step back, disengage himself consciously, or for unconscious reasons, simply not participate. But eventually, he must become aware of the struggle and the issues; if not, the resolution is incomplete—it remains as unfinished business, residuals of countertransference.

*Searles:* Yes. I get restless. One reason is that I grow very resistive to crediting my training analysis with good results. A factor in my present resistiveness is that I have made so many expressions of gratitude to Ernest Hadley in past years, and have said a great deal about what it did for me, whereas in more recent years I have felt much more conscious of what my analysis did *not* accomplish.

Another thing that I get restless about is that I feel, from my reading of your book (Langs, 1976a) in the last several weeks, and in taking that along with what you are saying regarding disruptions in the boundaries of the bipersonal field, that you speak of them often as *disruptive,* as tending to be *injurious* to the patient in analysis, for instance; and now you're speaking of them—I think very rightly; both are very right—in *positive* terms. I think that was one of the things that your book could have emphasized more—the positive potential of such things.

*Langs:* That is an excellent point, as long as its implications are understood. First, rectification and proper analytic work can turn such incidents to good stead; secondly, even in the face of unrectified deviations and the negative analyst-introjects they evoke, a given analysand may turn such experiences into constructive interludes with great creative potential. I also think that most analysands, particularly those who were analysands in that true sense—originally, this was the term for the analyst in analysis—tend to consciously overidealize their analyst and their analysis. It takes some years of working-through within ourselves to really acknowledge that there were constructive and destructive aspects—that there really was good and bad, if I may use such terms. I certainly found this to be the case. Only in recent years have I begun to realize, now that I understand the things that I have written about, where the more destructive side was and how this related to the residuals it left me. The positive thoughts had really set most of the other rumblings aside. I think that analysts tend to deny these residuals, try to cover them over; yet it is so crucial to have a balanced picture. But as for your point, I have indeed tended to overemphasize the negative aspects of errors, deviations, and things of that sort. I've done so, though, for many reasons—beginning with the extent to which analysts have denied so many of the consequences of their mistakes, and even their very existence. Many questions have occurred to me in this regard. Now, I fully recognize that if you do something hurtful to the patient, it can be a stimulus for growth. The question that I have—and I have labored with this a long time and I don't have a full answer at all—is this: Would the same or more effective growth occur in a more solidified or less complicated way, without the damaging element, if the error did not occur and if the self-expansion occurred on the basis of less traumatic impositions by the analyst? I've thought that probably there is some residual of hurt in addition to the growth under conditions of error, and that certainly at the very least, we should strive to help our patients grow to the greatest extent that they can, without those negative inputs. We will never ever entirely eliminate them, and oddly enough, they often are a powerful stimulus for creativity—though I would stress that deliberate errors are probably far more purely detrimental than inadvertent mistakes.

Some of my critics have said that I come across as moralizing, and I think that this is really a distortion based on my frank discussion of these very issues. I very much write of these matters in a nonmoral sense—as part of a search for the truth. And while I've emphasized the hurtful part, I have also—for example, in my misalliance paper (Langs, 1975b)—I have also stated that these can be extremely moving and insightful experiences for both the patient and the therapist, and if properly handled and analyzed, they can lead to growth for both participants.

*Searles:* Yes.

*Langs:* But you are quite right. Now, this is what I was thinking about as I read over your material. I want to find a specific reference to just this very question in one of your papers. It has to do with the woman that you told that she is no longer your favorite patient; it was at the end of—

*Searles:* I think that is something more recent.

*Langs:* Yes, you are right: it is in your paper on the analyst's participant observation as influenced by the patient in transference (Searles, 1977a). Let me read this and let's discuss the issues involved—they come across so beautifully:
"Several months ago I confided to a middle-aged female analysand that she was, and long had been, my favorite patient; I told her this because I knew that this phenomenon, although in various ways

pleasant to me, must indicate one of her major problems. My sharing with her this information (information which represents, obviously, an aberration in my customary participant-observer functioning with my patients collectively) had highly constructive results in terms of the emergence of a wealth of newly remembered transference material. She recalled, with intense feelings of murderous rage and grief, how all her life she had felt it absolutely necessary to be pleasing other people generally and, above all, to her mother. Her negative mother-transference feelings toward me, largely repressed for years in our work, now emerged with an intensity which I found at times frightening and awesome. With all this, she began manifesting a coherence and a purposefulness in her ego-functioning which had been largely lacking before" (p. 371). Now, should I make the first comment on this excerpt?

*Searles:* Well, I get thinking as you say how applicable that is to our feelings toward our training analysts. I hadn't thought of that connection. That is, that we do so commonly idealize them as I had been idealizing her. What are you doing now? You are trying to see if I have in mind the same thing you have?

*Langs:* Oh, no, you already have it in mind; that's not the problem at all. I was just thinking that the counterpart of the attitude you describe with your patient is the analyst's idealization of candidate analysands, which can create a misalliance—

*Searles:* Yes; right.

*Langs:* In which some aspect of the negative transference never gets analyzed.

*Searles:* Yes; oh, yes. Have I ever seen examples of that! The narcissism, the unresolved narcissism, that one sees in some training analysts in their way of working on the education committee of the analytic institute—specifically, in pushing the careers of their favorite, former training analysands. To a degree, such favoritism is quite understandable; but such training analysts show at times a really maddeningly bland refusal to acknowledge the possibility that they are, naturally enough, speaking from a favorably prejudiced position. The part that I find most exasperating is the training analyst's obvious, however denied, unanalyzed idealization of the former analysand. One has no doubt that the unanalyzed idealization is mutual and that there is, therefore, a kind of happily shared narcissism, with the more negative feelings being instilled into the other education committee members who must listen to one of their members extolling the virtues of this former analysand of his, this former analysand who is now, in his training analyst's opinion, obviously the best-qualified society member to be elected president at the next election.

*Langs:* Yes, but this is what I always do: search both sides of the interaction. And this is what you characteristically do, as well. That's why I like the bipersonal field concept, because once you think of the analytic experience as taking place in a field, you can never consider an experience in the field without trying to identify the contributions of both participants—and I think that's so crucial.

*Searles:* Yes. That certainly has much in common with the Sullivanian approach. I don't mean that your bipersonal field concept and Sullivan's interpersonal relations approach are identical, by any means, but rather that your concept is very congenial to one who has been used at all to thinking in Sullivanian terms.

*Langs:* Now, your vignette also raised another question: you are describing here a modification in the frame.

*Searles:* My having told her this.

*Langs:* Yes. In other words, you modified both your neutrality and anonymity. You have written in a number of places that you will reveal to your patients, at selected moments, aspects of your subjective feelings toward them. And most of this, of course, involves schizophrenic patients, which leads to this question: Do you do this at selected times with neurotics? What is your attitude toward that? I don't think you indicated whether this particular patient was schizophrenic or nonschizophrenic.

There are, of course, any number of analysts who do this. Little (1957) in her work with schizophrenics certainly advocated this kind

of selective self-revelation—though she later modified her position—
and Winnicott had a similar approach. His 1949 paper, "Hate in the
Countertransference," reflects that position.

When I say 1949, I must share with you how long it took me to fully
experience that your own paper was written in 1949, and not in 1969.

*Searles:* Which paper?

*Langs:* Your paper on transference and countertransference
(Searles, 1978-1979). After all, I had gone through the literature
chronologically, and established a time sequence in my head. And to
reorganize that sequence in so many important areas so as to allow
room for your contribution required a major readjustment. Winnicott's 1949 paper is recognized as a landmark paper; it was a bold
and brilliant essay at the time. And you had already written something quite similar; your paper has all of these innovative qualities,
too. It is still a very original contribution today, some thirty years
later. I just had to share with you the amazement, really, in terms of
the gifts that are revealed in that first paper.

*Searles:* Well, let me just tell you how I am reacting today, so far. It
may be obvious to you and quite visible: I feel that you are going to
destroy me. You're starting to put the squeeze on me. It is similar to
what I feel you did with some of these poor bastardly therapists in
*The Bipersonal Field* (Langs, 1976a) and, my god, I dread it and I
cringe and I can't supply these answers. I can't tell you what
determines at what juncture I might do, with a neurotic or borderline
patient, the kind of thing that I much more commonly did with the
chronically schizophrenic patients. I have told many audiences that,
in my work with nonschizophrenic patients, at one or another
juncture, relatively infrequently, I express feelings with an explicit-
ness which is relatively commonplace in my work with schizophrenic patients; but what determines my timing of my doing so I
cannot, I can't possibly—and I can say, too, I've told you before—
papers that I have written I treat something as bastard children. You
see, I don't want to be held responsible for them in a really grindingly
searching manner.

*Langs:* I understand what you are saying. That is one of my problems: I get this from the people I teach all the time, as you can well imagine. I know that this can be hurtful, but that is not why I do it. I am trying to establish a sound understanding of the therapeutic interaction, to identify our errors and how they can be detected. I really feel badly as to how threatening this can be, but I do feel that this quality lies in the nature of our field of study and in what and how we must truly learn in order to grow. I am indeed coming back to the issue of the frame, and to how deviations evoke active material from the patient—something we did not fully discuss last time.

I am a stickler on methodology: there is a listening process, intervening, and looking for validation. I disagree with the notion that if you get seemingly productive material it means that the intervention was valid, because hurtful interventions are powerful adaption-evoking stimuli.

*Searles:* But you react to that. I thought that you do hold to that, do you not?

*Langs:* No, I don't.

*Searles:* In your book? Oh, not merely productive material, but material that has to do with helpful figures.

*Langs:* Yes: I look for specific indicators of constructive productivity. In other words, I feel that you can have seemingly productive material based on a hurtful behavior of the analyst. Now, you say that this patient ultimately showed an increased level of ego integration.

*Searles:* I cannot say what the final result was, for she is still in treatment. She showed an improved level of ego integration after, and seemingly in part as a result of, the events which the passage you quoted touched upon, and that is still true now, some couple of years later. I regard that intervention, and its aftermath, as being among the most durably favorable turning points in my work with her thus far.

*Langs:* All right. Let me spell out my thoughts. Here is a deviation in the frame. Now, I must say that my position on the frame has so extensively and consistently been validated that it has really hardened. In fact, you have helped me in this regard, through your concept of therapeutic symbiosis, which lends theoretical support and affords further clarification to my ideas. I am convinced now that maintaining a stable and secure frame is vital to establishing what you allude to so nicely as an optimal holding environment. As you say about the patient in the early autistic phase, the maintenance of that hold is the analyst's basic task.

*Searles:* You're not forgetting that the patient becomes one's *own* optimal holding environment?

*Langs:* No. That's the other side of the holding functions of the frame. I thought that recognition of that side of the situation was exquisite again on your part. The only analyst besides myself to have approached this topic is Judith Kestenberg (1975) who, in writing on infants and mothers and holding, discussed how the infant holds the mother and related it in a general way to the analysand and his analyst. She wrote, too, of how the infant may facilitate being held. Based on her work and on other clues, I had written about the holding qualities of the ground rules—and of the patient—for the analyst. And I was quite struck by the fact that you make this point very explicitly in terms of the patient's hold of the analyst. I would like to ask if you have had further thoughts about this subject— have you expanded your thinking about how the patient holds the analyst?

*Searles:* No, I haven't thought about it in those terms. I'm struggling with the fact that I have so much to say about your book, you see, and I'm afraid it won't—

*Langs:* All right then, let's get to it. Let me finish this point, because it does serve as a transition to *The Bipersonal Field* (Langs, 1976a). In regard to modifications in the frame, it is my belief—really, my finding—that the frame as defined by the ground rules, the usual ground rules of analysis and therapy, offers the optimal hold for both patient and analyst or therapist—what you call a therapeutic symbiosis.

*Searles:* Yes, it makes sense, right, immediately.

*Langs:* And I have found that as soon as you modify the frame, there is an inherent invitation toward a pathological symbiosis. That is one of the ideas that I wanted you to respond to.

*Searles:* Oh, a very neat idea; right. I have a whole bunch of positive things that I will mention in brief, to give you at least an example of some of the things that I have valued a great deal about the book, and then a relatively few suggestions that I wanted to make—Okay?

Where you say on page 11, "I conceive of this volume as a major contribution toward the integration of the interactional dimension into classical psychoanalytic theory and technique," I frankly thought you were being grandiose; but by the time I completed the reading of the book I regarded this statement of yours as fully justified.

*Langs:* Well, thank you. I like to be straightforward, even though it means taking risks of that kind.

*Searles:* Now in the second paragraph on page 26 here, I thought you provided an excellent definition of projective identification, the clearest that I had come across. The one suggestion that I had, there, was that I thought it might be emphasized a bit how unconscious the patient is of this. But nonetheless, your discussions of projective identification are the clearest that I have come across and the most helpful to me.

*Langs:* Could I ask you another question, if we can pause from time to time. I noticed that you do not use the concept of projective identification. I believe that instead, you use the term projection in both senses: the intrapsychic and interactional. I can show you examples where you talk about projection as an interactional mechanism, such as when you write of the patient projecting into you qualities of figures from the past which you then experience. There, you are referring to an interactional effect, which I think really is projective identification. In other words, I wondered, had you been familiar with the term? Was there some reason why you didn't use it?

*Searles:* No; I had not been familiar with the term, really, until

recent years. Through reading Kernberg's writings I started to feel
required to try to get used to thinking in those terms. I still don't. One
reason is that I don't feel that there is such a thing as projection in the
way that term has customarily been used, as though it had no ground
in reality. In support of my position I refer to Freud's (1922) statement that projection occurs not "into the sky, so to speak, where
there is nothing of the sort already," but rather onto persons who in
reality possess an attitude qualitatively like that which the projecting person is attributing to them. So that what I talk of as projection
is, I think, what most people would talk of as projective identification.

*Langs:* Exactly. Some analysts, such as Grotstein (in press), feel
that every projection has an *interactional* component—even if it is
directed toward an internal object.

*Searles:* And what most people talk of as projection is, to my mind,
simply not a phenomenon that exists. Something that is totally
projected like onto a movie screen—I don't think that happens.

*Langs:* Yes. My impression was that you use projection primarily
in the sense of projective identification.

*Searles:* Now where you say, in paragraph 2 on page 28, that "the
therapeutic bipersonal field, in which the patient and therapist will
interact, depends on the secure and clearly defined framework," That
is a very nice concept—very basic to the book.
   I can give you dozens of things that I admire about the book. I don't
know whether this is the place to go into that, you see. What you said
about the value of one's not having heard a patient's history before
one sees him in consultation seems to me very sound and it is
something that I relatively seldom have followed in the past. I've
usually been accustomed to hearing a history, and on the basis of
having read this statement of yours I have become determined to
depart more and more from hearing the history. The last time I went
to NIMH, a couple of weeks ago, I arranged with them not to give me
the history, ahead of time, of the patient I am to interview.

*Langs:* What sort of experience was it for you?

*Searles:* I haven't started yet. I am going to be doing it this new way next time; but I have done it without a history, actually, a few times at various institutions, and I think it goes better, really. There is always the anxiety that one would miss some very major thing in the patient's recent history, for example. But so be it. And I think that one has cleaner hands in a way, then, in doing the interview without having heard the history.

And what you say of introjective identification, I also found very well said.

*Langs:* In your writings, it seems to me that you also use introjection primarily in an interactional sense.

*Searles:* One of the main things I like most about the book is the appreciation of the patients' creativity, their providing unconscious supervision to the therapist, their providing the material needed for him to make interpretations.

*Langs:* I want to remind you that much of that was inspired by your own papers. Once you put me on the beam, I think I did some nice things with it; but I have no idea how long it would have taken me without your contributions.

*Searles:* Now I have in my work with patients suffered a great deal from a fear that I am basically, when all the rest is said and done, diabolical. And I found it very helpful in your book here in paragraph 2 on page 51, for example, where you say, "We see here something that is absolutely characteristic of both the patient and the therapist, although hopefully it will be in different proportions for each of them. There is the wish to cure and be cured, and there is the wish to remain ill and do harm. In fact, even in the patient's or therapist's most destructive communications and hurtful interactional efforts, there is a kernel of therapeutic intention and hope."

You see, I've got too many things to say positively to cover them all.

*Langs:* Perhaps you can skim along. Of course, I'm more interested in the critical side.

*Searles:* You introduced many good terms here that have seemed to me to be very succinct and to the point.

*Langs:* Many of them are developed from terms coined by others. One reviewer (Seitz, 1978) called them neologisms; since the review was unfavorable to the point of being abusive, I suspect he might have meant it, on some level, in the psychiatric sense. Perhaps I'm being oversensitive, but to me he seemed to imply that new terms are psychotic per se. They were certainly not evaluated vis-à-vis the data I presented.

*Searles:* I find that your descriptions of framework cure very helpful.

*Langs:* Yes, I think it's a very useful concept. But it hasn't been picked up by many analysts or therapists as yet.

*Searles:* And your description of the analyst's unconscious contribution to the patient's acting out is, I think, eminently sound.

*Langs:* You have a term for that too: I think you call it *introjective acting out* (Searles, 1958). I call it *interactional acting out* (Langs, 1976a, b).

*Searles:* Toward the bottom of page 79, you say that "the therapist's appropriate love is expressed by maintaining the boundaries," and you indicate that his further appropriate expression of love would have been an accurate and well-timed interpretation, in the particular instance under discussion. That very much needs saying, that kind of thing. It helps me to keep straight in my work.

Well, I am up to page 96. I have starred and written "excellent" in the margins at a very great many junctures—far more that I'll be able to cover here, really. What you said there in your introduction, that statement which I at first thought grandiose, seemed to me, by the time I had finished reading the book, fully justified. That is, the book is a major contribution, the most major that I have ever encountered, toward an integration of what you call the interactional dimension (or what the Sullivanians call the interpersonal dimension) into classical psychoanalytic theory and technique. In one place I wrote across the top of a couple of these pages that you were pointing up, here, in a most effective way, the deficiencies of the classical psychoanalytic viewpoint. What you are presenting is something in my mind vastly superior to that.

Shall I tell you some of the suggestions I had? There were only about a third or a quarter as many of these as there were of my more positive comments. But again, to save time, I may have to limit myself to a few examples. I will get them said in brief, and I would assume that you have heard eighty percent of them already, because you have had so many discussions of your work. But I think there may be a few that you haven't heard before.

*Langs:* I would like to hear them.

*Searles:* Now, on page 98, "The interface has a location in the bipersonal field that tells us which of the two participants, from moment to moment, is exerting the greater influence on what is being communicated." I felt that this gets close to my ideas about the therapist's immersion in the patient's autistic world, and as to *who* is immersed in *whose* world, you see. I don't know where to carry it from there; but that was a note that I made and that was why I appreciate your having read one of those reprints (Searles, 1973a) I gave you recently, because I thought it linked up.

Now here is something I'm sure you have heard before; but I doubt very much that you realize how pulverizingly critical and condemnatory you are being, at least verbally, to the therapist. I marvelled, in some instances, that the therapist was able to go on reporting after the degree of condemnation that you had apparently been giving him—at least as judged by your words. It seemed to me that the fact that he did go on, and constructively so, as the seminars proceeded with the same therapist, indicated that nonverbally you're much less unkind than your words would indicate.

*Langs:* Yes; I rely on that, and on the very positive spirit with which I teach. Is there anything further you could say about that?

*Searles:* Yes. I will say something about it.

*Langs:* I would like to hear more about that because I do adopt a

very direct teaching approach, because that is the patient's unconscious position. But from what I can gather, my efforts are rather
unique in this respect. Many of my supervisees do experience this
mixture of threat and support or promise.

*Searles:* I was reminded of the harshness that one heard, here in the
Washington area years ago, to be characteristic of Sullivan in his
doing of supervision. I never had the experience myself, of being
supervised by him; but he was notorious for the severity of his
comments to supervisees. Nonetheless, they went on and got a great
deal from him; so it was evidently worthwhile.

A couple of papers that I wrote about supervision (Searles, 1955,
1962)—which I know you've read; I guess you've read everything I've
written—have some relevancy here. In those papers I describe what I
call the reflection process, wherein one finds that, in the supervisory
relationship, there are reflections of the same difficulties, basically,
as those which are troubling the treatment relationship itself. Now,
it seemed to me in reading your book, that one saw this kind of thing
going on, on occasion—when, for example, you seem to be, in
effect—judging by your words—castigating the therapist for his
being so harsh with the patient. You see, it is the same thing going
on. The patient was undoubtedly doing things that evoked this harsh
and condemnatory response from the therapist, and he would bring
it into your supervisory seminar and do things that gave you no
alternative but to be severe—and I, too, would find myself shocked at
some of the things the therapist had done.

*Langs:* Your goal, then, would be to become aware of what it was
in therapy that was being repeated in the supervisory field?

*Searles:* Right; yes.
Another way I thought of it was that you very much need to
integrate the unconscious supervisory psychodynamics into your
manifest supervising.

*Langs:* Right. I am doing a piece on supervision now, and I do
attempt such an integration (Langs, 1978b, 1979).

*Searles:* I've learned a great deal from this book and have devoted more time to it than to any other I've read in years. I am checking all of the things I've already mentioned.

Here I notice that at one particular juncture, in contrast to what I've been saying, it is evident that the therapist is relatively little hurt by your so harsh-sounding criticism in the previous seminar meeting. The way he turns up at this next meeting, he is functioning in such a way that he clearly has not been appreciably hurt by your recent criticism—and, you see, the book doesn't explain why. It may well be that there's nonverbal stuff going on that's quite at odds with the verbal.

*Langs:* Some people have read this book and find an enormous sense of compassion in my efforts, while others read it and believe me to be rather destructive. I react to the latter in a naive way: I believe that I am stating, in as kindly and supportive fashion as possible, what must be said. I also suspect that most supervision is woefully inadequate.

*Searles:* I notice that as time went on, in my reading, your compassion became evident to me. After you have told the therapist a great deal in a harsh-sounding way, then your compassion becomes very evident.

Now I am sure that it has been recommended to you—and that you, for your own good reasons, have elected not to act upon the recommendations—to use material from your own patients. That would make all the difference.

*Langs:* Right.

*Searles:* It would remove completely any aspect of this book as having been written in terms of your opining from a superior position. If we readers had a chance for you to share with us your own mistakes, then you would no longer be subject to that kind of criticism.

*Langs:* The reason I don't present my own material is related to my commitment to the frame and to my patients.

*Searles:* Well, I find the problems of disguising of patient material so difficult as to make it next to impossible for me to use material from my own patients. One reason I had been able to, in my work at the Lodge, was that those people were so very, very ill that I felt that if any one of them becomes sufficiently well to ever encounter an article that I have written, containing material about her or him, and be able to read it, he or she would have no real complaint coming. But when you are working with less disturbed people, many of whom are colleagues in psychiatry or related disciplines, it is an almost impossible problem. But even if you were to put in a few examples, that would take the onus off, you see.

*Langs:* Let me explain my position a bit more. When I wrote my first book, *The Technique of Psychoanalytic Psychotherapy* (1973, 1974), almost all of the clinical vignettes were derived from supervisory experiences, though I did not exclude a rare, highly disguised vignette from my own clinical work. And I found that the most technical books circulate among lay people, and I accepted direct, and especially indirect, material from my patients who learned of those books or who knew of them before coming to see me, as what I now call *commentaries* (Langs, 1978a) on that deviation—a modification in total confidentiality and, in some sense, neutrality and anonymity as well. And I quickly realized that they rightfully let me know that this really damaged the basic hold that I offerred as a therapist and analyst. It also generated an image of me as someone who utilizes the work with my patients in some form beyond their basic need to be helped—for some unilateral need of my own, which was a disservice and hurt to them. Basic trust was impaired and I was experienced as evoking damaging, hurtful introjects—negative introjects—that could compromise therapeutic outcome. Once I appreciated all of that—and why am I one of the first analysts to do so?—there was no choice: my first and most fundamental commitment as a therapist is to my patients. I would never knowingly do anything to harm them or impair the therapeutic setting and hold that they need for a truly adaptive cure. I firmly decided to never, ever again make any use of the material from my patients except for interpretive work in their sessions, and to maintain strict and total confidentiality and the rest.

*Searles:* I see. That's very interesting. Yes.

*Langs:* And I made this statement publicly in one of my papers (Langs, 1975b) to clear the air. On the other hand, my justification for using supervisory material is based on my position that there are only two reasons to modify the frame in regard to total confidentiality. The first is based on a therapist's need to get analyzed; you have to tell your analyst everything that comes to mind. The second is that the only way you can learn to do therapy or analysis is directly from supervision. So, I use only material from the latter situation which must be made public for supervisory reasons, and I then disguise it as I would for any patient. I feel that I am not for needs of my own, the prime reason for the public exposure of the material, and that therefore I could reasonably use that material in my writings.

*Searles:* Yes; that's right. Oh, yes, I don't question your using this material; I don't feel that your using it was harmful. And I think that I understand better now why you don't use material from your work with your own patients.

*Langs:* There are many who don't understand the point, and mistrust my failure to present my own clinical data.

*Searles:* Yes; I'm sure that they did. Okay, I don't think it will take much longer here.

On the middle of page 298 you say, "In addition, there is another point to be made. Her comment about not accepting help from others is also based on an unconscious perception of the therapist's failure to accept the help she is attempting to offer him. This too is a cause for depression for patients," and so on. Now, here I felt that you should apply your own logic—that you are using in the book—to an understanding of the therapist's unconscious "failure" or refusal to accept the patient's supportive psychotherapy. That is, according to your own logic, supportive psychotherapy tends to be damaging and not really helpful, you see, so that a therapist naturally would tend to ward off that kind of therapy. It simply is an extension of your own logic into an understanding—

*Langs:* If it was a true effort at support rather than an interpretive moment, I would agree with that. That is an interesting distinction you make there.

*Searles:* Okay.

*Langs:* Let me just add that I think that most often your point applies to patients' conscious efforts to be therapeutic, as compared to their unconscious efforts.

*Searles:* Yes, that makes sense.

*Langs:* I think that when they try to do it consciously, it is usually not helpful and has a different unconscious motive as compared to when these endeavors are undertaken without conscious awareness.

*Searles:* Okay, fair enough.
Now on page 311, in the lower half of the page, I was starting to get a sense that you are implying that any responses from the patient which are primarily nontransference in nature are based on perceptions of illness in the therapist—that is, as though it were either one or the other of those two possibilities. Do you see what I mean?

*Langs:* No. Could you clarify your impression?

*Searles:* Well, you talk, rightfully enough, of transference and nontransference elements. And your book contains (in its treatment of the nontransference, accurate, realistic perceptions on the patient's part of the therapist) so many examples of where the nontransference elements from the therapist are manifestations of *illness* on his part—that is, depression, you see, or unconscious sexual aims toward the patient, or whatever, so that the impression tends to grow on the reader that anything that is nontransference on the therapist's part is apt to be something bad. I think that needs something said about it.

*Langs:* Yes. That should have been said very explicitly. Those unconscious perceptions are a function of the therapist's conscious and unconscious communications—constructive or destructive. Your impression is primarily a function of the empirical nature of the book and the nature of the actual interventions or failures to intervene—most of which happened to involve countertransferences.

*Searles:* Because that's what classical analysts are afraid is the case, isn't it? That's what would tend to make them defensive and want to regard everything as transference.

*Langs:* Right.

*Searles:* When the reality of themselves must be (according to their unconscious and exaggerated fears) something bad and noxious.

*Langs:* Right. As I said, your impression stems from the actual work of the presenting therapists.

*Searles:* I understand; I thought of that—that they are people who are early in the field and there are a lot of problems tending to interfere a great deal with their work.

*Langs:* I am aware of the need to present examples of valid interventions and demonstrate the positive introjective consequences of such work.

*Searles:* Here is another comment I am sure you have heard many times before: oftentimes, what you were telling the supervisee was very, very perceptive and accurate, but too much for a supervisee, especially a supervisee who is not in analysis, to be hearing.

*Langs:* Oh, yes. There are two points about that. One is that I edited the book and added many elaborating comments that hadn't actually been made in the seminar. But the other is related to a basic supervisory issue: What do you do with a supervisee when these issues are apparent, and though he is not in analysis, the patient needs his understanding and some resolution of his countertransference? My justification for all of this has been that this is what the patient is in reality struggling with, and the therapist must know something about that. Now, what do you do?

*Searles:* Well, I'm not sure; it is, of course, a difficult thing. I tend to think, as regards telling a therapist anything as bluntly as you evidently frequently do, that it is something in the nature of a premature interpretation, and therefore I don't think it is going to help the patient whom I'm concerned about. If I give the therapist a very major, very premature interpretation, it will upset him. It will not help the patient to have the therapist more upset than usual, so that it isn't an either-or thing. Rather than make a blunt, and probably premature, supervisory interpretation, I try to *intimate* something about that same realm. I think, now that you have asked that, I would recommend to you that, in your work with the therapists in your seminars, you utilize something of the same allusive subtlety that you recommend they utilize in their work with their patients, as regards any implied acknowledgment of the therapist's psychopathology as it becomes revealed by their work with their patients. That is, I recommend that rather than your interpreting explicitly that they have this or that countertransference problem, that you phrase your supervisory interpretations more implicitly, so as to convey an implicit commentary upon the countertransference difficulties you perceive in them. In that spirit there is something kind of implicit, you see, not quite as blunt because in this more indirect style, you would be tossing it out for them in proportion as they can start hearing it.

*Langs:* Yes, that's interesting. I think that my more recent supervisees, who are better put together than those who worked with me earlier, actually tolerate my straightforward approach quite well. I believe that patients are characteristically quite blunt with their unconscious communications about the therapist and that supervisors tend to back away from, or often fail to develop, truly comprehensive formulations. Still, you touch upon a major issue that I don't know how to fully resolve.

Pertinent to this point is my failure to fully appreciate how divergent and perhaps revolutionary much of *The Bipersonal Field* is. I failed to sufficiently anticipate how disturbing my ideas could be for experienced analysts and others. I tried to discuss this in my preface, but I should have said a lot more.

*Searles:* Yes, I think a few pages of explanation about why you don't use material from your own patients would have minimized a lot of potential opposition.

*Langs:* There are two sides to this issue. One side is the observation that these valid and extensive unconscious perceptions and commentaries will be in the patient's unconscious communications, and I am reluctant to deliberately avoid expressing directly what the patient is conveying indirectly. And I do use discretion and modulation, but I like to be right where the patient is at. I do this in supervision. I think you're right that the supervisee often is poorly prepared for it, so to me it's a dilemma: the patient saying it, is struggling with it, and adequate therapy depends on the therapist's appreciation for the truth of the situation. It is not me that disturbs the supervisee, but the patient; I am trying to be open and helpful.

*Searles:* Yes; it is a dilemma. I think maybe we can start getting a little more light on this with something which I hadn't thought of—how it links up—until now. I have come to a place here on page 338, just below the middle, where you are saying: "It was at the very moment that the patient said in this session that she felt that he understood her because of his empathic response, that the therapist interrupted her associations to ask, if I may paraphrase it, What the hell have I been doing for the last three months?" Here I postulate what I call intrapsychic jealousy on the therapist's part. That is, it's as though he is in two parts here. He is in one part which is receiving this acknowledgment from the patient of how empathic he is. But let's say the greater part of him has been the one who has been functioning in the last three months and feels jealous of this part of him that is getting the acknowledgment, so that he is jealous of himself, in a sense, and I think that jealousy-phenomena helped to account for some of the dilemma that you and I have been discussing, concerning the doing of supervision.

I'll speak for myself, and tell you that when I'm working with a therapist in supervision and he is doing something beautifully in his work with the patient, I'm subject to feeling jealous of him because, say, he is doing better with the patient than I feel I could do if I were in his position, or I will feel jealous of the patient for receiving from the therapist something that I'm not receiving from him and did not—so my memory serves me—receive from my therapist; and so on, you see. And at times when I might be harsh—and I am sure my supervisees find me oftentimes harsh; I don't question that for a moment—but I think that *some* of the times when they are finding me harsh, I am speaking out of jealousy.

*Langs:* Yes, there is also the jealousy in the supervisee of the analyst who understands the patient when he is unable to do so. But you are talking about this in respect to your own introject, which I think is a much neglected aspect of the supervisory interaction.

About your concept of jealousy, you refer to Melanie Klein's work in your writings on this subject. I have the very strong feeling that you don't move enough into the issue of envy, which is much more primitive and destructive than jealousy. I think that when you use jealousy you are using it to refer to both jealousy and envy. You alluded to her definition of jealousy in terms of whole objects and often, three-person rivalries. I believe that you feel—and I think rightfully so—that you are studying here a very important emotion that is a dimension of many, many interactions, including that in therapy and analysis. It has been a relatively neglected subject.

The Kleinians emphasize envy as one of the most powerful destructive forces in the therapeutic experience. As you said, it is often related to the negative therapeutic reaction. But their concept of primitive envy carries with it a greater impact than the notion of jealousy, and I think that what you are into is also more powerful than the emotions and experiences implied by jealousy. I think that in addition to the jealousy that the patient, for instance, has of this supervisee who has made this nice interpretation, there is the envy directed at the supervisee and the concomitant wish to destroy his power and potency, and all the rest.

*Searles:* I guess I have trouble distinguishing between primitive envy and intrapsychic jealousy, because the primitive envy Melanie Klein links to the patient's—the child's, the infant's—envy of the breast; so that seems to bring in a jealousy-triangle kind of constellation.

*Langs:* You see, here again I think that you are using jealousy in the same sense that they use envy.

The other response to your comments about the intensity of this book is related to my work. I was writing *The Therapeutic Interaction* (1976b) based on a concentrated study of the literature, and I desperately wanted to include some clinical material to complete the picture. I couldn't include it there, so I decided to develop a separate, related book. I had kept a file of the tapes of these seminars, so I simply selected five tapes that I had marked with an "X", meaning that they were more interesting than the others. This was the only basis on which I picked them, after which I had them transcribed and I reworked them—primarily to update my ideas, which were expanding rapidly at the time. These seminars took place during the height of my clinical discoveries—personal and perhaps, general—so there was a tremendous upsurge of new ideas.

*Searles:* Yes. One of the many things that I liked about the book is that you brought in how your concepts have been changing, just in very recent years, in very major ways. That brings into the book a note of modesty that helps to offset the somewhat alienating effect, upon the reader, of those times when you're pointing out, to the therapists whom you're teaching, their mistakes. So the fact that you are able to speak of your own growth and your own discarding of previously held positions—

*Langs:* Yes, but that sense of discovery is one of the reasons why the book is so intense, that's what I wanted to say. With discovery comes frankness, openness—it is difficult to be otherwise. I think of my current supervision, and while there is still a good deal of direct work, it doesn't have the same intensity. In part, the residents' anxiety seems to have been heightened because I didn't have complete mastery over what I was teaching. I thought they would share with me the excitement of discovery, of fresh perspectives—so much of it unfolded from minute to minute in the supervisory situation, where I was once removed from the patient and much freer. I think the creative potential of supervision has been terribly overlooked. There, you have a certain freedom to play with the material and to create that you don't have in your own immediate clinical work. But where I thought they would share the excitement of actual moments of innovation, they seldom did so. New and different ideas are experienced by almost everyone—seasoned analyst or novice—as dangerous, frightening, a threat. And to make matters worse, there is a kind of seemingly merciless focus on the therapist, because of the many errors and because of the patient's focus.

*Searles:* Well, that really is what does the job, though; it has to be said. That's what does the job in the book; that's really what does it. It very forcibly and lastingly conveys the therapist's or analyst's—and

the reader inevitably gets that message, that this kind of thing goes on
at the hands of experienced analysts as well as at those of beginning
psychotherapists—

*Langs:* A lot of people have denied that point, claiming that I took
such terribly disturbed beginning therapists, that the book is not
representative of the usual analytic and therapeutic work. The more I
read and hear, the more I feel the absurdity of such an attitude.

*Searles:* It's nonsense.
Now I have a very few more comments; I'm nearly through. At one
point on page 403, I made a note that on the preceding page, the
material suggests that the therapist is unconsciously competing with
his patient for treatment from you. And repeatedly in the book you're
evidently—as you later make explicit, toward the end of the book—
working with therapists who are not in analysis, and you repeatedly
recommend to them self-analysis, which we know can be very lonely,
very limitedly useful to them. So your way of doing supervision with
them inevitably must be arousing greatly their needs for personal
therapy, and you're available for the time being and have the ability
and all, so that there must be a lot of their seeking treatment from
you, and of their being jealous of the patient for his or her being the
object of your compassionate concern—to the extent that the patients
are, in the book, you see. I don't mean that you should clam up, but
rather that it would be well for you to keep that dimension in mind.

*Langs:* Yes, your point is well taken. I think what you are also
saying is that the supervisees will do things with their patients in an
unconscious effort to evoke a therapeutic response from me, in order
to reveal some need of that kind. This is part of the rather neglected
interaction between the two bipersonal fields.

*Searles:* The two being the therapy and the supervision?

*Langs:* Yes, I am doing a book on it (Langs 1979). I was going to
call it "The Tripersonal Field," but it isn't a single, tripersonal field,
it's really two separate bipersonal fields that interact in very interesting ways.

*Searles:* Now, at the middle of page 413, you're saying, "In his own way, the therapist is attempting to have the patient mobilize ego capacities that she lacks in dealing with the boyfriend, and it may well be that he has chosen this patient not only to assist himself, but also to become an assistant therapist to the boyfriend." You remember all of that, I'm sure. Now, I felt that this kind of thing contains an example of what I call the reflection process, that in the supervision, my guess was, that you were unconsciously feeling—no, let me express this, instead, from the therapist's point of view—that he would tend unconsciously to feel that *you* are the patient's therapist, not *he* but *you* are, and that you are trying in that regard—if there is any truth in this view—you are trying to enlist the therapist as your assistant therapist, you see. So that's getting spelled out in the treatment.

*Langs:* That's interesting.

*Searles:* Whether that's true or not, that is the kind of thing I was trying to suggest in my two papers about the supervisory dynamics.

*Langs:* Will you bring that up with the supervisee at times or will you just use it for your own understanding?

*Searles:* I use it in either way at different times.
Here is another aspect of one of the things I was commenting about, where I sensed that your type of supervision greatly stimulates this therapist's need for therapy and that the therapist then unconsciously turns to the patient for therapy because even she, the patient, is less tabooed than are you in the supervisory seminar context, you see. So that on the one hand, I think, you stimulate the therapist's need for therapy, a need which he has, but which you tend to bring to the surface. But on the other hand, there is also, in the supervisory setting, evidently a strong taboo on his turning to you, in any explicit way, for therapy—a taboo based in part upon the realistically-feared, potential jealousy on the part of his fellow seminar-members, as well as upon the realistic limitations of the supervision—frequency, and so on.

*Langs:* Well, I don't become involved in any type of therapeutic effort toward the supervisee. I define the field as a learning field, rather than a therapeutic one.

*Searles:* But your style of supervision inevitably is confronting the therapist, time after time, with his very clear need for treatment. So that's a part of what is often called treatment: namely, confrontations.

*Langs:* Perhaps in its broadest sense. I meant therapy in terms of conscious and direct interpretive efforts; you're talking about in its broadest and less precisely defined meaning—there are many kinds of experiences with therapeutic potential.

*Searles:* One other thing and then I'm through, and I appreciate your allowing me to get this off my chest.

*Langs:* I appreciate your giving it so much thought. I am really very honored.

*Searles:* At the middle of page 437, you say that "most psychoanalysts have been analyzed under conditions in which the framework of their own analysis has been modified"—as was the case in my instance, do you remember?

*Langs:* Yes.

*Searles:* And you continue, "and I think that this accounts in part for the extensive general blind spot in regard to the meanings of the framework, and the neglect of the vast implications of erroneous interventions, that prevails in the psychoanalytic literature." Now, you gave me to think that your training analysis had been highly classical, and had been largely devoid of the departures from the classical analytic position that my late analyst on occasion indulged in; and at the time I told you about those you seemed, time and again, on the shocked side. I wondered if your training analysis—let's assume that it was, indeed, very largely free from such departures by your analyst. I want to raise a question whether you are putting too negative a connotation upon such departures, as a way of dealing with possible envy on your part, you see.

*Langs:* Yes, the deviations in my analysis were not as gross as the ones that you described, though my analysis—as I've gone back over it—was filled with the more controlled and subtle departures that are typical of so-called training analyses: reporting to an education committee, making extraneous comments, noninterpretive interventions.

*Searles:* You see, what I am trying to suggest is, again, on the positive side of these disruptions of the field.

*Langs:* I understand, but I don't believe that envy has distorted my evaluation of the relevant clinical data.

*Searles:* And I had another thought; this is not in the realm of criticism but a different way of looking at the bipersonal field. The frame of the bipersonal field is the area in which the patient's difficulties and the therapist's difficulties may first become manifest—in the frame, or boundaries, of the field. Now, that way of looking at it is, I think, free from blame. Looking at it that way, one is not blaming the therapist. It is a little different way of looking at it. The way that your book tends to look at it is that because of the therapist's failure to develop and maintain a secure frame, the patient's symptomatology worsens. That is true, but looking at it that way tends to carry the blame-onus with it, whereas this other way of viewing it does not. The view I am suggesting would emphasize that one reason why it is so important to be attentive to the frame of the bipersonal field is because it is there that the patient's difficulties will become manifest.

*Langs:* They will impinge there—right. Yes, the frame is, indeed, a major arena for the expression of psychopathology—for both patient and analyst.

*Searles:* And that isn't blaming the analyst at all, to suggest that he attend to the frame as being the area where his own difficulties, as well as those of the patient, will become manifest. It needn't be said in a blaming way.

*Langs:* If that quality is present, I certainly want to eliminate it; your points are very well taken. I think that inevitably some of the earliest issues in therapy do come up related to the frame—communications, behavioral pressures—and that both the therapist and the patient will have to explore, manage, and interpret. It comes back to this point: it seems to me the fair way to say this is that there is an inevitable or inherent need in both the patient and therapist for alterations in the frame, for the pathological symbiotic gratification and defenses that it affords both of them—as well as a need for its mastery. But, if the therapist is aware of this wish, and manages his own propensities in this respect and resolves them—gets them insightfully under control—he will, as a rule, adopt a general attitude toward the frame which is in the direction of its maintenance. And it will be supported by the material from the patient—the indirect material.

I was reacting primarily to my own empirical findings, to the patient's derivative responses which, in contrast to his conscious comments, were uniformly critical of a therapist who altered the frame and which reflected positive introjects when he maintained it and interpreted the patient's wish for a deviation. There is a strong tendency among therapists to accept modifications in the frame, to think of my viewpoint as rigid and to dismiss it on that basis, because flexibility must be the hallmark. Why that concept has to necessarily mean the best technique for the patient, I have no idea. It goes along with an approach to these issues that stresses looseness and the patient's manifest reactions, while either ignoring his derivatives or treating them as inherently distorted and pathological—as fantasies rather than *commentaries* which contain quite valid unconscious evaluations and perceptions, as well as distortions.

There is almost no literature on errors in technique. It is implicit in your work, since you deal with the kinds of things that can go on between the analyst and his patients, and the ways in which errors may come into it. Now, here too, you might suggest that the concept of errors already has this kind of blaming, condemnatory quality.

*Searles:* Yes, it does.

*Langs:* Yet at the same time I feel that there is a need to define a correct, as compared to an incorrect, intervention. Sure, there is always a continuum, and a gray area in the middle—but I do find that the patient's unconscious responses is a reliable guide. I don't agree with those analysts who think that any one of five interventions can be made at a particular moment. I really believe that there is an optimal intervention and a correct moment or two for it to be given.

But once I introduce the concept of errors, there is a question of the tone, and the need to be quite clear that there are no moral or condemnatory implications to my ideas and comments. Greenson's (1967, 1972) unique discussion of errors refers to rather gross errors, where the patient points out to the analyst something that's obvious and quite conscious—for example, a disruptive attitude that he hasn't mentioned for years, an angry tone of voice, and things of that sort. The kinds of countertransference-based expressions you are writing about, and that I get into, are much more unconscious, sometimes on both sides, and many, though by no means all, are much more subtle.

But, the literature on errors, limited as it is, alludes almost entirely to the analyst's verbal interventions and interpretive efforts. You, once again, are an exception because you refer in one paper to possible errors in the area of limit-setting, which you discuss in terms of private practice. You make the point that your model, as mine, had been that the analyst interprets, that his verbal interpretations are the key to his being a good analyst, and that the limits that he creates— you see, a frame experience—

*Searles:* —Are something that is kind of pedestrian, or a chore— a low-class chore—by contrast to the analyst's function, much more highly-touted in our training in past years, of providing interpretations.

*Langs:* Right. You state that you came to realize over the years that this, too, was a significant part of your functions as an analyst.

*Searles:* One patient in particular brought that home to me. This woman I worked with for several years—borderline woman—got that across to me.

*Langs:* Yes. So you were able to learn from her that the creation and maintenance of the frame can be every bit as important as the analyst's usual verbal interventions, you see. And that is in contrast to the usual classical analyst who concentrates on words and fantasies, and their interpretation, not recognizing there are other reality dimensions to his interaction with the patient, and that they are quite crucial in many ways. So the frame area, you see, was set aside, or never carefully investigated.

*Searles:* Yes. One of the many things that I liked about the book was what you said about supportive psychotherapy, as being rife with misalliance cures and as being, essentially, a myth. I think that was very, very well said.

*Langs:* In that connection, a similar attitude is reflected in your remarks about medication—as being quite anti-analytic and anti-therapeutic.

*Searles:* What you said about the patient's wanting drugs, that was awfully good to read. I refer to your saying, on page 155, "The request for medication, virtually without fail, comes at a moment when the therapist has been hurtful, and in addition, hasn't made the inter-pretations that the patient needs."

*Langs:* Did you see that there is a study now out of Michael Reese Hospital on schizophrenic patients, showing that since the advent of the phenothiozines and other tranquilizers, and all the rest, there has been no significant change—

*Searles:* That's right; I did read that, and saved it. I've got it filed away in the file of one of my chronic patients with whom I'm still working. They studied only about 150 patients, I hink; it was a very small number. But still it was interesting to read.

*Langs:* Very dramatic.

*Searles:* I took it as strengthening my arm a bit in not using the drugs.

*Langs:* Exactly. That's why I thought of it. I think that therapists have been looking in the wrong places in their wish to offer better means of therapy. I have a brief paper on a frame issue in an in-patient setting from a social worker at Hillside Hospital (Uchill, 1978-1979). And she suggests that the time has come to look at the in-patient team approach, and to look at the modifications in confidentiality that are involved, the openness of the setting. We must wonder whether this isn't detrimental to the patient, rather than otherwise, and if it isn't an expression of the pathological needs of therapists who are working with schizophrenic patients that have frustrated and frightened them, and who are difficult for them to understand or maintain boundaries with. Her single vignette raises many questions in these areas.

*Searles:* One of the questions that I've asked myself is whether my schizophrenic patients—let's say them, at least, not to mention my patients generally, quite a number of whom I don't write about mainly because they are professional colleagues—would have done better clinically in psychotherapy if I had never written a thing. I think they would have. I think that enough of my energy and hope was shunted off or drained off into this other field, which proved to have an awful lot of gratifications for me, far more than sitting with a mute patient year after year was providing, so that it kept postponing, on and on into the future, the day when I would say to this patient, "You miserable son of a bitch! Why should I spend my life with you?"—you know, that kind of thing, which such a patient may have needed as the only thing that could energize him.

*Langs:* You've just crystalized something for me that I've been working over in bits and pieces, and I agree with you there: there are such risks in writing and we must be cognizant of them and not let them get out of hand. Now I'll show you the other side of it though, the positive side: I really believe that if you hadn't written, you would never have crystalized the insights that you've developed which you were then able to utilize to better help your patients. Writing may also help to lessen a tendency to overinvest in one's work with patients. It is difficult to strike a sound balance. I think you are quite right that when you have such a major area of professional gratification it does lessen struggle.

*Searles:* And it takes away from it and it gets set up as a rival of it. Now, this woman whom I've worked with nearly twenty-five years— we might look forward to your hearing a tape of one of my sessions with her during one of our later discussions. I went through several years with her—a phase that has come to a close only a couple of years back—of feeling a recurrent anguish of guilt about whether I cherished more the patient herself as a person, or her schizophrenic illness. And I kept having to ruefully—that's putting it much too mildly—face the fact that my fascination with her illness kept coming out ahead. During the past couple of years, I have felt confident that this particular, deeply guilt-provoking conflict is now behind me in the work with her. I no longer experience doubt as to my concern for and caring about her, and my interest in her illness now feels to be—no matter how many valuable papers I could write about her illness—in the service primarily of helping her to become free from it.

*Langs:* To complete my thoughts about the frame, analysts have not, after altering the frame, listened to all of the subsequent material as a *commentary* on that modification.

*Searles:* I know; your discussions on that topic, in your book, will have a lasting effect upon my work with patients, I'm sure. That's one of the kinds of data I shall be sure to listen for, from now on, more attentively than I used to.

*Langs:* What happens typically after such an intervention is that we find a major split: the patient directly says, Thank you—he welcomes it—it is very nice of you to be so kind. Then you listen to the continued associations, and you hear of somebody—often himself because of the introject involved—who is trying to overwhelm another person, corner or destroy him, or of someone being seductive, autonomy is lost, boundaries are not being maintained. These are frequent themes. And only rarely is any of this related by the analyst to the altered frame.

*Searles:* This brings me back to the excerpt you read to me earlier today. If I may, I will read it again (Searles, 1977a):
"Several months ago I confided to a middle-aged female analysand that she was, and long had been, my favorite patient; I told her this because I knew that this phenomenon, although in various ways pleasant to me, must indicate one of her major problems. My sharing with her this information (information which represents, obviously,

an aberration in my customary participant-observer functioning with my patients collectively) had highly constructive results in terms of the emergence of a wealth of newly-remembered transference material. She recalled, with intense feelings of murderous rage and grief, how all her life she had felt it absolutely necessary to be pleasing to other people generally and, above all, to her mother. Her negative mother-transference feelings toward me, largely repressed for years in our work, now emerged with an intensity which I found at times frightening and awesome. With all this, she began manifesting a coherency and a purposefulness in her ego-functioning which had been largely lacking before" (p. 371).

So, you see: judicious deviations of this kind may ultimately prove to be constructive.

*Langs:* You are here illustrating two of my findings regarding modifications in the framework (Langs, 1975b, 1976a): (1) that they evoke intense communicative responses and (2) that there is a typical split in how patients respond—manifestly appreciative and latently angry or questioning. The rage and grief may well reflect a valid unconscious perception and introjection of processes within yourself that prompted your self-revelation. In addition, I would postulate that in derivative form they express the patient's feelings toward you for your comment. I would need more material to validate these ideas; for the moment, they may serve as representative of findings under such conditions.

Your consideration that the genetic material must reflect primarily transference responses brings me back to our discussion at the last meeting, and to a point I wanted to clarify. When the analyst deviates, the patient is usually quite stirred up, and virtually always, these are important genetic links.

*Searles:* Genetic, in the sense of her family history?

*Langs:* Right.

*Searles:* The word *genetic* tends to throw one off because it is about genes. I think we might use a better word.

*Langs:* Yes. You had said at our last meeting that one of the ways that you try to safeguard against countertransference expressions in your work with patients, and try to measure the extent to which the patient is involved in transference and distorting responses, is the presence of a connection between his view of or reaction to yourself and an earlier life figure, an earlier genetic figure. And I should have said to you then—and I don't quite know why I missed it, I was thinking about it—that a genetic link is not a suitable criterion for distinguishing transference and nontransference, or for identifying the presence of countertransferences. I tried to show in *The Biperson-al Field* (Langs, 1976a) that nontransference reactions—responses to traumatic, countertransference-based behaviors by the therapist or analyst—also have their genetic antecedents. This is where Racker (1957) comes in; he stated this quite clearly. The distinction between transference and nontransference is quite crucial in this regard: when a patient's response is truly transference-based the analyst has not in actuality repeated the past trauma in some form.

*Searles:* Has not?

*Langs:* Has not. When it's nontransference, the analyst has done just that, and the genetic figure then comes up, not because the patient errantly introduces him, but because the reality tallies in important ways with past realities and with the current pathological inner mental world of the patient.

*Searles:* It's very good; yes, I've started to get hold of what you're saying.

*Langs:* Everything has to be appended to the actualities of the analytic interaction, you see. Interpretations must unfold around the unconscious implications of the actual communicative interaction between patient and therapist or analyst. I am quite convinced clinically—and your comments last time helped to clear the way for me—that there can be no valid interpretation in analysis or psycho-therapy without some connection to the therapeutic interaction as it exists at that moment. Brenner (1969), among many others, wrote that the analyst should be able to validly interpret the implications of experiences outside of the analysis. They are certainly important too. However, clinically I have found that there is always a crucial connection to the analytic interaction, but you have to then know the prevailing unconscious actualities. The analyst must ask himself if he has on any level behaved in a way that is in keeping with a past pathological interaction. If so, the patient is actually experiencing a repetition of that past trauma, you see, which he is working over. Such an experience repeats the past and confirms the basis for the patient's pathology, rather than being discordant with it. As Racker (1957) pointed out, the patient experiences a different reality only when the analyst doesn't behave in keeping with it. So, that the fact that a genetic figure appears in the material—a person from the past—

*Searles:* Oh, no—I don't think that I had meant to say that if a genetic person appears in the material, from the past, that it means that one's own hands are clean—to use that image again.

*Langs:* We both allowed that to slip by in that form.

*Searles:* Yes.

*Langs:* The analyst must determine the prevailing conditions: if he is repeating the pathological past, his verbal interventions will fail to have their intended therapeutic effects and the disruptive influence of his behaviors will prevail. If he has not acted in that way, he is in a position to offer valid interpretations that will have salutary consequences.

*Searles:* Well, but I still think that if the analyst has a sense that what is happening between him and the patient is part of the warp and woof of the patient's history as he, the analyst, has by now come to know it, this is a very large safeguard. Whereas if he becomes involved in what he might wish to think of—erroneously—as a therapeutic symbiosis with the patient, but which the analyst experiences as being brand new in the patient's life, feeling that here, at long last, the patient has found a loving person—namely, the analyst—all this has the quality, in my estimation, of a *folie à deux*.

*Langs:* Yes. It's a somewhat different issue. You are talking about the failure of analysts to appreciate the extent to which a reality may have a counterpart in the past, even when it's related to a healthy development. What I am saying has much more to do with the unconscious meanings, functions, and implications of your interventions—with what has been unconsciously communicated to the patient.

*Searles:* Like, for example, my intervention of telling this woman she had long been my favorite patient.

*Langs:* Yes. And her response was rather typical: it was relatively uncontrolled; you said that it was frightening and awesome. And I suspect that one of the factors was that you had made a direct self-revelation. Now, you were able, somehow—again, you are an exception here—to understand what was happening and to interpret it. Racker (1957) makes the point that if you get into a vicious circle of this type, you will often be so much a part of it that you will not be able to interpret what is really going on. And then you are even more like the earlier figure, who also was, as a rule, quite uninsightful. But you were quite sensitive to the situation and your subsequent interpretations can reestablish the necessary therapeutic difference between yourself and earlier traumatizing figures. It seems to me that you characteristically make noninterpretive interventions like this one, that are somewhat traumatizing, but you are sensitive to their presence and effects. You are therefore able to interpret the unconscious aspects of the traumatic experience, which now makes you quite different from the earlier figure. This provides insight and a positive introject to the patient, and leads to ego integration.

*Searles:* No, I do not agree with your impression that I characteristically make noninterpretive interventions. I feel that, if time allowed here for a sufficiently detailed study of sample clinical situations and their long-range contexts, I might convince you that my interventions are interpretative in their intent. I do think that you are much more dominated than I am by anxiety lest the patient be at all traumatized by the analyst's intervention. But enough of that issue for the time being.

As regards dealing with the effects of one's intervention, I'd like to mention, once again, the demonstration-interviews I do at various hospitals. Oftentimes the residents who have seen my interviews, when they attempt to emulate my way of rather bluntly confronting a patient, are not at all prepared for, or able adequately to deal with, the results of their confronting their patients in a style superficially similar to mine. I feel better equipped, by reason of much past experience, to deal with the results of my confrontations and other interventions.

Now, as for any modification of the field in my telling this woman about her being my favorite patient, I think that one could argue: Where is the field modified, though? I mean, the field was modified long earlier through her having become my favorite patient without my telling her anything of it, and in telling her of it, I was not so much modifying the field as trying to set it right, you see, that was my conscious feeling.

*Langs:* Yes, but I would say that the way to set it right is to come to a point, partly through her unconscious help no doubt, partly through your own self-analysis and working through, where you have resolved this piece of countertransference. And I'll use your own remarks as my model (Searles, 1975): the results of such therapeutic work can best be acknowledged *implicitly* by conveying the difference in your attitude through the way in which you intervene.

*Searles:* Well, you're the one who describes that.

*Langs:* But you said that yourself in your paper on the patient as therapist to the analyst.

*Searles:* Yes; so I might not have told her this so boldly, so bluntly.

*Langs:* I have found that there is a crucial difference for the patient between implicit and explicit communication from the analyst. The latter constitutes a modification of the frame, a self-revelation which the patient then experiences as pathologically exhibitionistic, as an unneeded confession—as some type of countertransference-based expression.

*Searles:* Yes. My way of doing it surely burdened her with my guilt, didn't it? It is inconceivable that I could have said that to her in a nonconfessional way; it had to have some element of a confession.

*Langs:* You say you are still seeing her; her reactions to all of this are still in the material. This type of response goes on and on.

*Searles:* Well, she went on vacation. I got a postcard from her. Most of my patients don't send me postcards. Occasionally they do, but most of them don't.

*Langs:* I call that Langs' law—if you will forgive me: one deviation begets another. That is so typical.

*Searles:* Yes, yes.

*Langs:* You confirmed my ideas in one second, didn't you?

*Searles:* Yes.

*Langs:* Now I would like to show you how it affects the field, the communicative properties of the field. I have now gotten into some new ways of thinking; I would like to tell you a little bit about it. It has something to do with your comment that there is a difference in the way in which the patient and you communicate in the autistic as compared to the symbiotic phase. Let me tell you something about this. It started when I developed the concept of the adaptive context (Langs, 1973, 1978); for me, that is the key to everything.

*Searles:* Yes—"central adaptive context"—right?

*Langs:* Yes.

*Searles:* This is a concept you introduced, isn't it?

*Langs:* Yes, it comes from Freud's (1900) day residue concept; I acknowledge that immediately. The day residue and the dream is I think the model for all mental functioning, the interplay between reality and fantasy (Langs, 1971).

*Searles:* A beautiful concept. I don't think that your book adequately makes clear that it is original with you, though. You see, I, like many analysts, haven't read much about psychotherapy, and because the material in your book is derived from psychotherapy, I didn't know whether maybe there were a number of standard textbooks about psychotherapy which discussed the central adaptive context.

*Langs:* Well, in the listening book (Lang, 1978a) I'll be sure to clarify these concepts. In the first technique book (Langs, 1973), I defined the adaptive context and discussed its importance clinically—it is the key to the adaptational-interactional approach that I advocate. In time, I have discovered that the most crucial adaptive concepts occur, of course, within the therapeutic interaction, once the patient is in treatment or analysis. The goal is to identify the meaningful intrapsychic adaptive contexts, and to then listen to all of the material that follows or surrounds it as a commentary on that context—a mixture of perception, introjection, and truth on the one hand, and distortions on the other. It opens up the whole bipersonal field for new observations.

Now, on that basis I've defined three styles of communication in patients and analysts. I began with a classification of the patient's material and of how therapists and analysts listen. There are those who attend to manifest content alone; for me, that is not analysis or analytically oriented therapy. It denies unconscious contents and processes.

Then there are what I call Type One derivatives, and I think that most therapeutic and analytic work is done with Type One derivatives, which are inferences drawn from the manifest content based on efforts to decipher unconscious meanings. This work is not adaptively framed. For example, an analyst hears a dream and he tries to understand what the dream means, what are its latent contents. He may use symbolism, or base his thinking on what he knows about the patient. If there is a reference to a doctor, a teacher, he thinks of himself, usually in terms of distortion, displacement, and the like—so-called transference. These are all Type One derivatives, the reading of unconscious content in terms of isolated segments.

Those formulations are not organized around an adaptive context. Once you bring in the adaptive context, you then have what I call Type Two derivatives, in which you are consistently linking the material to a particular adaptive context. On this basis, you can more readily make the distinction between unconscious fantasy and unconscious perception. Because if you are just thinking of contents, you don't know whether they are valid or distorted; it is more difficult to decide without the precipitant for the response.

*Searles:* Yes. That's very interesting. Yes.

*Langs:* That was the first step. The next came in terms of the kinds of communicative bipersonal fields that can be identified based on that first distinction. How can we characterize the communication between patient and analyst? In this effort, I got help, from you, from Bion (1977). I identified three analytic fields. I call them A, B, and C. I like to label things; I find it helpful in organizing clinical concepts.

The Type A field is the one that most analysts assume exists in most analyses, which is far from the truth. And by the way, Masud Khan has a paper in the 1973 Chicago *Annual of Psychoanalysis* which is very much comparable to two-thirds of my delineation. He does it in his own way, and I found his paper after I had been writing my own. But he really has said some of this beautifully. The Type A field is one with a transitional quality, a play space—Khan got that in part from Winnicott (1953). Language is used primarily for symbolic communication. This is what I would term a field with analyzable derivatives; both the adaptive context and meaningful indirect responses are present. In your terms, this is a form of communication through unconscious fantasy which is characteristic of the symbiotic field, you see?

*Searles:* I think so, yes. I'm having a little trouble keeping up with it; but it's okay.

*Langs:* Yes, I'm sorry—there is a lot to this. I refer to your concept that when the patient shifts from autism to therapeutic symbiosis, the analyst now has material to interpret. That's what I call analyzable derivatives: adaptive context and meaningful disguised responses.

*Searles:* Yes; right.

*Langs:* That's symbolic communication. The field, then, is a play or transitional space, and illusions are characteristic.

Now, the classical analyst tends to believe—to assume—that the patient is communicating to him essentially in the verbal sphere, with symbolic communication except when there is so-called acting out. He expects largely to interpret the patient's defenses and fantasies—contents and mechanisms. He does not really think that there could be another kind of workable communicative field, and will usually say that anyone who doesn't communicate such derivatives is not analyzable.

*Searles:* Yes; I know.

*Langs:* But instead there are two other fields.

*Searles:* Concurrent, simultaneous—right? Is that what you are saying?

*Langs:* They could alternate, but I think both patients and analysts have a preference for a particular type of communication—the fields are an amalgam of the two individual communicative styles. It gets complicated: it depends on the analyst, it depends on the patient. And the use of words is no guarantee at all of a Type A field.

The second field comes from my study of the Kleinian literature (Langs, 1976b) and especially Bion (1977). It is a field of action and discharge. There is a tendency toward acting out, but there is more: language itself is used not for symbolic communication, but to get rid of inner tensions and disturbances. As Bion stated this in a different context, the goal is to get rid of accretions of stimuli, to projectively identify, to put things (contents, mechanisms) into the other person—let's say the patient toward the analyst—not so much in order to understand them, but to just get rid of them and to plague him with them, to get rid of tension, you see. It is a discharge oriented field. Khan (1973) also described such patients.

*Searles:* Yes; but I think Rosenfeld (1965) may say a little of that kind of thing also.

*Langs:* Oh, I'll have to look for that. So that's the second field. Now what's interesting about that field is that you can be using words and still aiming only for discharge. The analyst, for example, can believe that he is being interpretive, and he can still be discharging disturbing contents into the patient.

*Searles:* Very neat; excellent.

*Langs:* And I think that a lot of analysts actually do just that, you see.

*Searles:* Very neat, because there is no one more sanctimonious than the classical analyst interpreting.

*Langs:* Right, and it turns out that often he is projectively identifying aspects of his own pathology into his patient, and then he doesn't understand why they are acting out or why the analysis is not going well.

*Searles:* Beautiful.

*Langs:* Any modification in the frame is a movement toward a Type B field; that's another way of putting it.
Now the third field is related to your autism phase, in which the patient comes mainly to be held, not to be interpreted to, not projectively identifying into you—he is not dumping a ton of stuff into you—he is not giving you stuff to contain, as Bion (1977) puts it. They just want to be held, something static, almost nonrelational.

*Searles:* Well, maybe they do. I kind of think that they come in in the hope that *you* will want *them* to hold *you*. You see, that's a big part of it, I think. I think it lowers a person's self-esteem to work with him on the assumption that he is *seeking* something—whether being held, or whatever—*from* you, period. Anyone who is markedly autistic possesses already only a very, very low self-esteem. I don't see how he could come to an analyst and have an experience of feeling lovingly held unless he had gained some greater sense of self-worth.

*Langs:* Through holding.

*Searles:* Yes, particularly when we consider that these persons are adults, and that even a little child—but surely an adult—is seeking for the fulfillment of some hope that *he* can be caring *towards* someone. If he feels *cared for*—this is one of the many things I learned at Chestnut Lodge—if he feels cared for, period, it tends to bring to light his guilt, his guilty doubt that he is capable of loving anyone as much as his therapist or analyst evidently loves him, you see? So he can't simply passively accept the being held.

*Langs:* Yes, you are already extending my thinking in an important way. I don't have a clear picture of all of this as yet. It is a characteristic of these patients that they don't experience the therapeutic relationship in a positive way. You are quite right about it. They come in; they are not communicating analyzable derivatives; they are not dumping into you.

*Searles:* I'll give you an example of a hebephrenic man with whom I worked for a year and a half in the same room with another Chestnut Lodge therapist and a second chronic, manic-depressive patient—and then we parted company for various reasons. I went on working with the hebephrenic man and my colleague worked with the other man for several years subsequently. I worked with this hebephrenic man for nine years after the foursome had split up. This man was hopeless in the extreme. He had spent ten years in a V. A. hospital without *any* specific form of treatment before he came to the Lodge, and then he had a total of about five years with two previous Lodge therapists before my colleague and I undertook the conjoint therapy with him and the manic-depressive patient. This man whom I'm describing had already had, that is, by the time the conjoint therapy began, fifteen years of chronic hospitalization, and he had been for years and remained for years longer, largely mute. And he was dilapidated; he looked like a hopeless hobo kind of person. What I want to emphasize to you is that I came to cherish being in his company. All he had to offer was a holding environment. I feel very, very moved as I say that. I'm very moved. That's all he had to offer. And, you see, anybody in their right mind would be ashamed to accept it. You see what I mean?

*Langs:* Yes.

*Searles:* It was only over the long course of time—perhaps eight or nine years—that I became able to accept it, and I speak of him because he had an enormous impact on me and because I've thought of how I'd like to go to visit him, just to be with him. He remembers me, I know, because when I went to the Lodge a couple of years ago to see a briefly-hospitalized patient, he managed to place himself sitting right next to the door where I would walk by when I left, and I spoke to him. It was obvious that he remembered me. I can't go to spend time with him for various reasons; for one thing, I'm afraid it would interfere too much with the treatment that he is still having. But, to reemphasize the point of all this, that was all he had to offer; that is, mute and motionless. Such a person does tend thereby to offer a holding environment.

*Langs:* I think that many therapists and analysts would not experience this as a holding environment, that this is a special capacity or form of therapeutic relatedness that has important individual determinants in the analyst.

*Searles:* I didn't at first with him; I didn't. It took me a long time to come to experience it as a holding environment, and it is very startling—to put it mildly—to find that one is looking forward to being with such a person. It doesn't start off that way; it has all kinds of resistances to go through to start to treasure it. You feel silly, you feel crazy, you feel embarrassed.

*Langs:* Yes, I see. So it takes something that you had to work out in order to experience it that way.

*Searles:* That's right, and I believe that it typically is difficult for other therapists as well, there at the Lodge—that is, to become relatively fully aware of and accepting of the extent of their positive feelings toward the patient and their reacting to the patient as an early mother. I mean—there are different ways of conceptualizing this—that such a patient's ego development was largely severed very early in life, when he had to leave a relatively good holding environment, and he hadn't had any chance to carry it further. But he *identified with* that—see, that, at least the beginnings of—a good mother, and that's what he has to offer people. But it's not verbal, just a nonverbal presence. But he couldn't come to accept *me* as *offering* a holding environment, I'm sure, without my first being able to do so with him.

*Langs:* Yes. You are stressing a spiraling sequential interaction that has been quite neglected—even by those analysts such as Modell (1976) and myself (Langs, 1976a,b) who have written on the subject. I have discussed the patient's hold for the analyst and described related functions for the frame, but you are taking the subject even further—and quite rightly so.

*Searles:* You see, if I hadn't found the courage to get to know that he was providing me with a good holding environment, how could I expect him to get the courage to attribute such a positive quality to me? He had more reasons than I to be resistant. We really ask so much of a patient. A neurotic adult patient, maybe we can reasonably ask him to regard us as basically good, basically healthy, basically oriented toward giving him something; but I think that's asking an awful lot even from a neurotic patient—to ask him to be the patient and to receive good supplies from us.

*Langs:* Yes, you've made that point in your writings. I am reminded of your paper, "The Patient as Therapist to His Analyst" (Searles, 1975); there you said that the vicissitudes of this type of curative thrust are perhaps the most significant factor in mental illness that you had come upon. Winnicott (1965) stressed that it is the holding environment offered by the analyst that contributes to the patient's courage to regress. You're really saying that the patient is not able to experience that hold as a good one, however, unless he can offer some type of holding to the analyst himself.

*Searles:* His own goodness gets confirmed, at least in pace with it and I think somewhat ahead of it, because otherwise it only would make him feel an intensified sense of how bad he is, how incapable he is of *giving* love.

*Langs:* This is so crucial, because what you are implying is that you cannot really conceive of a cure of the patient without the patient's unconscious and successful curative efforts toward the analyst. Such an idea is unheard among classical, and even Kleinian, analysts. The little I have written on the patient's attempts to cure the analyst has met with a lot of resistance. The notion that there is only one person with curative powers, abilities, or interests, and that he is the analyst, is fiercely maintained—in large part because of strong countertransference-based needs. And here you are saying—and the point seems inherently valid, though I would, of course, want clinical verification—that the analyst's ability to benefit from the patient's holding and curative efforts, however unconscious, is essential to the cure of the patient.

*Searles:* Well, yes. This seems to me very congenial to your orientation toward patients in many ways—for example, in your book where you highlight patients' unconscious creativity, stating that every patient is a genius in terms of unconscious creativity.

*Langs:* Gill (personal communication, 1976) thought the book gave the impression that I viewed the patient's unconscious functioning as an independent omniscient intelligence.

*Searles:* Who thought that?

*Langs:* Merton Gill. I think you have only to hear such derivatives in the appropriate traumatic adaptive context—it's just amazing to me. This also means, of course, that we are really natural born analysts, and that a lot of things then interfere with its conscious expression—including our training. In a sense, we have to rediscover these gifts.

You also wrote a paper on how the patient's symptoms may serve as a transitional object for the analyst (Searles, 1976). There, you very perceptively tune in on the analyst's investment in the patient's pathology. That is another very important subject, because the prevailing idealized model of the analyst is, of course, that he wants only to help the patient to get rid of that pathology; few have acknowledged the investment that the analyst has in sustaining such pathology.

*Searles:* Your way of putting it gets me to thinking that it's a relatively commonplace concept for analysts to be aware that the patient's loss of symptoms is a loss, isn't it?

*Langs:* Right.

*Searles:* That's not earthshakingly new, that analysts realize the change for the patient is going to involve loss. So, it seems to me, the analyst's coming to develop a very considerable, conscious emotional investment in the patient's symptoms is all part and parcel of that, in order that *he* will know at first hand something of the *patient's* loss in changing for the better.

*Langs:* Still, I think analysts very much deny the extent to which they miss the terminated patient and experience his loss—though such emotions should be kept within limits. In your paper on oedipal love (Searles, 1959), I believe you make that point quite explicitly: that there really is a loss experience. And I think one of the ways in which analysts have maintained their denial of meaningful loss is through very frequent modifications in the framework during the period of termination. Unfortunately, that tends to modify the opportunity for the patient to work through the separation experience. It also softens the trauma for the analyst, by providing him a last moment of pathological symbiosis, you see.

There are some analysts who sit the patient up, for one thing. Other therapists and analysts will accept social relationships with patients after the treatment—or toward the end. And of course, that's a major problem in a so-called training analysis, where many realities serve to greatly modify the separation experience. That very aspect plays into and intensifies the budding analyst's need to deny the significance of the loss of the patient, some of which can be traced to an investment in keeping him sick and in maintaining his symptoms. However, I don't think this is familiar stuff to classical analysts at all.

*Searles:* I agree; from my very limited reading, I agree with that. I'm involved currently in a termination phase with a patient I've worked with several years who I feel has gotten a lot out of the analysis—and I have, also, from the work with this person. It has caused me to do some further thinking about the termination phase. One thing, I get the sense that the termination phase is highly individualized. My sense of this is in some contrast to the picture I have gotten from the limited reading I've done in the analytic literature about the termination phase. I don't think the literature about that phase sufficiently prepares one for finding how much the termination phase, and the way in which it goes, is a function of the patient's developmental history—and, I suppose, of one's own, also. And another impression I have about the termination phase is that there is a considerable intensification of the patient-as-therapist theme.

*Langs:* I have not carefully reviewed the literature either, but most of the papers on termination that I've read give the impression that there has been a kind of erratic course toward health and that the termination phase just kind of rounds it out. There is no question in my mind that this is really a myth, and that the termination phase introduces a new set of anxieties and problems, and a new regression in every patient.

*Searles:* And, I think, in the analyst.

*Langs:* Yes, I was just going to say: and in every analyst.

*Searles:* I think that to the extent that the work has been construc-tive, the analyst feels that here is—among other things—a fleeting chance for him to get some personal help that he isn't ever going to get elsewhere.

*Langs:* It brings up a lot of issues, yes. It brings up therapeutic needs for both, in very specific ways. This discussion is related to your participant observation paper (Searles, 1977a), where you use projection so clearly to allude to projective identification. I think, too, that since the term *identification* is so confusing in projective identification—in terms of implying that the subject remains identi-fied with the projection or attempts to evokes an identification in the object—the term *interactional projection* (Langs, 1976a) might serve better.

I will summarize your comments. You say here that transference data which emerged subsequently gave you an opportunity to note to your great relief how powerfully motivated the patient had been to project upon you the feelings of inadequacy which he had felt toward an older brother—an effort you had then experienced.

You were really describing interactional projection, which implies that there is no such thing as an entirely intrapsychic projection, that it always has an interactional element.

*Searles:* On page 290 in *The Bipersonal Field* (Langs, 1976a), you said, "I'm not talking about projection, which is an intrapsychic mechanism, in which somebody imagines a content within himself to be in someone else. That's an imaginary and internal process; it is not designed to evoke an interactional effect, or to stir up a response in another person. So projection is intrapsychic; projective identification is interactional." My marginal note is: "I am very dubious that projection actually exists, in this meaning of the term (purely intrapsychic)."

One of the things that gave me this orientation I now have about such matters is, again, this work at Chestnut Lodge, and I am thinking of a paper by Tudor (1952). Tudor describes her finding that an extremely, severely withdrawn schizophrenic patient was not a separate entity who had withdrawn and was remaining withdrawn from the staff and other patients, but that he was involved in a mutual-withdrawal process on the ward. Tudor found, in her research on the ward, that—lo- and behold—there was a lot of withdrawing on the part of the *staff* vis-à-vis that patient as well as on the part of his fellow patients *vis-à-vis* him. Tudor's paper concerning mutual withdrawal provides a very nice example of a principle which I believe can be stated as a valid generalization: an individual patient's psychopathology is part of an interpersonal process wherein the psychopathology is mutual in some very disguised way.

*Langs:* That's what I think is becoming quite clear now.

*Searles:* I'm just recalling another example of this same principle, from my work with my very chronically schizophrenic patient. It may please you a bit to learn that, since I've been reading your book, I find my work with her—and with others among my patients also—to be going differently. The example from the work with her, which I just recalled, occurred during one of her sessions about a week ago. She was talking voluminously, as she often does, and I interjected some comment, concerning something in what she had just been saying, which deserved to be called to her attention before it would become stale. I knew from past experience that if I were to wait even a few moments, the material would have become, for her, stale; she would have forgotten she had said it.

So I interjected my comment. She looked a bit interrupted for only a moment, and went on with, seemingly, hardly a pause or change in her course. But then, within at most two minutes later, I heard, in the midst of her voluminous talking (highly delusional, as usual), her describing how, at Chestnut Lodge, someone—a fellow patient, so I gathered—had thrown some explosive material into the television set. This was clearly delusional in content; but I felt sure it had to do with my having thrown in, as it were, that comment only a couple of minutes before. That is, this delusion of hers involved not simply the projection of something entirely intrapsychic on her part, but sprang in part from an interpersonal contribution from me—that is, the comment I had thrown in.

*Langs:* Her unconscious perception of it; yes, the explosive quality it had for her—and perhaps for you, too.

As we have been talking, I was thinking of a paper by Martin Wangh (1962), which I mentioned in *The Bipersonal Field.*

*Searles:* Yes, I read that—"The 'Evocation of a Proxy.'" I have a very poor memory for papers I've read. I read it a year or two ago in preparing a paper; I guess it was my paper (Searles, 1976) on transitional objects.

*Langs:* I think the Kleinians had emphasized the destructive aspects of projective identification, along with the placing of good parts of the self into the other person for safekeeping. And Wangh's paper, which I'm convinced is really on the same mechanism—he wrote about an interactional mechanism designed to evoke proxy responses in the other person—is very close in its line of thought to your concepts.

One aspect that was extremely meaningful for me in your work relates to something that I shared with you, which I think every analyst goes through. I refer to the experience—not always unconsciously—of the patient first as the enemy, as the person to be confronted (in the sense of attacked as dangerous and as a threat), and all of that. And I only fully discovered the positive aspects much later on—just as you experienced first the ambivalent aspects of symbiosis and then the loving aspects, the curative aspects.

I think you are saying that in *The Bipersonal Field* I hadn't fully found the balance in that respect, but I certainly was establishing both sides of the patient's attitude there: toward the analyst, he can be both intensely destructive, and loving and helpful. Analysts in general have especially missed the patient's positive and loving intentions, his constructive unconscious curative efforts on the analyst's behalf. But they also have failed to consciously appreciate the patient's destructive intentions as well. Your work, which again and again brought to the attention of the reader the patient's actual loving, curative, and destructive intentions from very early on, was the main exception (Searles, 1965). Your first papers in the late 1950s have the kernels of most of your later, more detailed studies.

In general, it was only in 1972 that Brian Bird, as a classical analyst, suddenly discovered that sometimes, as he put it, when patients are resistant, they are really trying to harm us as their analysts—that they really want to do us harm. Analysis isn't just a word of fantasy, you see. I don't think that he alludes to your work at all. Nor have I found that his paper has especially been picked up by other classical analysts. And it was like such a belated discovery.

Now, he says there—and I want to ask you about it—something to the effect that it is his belief that in the analytic interaction, the patient cannot really actualize the depths of his destructiveness. He feels there is a limitation on how much analytic work we can do in the area of the patient's destructiveness.

*Searles:* What is the word, "actualize"? I don't understand how that's meant.

*Langs:* The extent to which it can really be expressed and experienced in the analytic interaction.

*Searles:* By either patient or analyst, right?—is that what is meant?

*Langs:* I believe so; I am summarizing from memory. It was his opinion that the patient's transference reactions are unable to reproduce the full range of his destructive tendencies. I didn't understand his reasoning, and I wondered what sort of chord it would strike in you. Because it seems to me that in your writings, you describe the intensity of the patient's sadism, both strong sadistic and masochistic tendencies in schizophrenics and others, suggesting that their transference reactions quite extensively reproduce the range of their destructiveness. I think that Bird was also contrasting this with the libidinal side, where he felt that that full range of expression could be available.

*Searles:* I don't know. I don't concur at all fully with what he says; I don't. But I can't just discard it either, because of my personal experience as a patient in treatment. As I mentioned to you, the strongest emotion I had—out of many different kinds of emotions as the years of my training analysis went on—there was a lot of unlocking of feeling in me, for at the outset my feelings had been very largely repressed—but the strongest emotion I had was a murderous feeling *toward my father.* I had other strong feelings but I would say that that was the most intense one and, you see, it was felt not toward the analyst, but (during one of my analytic sessions) toward my father. So, at least in my experience as an analysand in training analysis, what Brian Bird says is true.

And now, when I get thinking of my work with my patients, I do have to remember an occasion when a patient of mine was—well, a couple of recent occasions in the last six months, say, where patients were giving voice to certain images they had of me as being coldly sadistic and impersonal and intensely inhospitable and so on, that I couldn't stand listening to; I couldn't. So that I have to say that there are limits on my ability to help a person come to know his or her own feelings, and now I can say that maybe if the treatment with these persons goes on long enough I can come back to it. I think that that happens in treatment. It's not only that the patient becomes more and more able to face strong feelings but that the analyst, through his experience with that patient, becomes better and better able to face them also and that he can't with his first interview with the patient. But I can't lightly discard what Bird says, either.

*Langs:* So, you can find something in his ideas. I'm thinking as you talk—I don't know why it comes up at this point, I think probably because you are describing the vicissitudes of your work and the changes in yourself, and we are talking so much about how our view of our work has changed through the years and all—I was thinking of Freud's (1937) comment about that impossible profession, analysis. That is, it is the nature of analysis that a true analyst will never be fully at peace with his work. Would you agree with that?

*Searles:* To a large extent yes, and yet I would greatly regret to think that that is true because, for example, years ago—

*Langs:* Just say, I mean total peace. I think that one can come to some sense of resolution, and to a feeling that by and large one has some sense of mastery and some perspective. And one can feel that something has really been accomplished, that much of one's work is going well, and the rest. But there will always be some area of discontent.

*Searles:* That makes sense, right. I was reacting against the idea that maybe an analyst had—we had to be resigned to the idea that an analyst is in a chronic state of seething discontent, for I can't accept such a view, and I would think that patients *must* have it otherwise— that they can't thrive unless the analyst has achieved a *reasonable* degree of self-fulfillment.

Well, let me say something that gets away some from what we are talking about now, but goes back to something that we were speaking of earlier, about analysis as the impossible profession. I am pretty sure I read that paper of Freud's; but I am very sure I don't remember it, if I did. But what I was reminded of is that these days—

*Langs:* The paper by the way is "Analysis Terminable and Interminable."

*Searles:* Yes. These days, with malpractice suits as prevalent as they are—relatively prevalent—there are more than there were ten years ago. And with insurance carriers having such a large place in treatment, as they do in the Washington area, a very prominent place, with the reports that are necessary to make to them. And with the peer review procedures—you see, these three factors, it seems to me, come very close to making it impossible to practice psychoanalysis. Now that's an overstatement; but it is a reality that looms very large, and it is a reality that works very powerfully against what I believe is the main message in this book of yours.

*Langs:* Exactly.

*Searles:* Because analysts are going to be very threatened at seeing their own subtle and heretofore unconscious, damaging, destructive ways of responding to patients. The times are against that kind of self-awareness. That is a very big factor.

*Langs:* I am interested in hearing how you come to this conclusion.

*Searles:* Well, I come to it through working with an occasional borderline patient who gives me reason to greatly fear lawsuit. I've never been sued for malpractice, but—

*Langs:* Nor I.

*Searles:* But there have been enough implied—or in some cases, explicit—threats in that regard so it causes me a degree of concern that it didn't ten years ago. Where that gives me great difficulty in my work with patients is that it works against the kind of candor that I had prided myself upon and that I think has had a most useful place in work with patients.

*Langs:* What you are saying is that third parties have a significant constricting influence on you.

*Searles:* Yes, in fact, it even constricts candor in communicating my clinical work to colleagues and in my writing of papers. It gives me pause.

*Langs:* What about with your patients?

*Searles:* I've already mentioned that, that's what I meant when I said—

*Langs:* You meant as a primary place?

*Searles:* Yes. Now, your book provides a way of dealing with that, I think, where you recommend that the therapist or analyst had best not explicitly say that he loused up the field, but that he acknowledge this implicitly in his interpretations. That, I think, offers a very effective way of acquainting the patient with one's own difficulties without putting it in so explicit a way.

*Langs:* Right. You see, there is an analogy there, too, to the mother who will implicitly convey certain problems, but when she does it explicitly it is a far more devastating kind of thing. But what you are saying brings me back to something I had in mind, but didn't finish. I had defined for you the three types of communicative fields that I am now trying to study and conceptualize. And what I didn't spell out fully is that when the frame is altered, you move away from an interpretable field in which symbolic communication prevails to a Type B or a C field, to a field in which you do not have analyzable derivatives, symbolic communication. You have discharge or barriers, pathological forms of symbiosis. And the only interpretive work that can be done then, that will have any meaning and find confirmation from the patient, will be with derivatives related to the alteration in the frame and to the kind of field it has created.

Analysts do not really have a concept of Type Two derivatives, those that are connected to a specific adaptive context. They do not really know how to listen to their patients, and very often miss the unconscious meanings—thinking of material, for example, as conveying fantasy when it is really much more a matter of perception and introjection. All this means that they can work in fields where an insurance company is involved and not realize that the nature of the communications from the patient and from themselves has been entirely changed, that the opportunity for symbolic communication has been significantly modified. Much of what they are calling analytic work is not what I would see as analytic work. They are not getting the kind of analytic validation that I would insist on. They often end up with uncontrolled analytic situations where there is a great deal of acting out and discharge that they are unable to interpret, because they themselves are unwittingly doing the same thing. They are releasing information. They are including third parties into treatment which sets up action fields or uninterpretable barriers, and which lead to other deviations. These are treatment situations where the patient will suddenly terminate, will suddenly act out.

*Searles:* When you say "action fields," what do you mean by that term?

*Langs:* Discharge fields where the purpose of the words, the purpose of the behavior, is not symbolic—

*Searles:* Understanding.

*Langs:* Right, not understanding. Words are not used for symbolic communication, but to get rid of inner tensions, to act upon the other person and projectively identify into him. And these factors create communicative fields in which you cannot bring the patient to the maturity of symbolic communication, you see. It is for these reasons that I also conclude that analysis will be impossible to practice under those conditions, because you cannot do true analytic work.

I have not completed an insurance form in years. When the patient comes in, I do not accept the insurance as part of the ground rules. I set a fee that they can handle without any third party. I don't refuse the insurance, I simply create the neutral conditions under which its implications can be analyzed. I never say yes or no; I never direct the patient. I also don't ask questions any more (see Langs, 1978 a,c). I really feel the patient will unconsciously direct the treatment from their spontaneous associations and put into the analyst all that he needs for his interpretations.

*Searles:* You don't take a history in the first interview?

*Langs:* Oh, except for the first interview, depending on the patient; and that's the only session where I would ask questions—and as few as possible. I take enough of a history as is needed to make recommendations, but I try to follow the leads from the patient. And if the patient is talking actively, I won't take a history—I'll just let the session unfold. But I do attempt to form a relationship through inquiry only in the first hour.

Now, if the patient has insurance, I simply say that this will be treated as everything else in analysis or therapy: it will be explored so that the patient can come to understand its implications, and the patient will decide. And by exploration I mean not only his conscious associations, but also his indirect responses—Type Two derivatives in the adaptive context of the insurance, commentaries with both reality implications and fantasy elements to them. I have not seen an exception; as long as I don't take that form, as long as I don't set a fee that is higher than the patient can afford on his own— which means I'm accepting the insurance, because that has got to be part of the basis for payment—the patient will always produce convincing derivatives that express their unconscious appreciation for the destructive implications of the presence of a third party to therapy or analysis—to the therapist's participation in a modification of total confidentiality.

There is a typical split: consciously, many patients will say this is crazy; other doctors—like you say in your book (Searles, 1965)—other psychiatrists do it, so you're crazy. Consciously, most will want the insurance and they will introduce it. But what is so beautiful is that when you have the adaptive context, you can just wait for the indirect communications, the derivatives. And if their implications are understood, the situation can be readily interpreted.

Some patients don't even mention the insurance until something really threatening comes up; then they bring it in to invoke a *framework cure* (Langs, 1976a). And there, too, if you listen to the indirect material in that particular context, the patient will always— really, without exception—communicate that this will destroy the treatment. The acceptance of insurance will destroy the openness of communication, will create conditions under which a therapeutic regression with this frightening stuff will not occur.

And I learned all of this from patients, by the way, every bit of this. I modified the frame in one way or another because it was what I had been taught to do by my supervisors. Once I learned how to listen, my patients taught me otherwise. At one time, I filled out such forms and tried to analyze the implications—but the frame was already modified and little was revealed. Much more came through after the frame was rectified and a Type A field established. The notion is that you can analyze anything—the presence of a third party or whatever— and that will be sufficient. That is an absurdity. The actuality of the presence of the third party has its influence regardless of what is said.

*Searles:* The financial realities of life are such that I cannot imagine—if a new patient comes to me who has insurance, I can't imagine setting a fee of, say, five dollars a session, which might be all he realistically could pay, without the use of his insurance. I can't do it.

*Langs:* No, I haven't had to do that. I've had to set a fee that is a bit lower than my usual fee. And that, of course, again since it is a lowered fee, that may be seen as another modification of the frame, but I do not present it as such. I select what seems to be a realistic fee, and try to stand by it, stating it as my fee—period.

*Searles:* Are these all persons who do not come to use their insurance? Is that right? They may do without it.

*Langs:* No. Consciously, they would like to use the insurance. Most people seem to think that I strongly influence the patient, I advise them. This is not the case. Certainly, there are indirect communications in my not immediately accepting the form, in my saying: let's analyze it as we would everything else. But that is essentially a way of creating basic conditions for analysis; it is not a directive in the sense of a manipulation. I hope that you get some feeling that I listen to patients and let the patient direct me and the analytic work.

*Searles:* Yes, I do get a lot of that feeling.

*Langs:* You have my assurances that this is what the patient himself comes to, if I simply don't participate right off. I tried to demonstrate some of these principles in *The Bipersonal Field* (Langs, 1976a) and summarized it in a chapter in *The Therapeutic Interaction* (Langs, 1976b).

*Searles:* Oh, *The Therapeutic Interaction*—the big book.

*Langs:* Perhaps you could read that chapter. I say there that there are three means of understanding the functions and meanings of the frame. One arises when you don't participate in a patient's proposed alteration of the frame and then listen to the subsequent material as a commentary. There, you have a field where the communicative properties are maintained, where you haven't enacted with the patient, you haven't gratified or defended yourself—that is the ideal way to learn, and to handle the situation.

After my initial discoveries in supervision, I learned a great deal initially by rectifying the frame with my own patients—again, through their unconscious directives. I had only to learn how to listen—they showed the way. Remarkably, it had always been that way—we simply hadn't heard them.

So, for example, when a patient handed me a monthly insurance form, I did not accept it; I didn't fill it out for the moment. I suggested that we should explore it, take a fresh look at it. Under those conditions, I got material that I had never ever heard before from the patient—not only did I hear more, the patient also, quite indirectly, told me more. It had to do with the meanings of this alteration in the frame, its actual unconscious functions which were so destructive to true analytic work. The patient left himself with but one choice: either eliminate the insurance or end the treatment.

Of course, the third and least desirable way to learn about the frame occurs with the analyst who is filling out these forms: if he will spend the session the day that he gets that form, or hands it back to the patient, listening to all of the material as a commentary on what just transpired, in a modified form he will get the exact same message. So, while I've had patients (and colleagues) claim, in one way or another, that I am totally insane in this respect, the indirect material always has been so powerful and so convincing that I am completely reassured. I always think that here's the patient who is going to show me I'm wrong, or: I'm going to lose the patient. I virtually never lost a patient on this basis; it becomes an opportunity for a patient to explore his motives for, and anxieties about, therapy.

You've written of the danger of getting stale as an analyst, of getting tired of your work, feelings that it is becoming monotonous. When a frame issue comes up, the liveliness of the interaction and of the communications from the patient is remarkable. It is therapeutic for me, in a sense. And I go through this experience of discovery every time. And you'll get dreams under these conditions, and you can safely predict that it will be about the frame issue. It never ever fails to be quite obvious.

To me, of course, it is a very exciting area. And I've taken such a different position from my colleagues, but one's work with patients is dramatically different—and far more effective.

A friend of mine, Gene Halpert (1972), wrote a paper which a number of Washington analysts tried to dispute. It was on the influence of insurance on analysis. He had two patients who had one hundred percent insurance, and found that the analytic work was paralyzed. There were no interpretable derivatives. The patients had control of the situation, were omnipotent. He didn't attempt to identify the broader meanings of his findings. He has nice clinical material there, exactly the kind of thing that I am describing. He is really saying that he had a Type B or Type C field, in which the patient was just dumping into him and he had nothing to interpret. And then when the insurance lapsed, it was an entirely different communicative field. So much depends on realizing how crucially the frame determines the communicative properties of the field; this is where it took me to.

*Searles:* Yes. I'm someone, as you know, who has seen patients and does see patients who have insurance, and I have sent in forms with the diagnosis, and I want to report to you that I am very struck— although not exactly surprised, but very struck—with the lasting impact upon the patient of one's having put a diagnostic label upon him. I can say that I see consequences of that for years after the action—years. I hear material coming in highlighting that he is trying to rub my nose in the diagnosis, or he is bringing in material that highlights how appropriate the diagnosis would be as applied to me rather than him, you see.

*Langs:* For what you did.

*Searles:* That's right—and, not surprisingly, all this is true of those very patients who most behaved, at the time, as though there were no sweat at all about this.

*Langs:* Right. This is the split.

*Searles:* There was no sweat at all. Then, "Why are you quibbling? Why are you making so much of it?" And I knew that this was a very mischievous thing for me to be entering into, but I entered into it, again and again, in the interest of earning a living.

*Langs:* Oh, yes. I think that this is where analysts have gotten into trouble again and again: when finances influence their clinical functioning and judgment.

*Searles:* I suppose another way in which this interferes so much in the analytic work is that the insurance agency—or the peer review committee, whenever that comes into the picture; I've never had any personal experience with peer review—comes on the scene as an object upon which both patient and analyst can project all sorts of malevolent omnipotent judgmental attributes.

*Langs:* Then it's very dramatic. You see, I'm thinking now that this is where your concept of a therapeutic symbiosis was so helpful to me; it is another way of finding that the frame is absolutely basic. Without a secure frame, you have a pathological symbiosis.

I must say, too, that I realize that the term "frame" has both value and limitations. It is a nonhuman term for a very human set of tenets and functions. It serves to hold and contain, to establish boundaries and conditions of relatedness and communication. I need a better metaphor. It's part of the basic symbiotic hold, you see. But what you are telling me is that not only does the therapist offer it to the patient, but the patient does it for the analyst as well. You see, I've wondered why the patient is so sensitive to this dimension—to the ground rules. I believe now that it is an essential part of the foundation on which growth can occur; and he knows this, he senses it. And what you are saying, too, is that a secure frame provides the conditions under which the patient can be helpful to the analyst in ways that he needs to be in order to resolve his conflicts and to grow. An altered frame interferes with that aspect of the therapeutic symbiosis, too. I wasn't aware of that point to the extent that you made me aware of it today, and I know it's there. I'm going to document it for you, to find the material to validate your thesis.

*Searles:* Material where? Where do you mean?

*Langs:* Any time I supervise at the clinic, I'm going to get it. I'll also confirm it privately in my own clinical work.

*Searles:* I thought maybe you were referring to some material in what I've been saying.

*Langs:* No. So the patient is that sensitive to the frame because it is so crucial. And that's what I feel is going to destroy analysis. I think they are selling themselves down the river because of their financial needs. And I think that as soon as analysts are involved with an overriding need of their own, it can be terribly destructive.

Paradoxically, accepting such modifications of the frame leads to a relatively unstable set of conditions for one's clinical practice. So, in the long run, the prevailing attitude is self-defeating. A most re-markable finding that I haven't mentioned as yet is that every alteration in the frame is a repetition of some meaningful piece of pathological interaction from the past. Deviations confirm the pa-tient's neurosis so that it can't be truly modified verbally. You will pick it up again and again, once you start to listen for this. You'll know exactly what I mean. And it's that very area then that can't be analyzed or modified.

Well, I think I've said enough on this subject. I wanted to return to the Type C field to see if we can clarify its relationship to your concept of the way in which the patient in the autistic phase communicates.

*Searles:* The Type C field?

*Langs:* Yes, and the fact that you don't see an opportunity to interpret, that you see an opportunity to accept the hold of the patient and to hold the patient in return.

*Searles:* How do you define the Type C field?

*Langs:* One in which Type Two derivatives are not especially present. These patients characteristically will give you an adaptive context and not give you the indirect material. Their associations don't go on to illuminate indirectly the adaptive context. Or they will give you dreams without a meaningful day residue, without an adaptive context. It is a static field, one of barriers—both intra-psychically and interpersonally. I felt that such a concept was implicit to your paper (Searles, 1973b) on unconscious fantasy, where you described two forms of symbiosis. One is based on the patient communicating a lot of unconscious fantasies—

*Searles:* Yes, yes.

*Langs:* And the other is the reverse. You're really saying that unconsciously, the patient can control the expression or unconscious communication of derivatives.

So, in the Type C field you don't have analyzable derivatives, nor do you have the patient especially acting out, discharging into you. The sessions are often flat and boring; they have a certain unpleasant quality at times because they become rather monotonous. None of your interpretations are confirmed unless you address what I term metaphors of the Type C barriers (Langs, 1978a). In general, one moment the patient will speak very positively of the therapeutic experience, and the next moment complain that he is getting nowhere. In other words, it is neither a symbolic transitional field nor one of action-discharge and projective identification. It's a very static kind of field, which I connect with the autistic field that you describe. And I think that the Type A field is the therapeutic symbiotic field and the Type B field is the pathological symbiotic field.

*Searles:* I feel that you are getting so far ahead of me with all of this that it is hard for me to keep a grasp of it. I want to urge you, when you write up these things, to give your reader very carefully a solid point of orientation that is grounded in concepts that are familiar to him, and go gradually enough into these concepts of yours so that he can follow you, because otherwise there is considerable danger of throwing him into stuff that is so new and foreign to him that he just won't be able to get with it.

*Langs:* I understand; I realize that. You know, I've done all of this work in isolation, in total isolation. I've shared it with my students, and now I have students who are more understanding and accepting of these ideas and quite stimulated by them. As for my colleagues, most of them have not tried to understand the language and, in addition, they are quite skeptical and aloof. And in some ways it has helped with my creativity, and in some ways, it may have made things more difficult.

The nice thing about my work—and I am sure you have gone through this cycle, too—is that when I finished *The Bipersonal Field* (1976a) I said to everyone: That's it; I'm done; my creativity is over; there it is and the rest will just be minor refinements. And I'm so pleased that that isn't true, that I've now gone on to what I sincerely believe are new insights. There was a lag of about six months or even more. But have you found similar cycles of bursts of creativity and then flat periods?

*Searles:* Oh, yes I have. There will be some times when—I always set down my ideas soon after I get them for future reference—there will be some times, as long as a few months, when I will get none. And then there may be several new ideas. I've never gone through the degree of self-doubt about my creativity that you have manifested about yours, earlier on. I don't feel that. I feel a sense of confidence that I always will—sporadically, at least—be having new ideas. But another thing about this is that with one training analysand whom I had in analysis for several years, I am reasonably sure that I never got a creative idea in the course of our sessions. I relate that partly to his very intense and open competitiveness with me—very competitive—so I felt that it was no coincidence that I was being denied the pleasure of some new idea. I mention my work with him as an example of the effects of one's various individual patients—whether negative or positive effects—upon one's creativity.

*Langs:* Right; oh, that's so interesting. I said this about empathy: there are patients who disrupt the analyst's capacity for empathy, patients who will interfere with your empathizing, and others who foster it greatly. But it is really true that there are certain patients that have really, quite unconsciously, repeatedly evoked creative thinking in me, and other patients who seldom, if ever, do so.

*Searles:* Some of my patients have been very productive and have led me to have creative ideas.

*Langs:* I can immediately identify that kind of experience. Once again it shows the complexities of the therapeutic interaction, where the patient is so unconsciously in tune with some of what you are working over. It is a reminder, too, that everything in analysis is an interactional product—even the analyst's creativity.

*Searles:* I hope we don't defer till very late our listening to that recording, because I think you will find—

*Langs:* I think we are ready for it.

*Searles:* I think you will find that it highlights so many of the things that we are talking about.

*Langs:* Yes, let's plan on it for next time. Thanks for a most stimulating and refreshing dialogue.

*Chapter 4*

# TECHNIQUES OF THERAPY WITH A SCHIZOPHRENIC PATIENT

*Langs:* Today we are going to hear the taped extract from your work with the schizophrenic woman.

*Searles:* Yes, an audio tape of a session held with a woman whose treatment is described in a fragmentary way in a paper (Searles, 1972) in the *British Journal of Medical Psychology* in 1972.

*Langs:* Yes. I know that paper quite well.

*Searles:* But first there is this bit of thing that I wanted to mention. You asked about what I wrote of pathologic symbiosis—how that relates to therapeutic symbiosis? Well, since we met last time, I did come across a little comment I made that has reference to that, on page 98 of my "Patient as Therapist to His Analyst" (Searles, 1975): "For him now as a chronological adult in psychoanalytic treatment, the crucial issue is whether he and the analyst can function in such a manner that (1) a transference-symbiosis can develop, a symbiosis which will at first be highly distorted or pathological, as contrasted to that epitomized by the healthy-mother and healthy-infant symbiosis; (2) the nuclei of reality in this pathologic symbiosis can become sufficiently evident to both patient and analyst that this symbiosis can gradually evolve into what I call a therapeutic symbiosis, which is essentially a mutually growth-enhancing symbiosis like that of normal infancy . . . ," and so on. I at least make some brief reference to that.

*Langs:* I found a reference in your 1972 paper, too, in which you stated something very similar. You refer to an earlier paper, and distinguish there therapeutic symbiosis from a *folie à deux.*

*Searles:* Yes, I'm trying to; yes. I repeatedly spoke of that.

*Langs:* On page 9 of the 1972 paper, you refer to your earlier papers, the '65 collection, and to this distinction. You're talking about some of the pathological components in a symbiosis which then get analytically and interactionally resolved, to create a more therapeutic symbiosis.

*Searles:* Right, now may we go ahead with this?

[*Background data and overall course of treatment thus far.*[1]Mrs. Joan Douglas (a pseudonym) has conveyed much information which indicates to me that she began to suffer from schizophrenia, unrecognizedly, early in childhood. But it was not until the age of 33, soon after the death of her mother, that she became overtly psychotic. (Her mother had been a highly unstable woman who, in the words of a brother of the patient, had "loved to dominate" the daughter.) At this time, the patient was herself the mother of four young children. An intimidatingly domineering woman, as her mother had been, she managed thereby to stave off hospitalization during two years of increasingly delusional and chaotic behavior, at the end of which time her relatives, having good reason to fear that she would kill someone, placed her in a psychiatric hospital. That hospital, although prominent, specializes in "eclectic" (to some degree psycho-

1. The material reproduced here in brackets represents pp. 1-5 of Searles's "The Function of the Patient's Realistic Perceptions of the Analyst in Delusional Transference," which first appeared in the *British Journal of Medical Psychology* (Volume 45, pp. 1-18, 1972). It introduces the reader to the background of the patient whose taped psychoanalytic therapy session is about to be presented. As should be clear from context, Langs was familiar with this paper at the time of our dialogue.

therapeutic, but largely somatic) modes of treatment. In her one year there, her paranoid delusions did not lessen despite—or because of—attempted psychotherapy, two courses of insulin-coma therapy totaling at least 70 comas, and two courses of electroshock totaling at least 42 treatments. A consultant advised that she be subjected to a lobotomy as, seemingly, the only recourse. But the family obtained a second consultant, who advised transfer to Chestnut Lodge for a last-ditch attempt at psychoanalysis.

[Upon admission to Chestnut Lodge at the age of 36, she was an attractive, well-groomed, healthy-appearing but actually highly paranoid woman who poured forth, at the slightest provocation, intensely threatened and threatening expressions of remarkably distorted delusional experiences. Her first analyst at Chestnut Lodge quit in discouragement after one year of work with her because of the proliferating, rather than lessening, state of her delusions, and her adamant resistance to treatment. His doing so was highly unusual behavior for a Lodge staff member, and one testimony of the formidable nature of her illness.

[A few months thereafter, in January 1953, I became her analyst and, having obtained by then several years of full-time experience in this work, felt strongly confident of my ability to help her become nonpsychotic. I am still working with her, and throughout all this more than 18 years I have seen her four hours per week (apart from brief vacations) for a total of some 3,500 hours at the time of this writing.

[For several years she steadfastly refused to come to my office and by the end of about ten and a half years had been there only some three or four times, when she finally began to come there with some regularity. She still had to be accompanied to and from the sessions by a nurse or attendant and when, six months later, I left the Lodge and established my practice in Washington some ten miles away, she was still so delusional and resistive to treatment that an escort had to accompany her in a taxicab. Only some five years later, about two years ago, did she become sufficiently collaborative to come in the cab, although still very delusional, without any escort from the Lodge. Throughout at least 16 years of the work I lived with the bitter knowledge that were I at any time to become sufficiently discouraged and defeated to quit, she would be far indeed from feeling hurt, disappointed, and grieved; she would count it, I knew, as simply one more triumph, and a not particularly notable one at that.

[The years have taken, and continue to take, their toll. Her husband, who from the first had visited no more than once or twice a year and had seemed to me quite unconvinced about any worth-whileness of the treatment, finally came to feel, after five years of my work with her, that his own conscience had been appeased and, liberating himself from his previously rigid ethical scruples, divorced her. From the first she had refused to acknowledge the existence of her children and had refused for prolonged intervals to open letters or gifts from them. A visit from the husband and the children prior to my becoming her analyst had been disastrous, and only after nine and ten years of our work, respectively, did each of the two older children visit. Each found her so disturbingly crazy that neither has yet returned, years later. My own feelings of comdemnation of her for her rejection of her children, and my own hurt at her unpredictably harsh maternal rejection of me, have been, for me, among the more difficult aspects of our work. Most difficult of all for me has been the guilt and despair evoked in me, in innumerable sessions, concerning my feelings of being, in effect, a bad mother to her.

[Meanwhile this once youthful and attractive woman has become, in appearance and in actuality, a grandmother, at times coming to express, indirectly, a poignant concern lest she become written off as a geriatric patient. Several years ago she needed to be fitted with an upper dental plate, and for several months it caused me a particular agony of guilt when, in the midst of a stream of paranoid reproach or declaiming, she would suddenly take out her uncomfortable plate and become years old in her toothless appearance, gesturing now with the dental plate as she spoke. I came subsequently to feel grateful to her that her own indomitable quality, persisting despite these ravages, helped me to become largely free from that guilt.

[For more than six years I have tape-recorded all our sessions—with her knowledge; this is one of the manifestations of her increasing investment in our work. I have saved all these hundreds of tapes, and occasional playbacks of various among them have convinced me of their priceless value for research in the psychodynamics, and in the difficult endeavor of psychoanalysis, of schizophrenic patients.

[This woman made, for several years following her admission, an enormous impact upon the whole Chestnut Lodge community, by reason of her powerfully coercive, delusion-motivated behavior, her rare wit, and her caustic warmth. At times her delusional behavior spilled over into the surrounding small city of Rockville, and at times even into the somewhat more distant nation's capital. An expert equestrienne, during one of her several elopements prior to my work with her (she made none thereafter), she went to Washington, hired a horse, and rode up Pennsylvania Avenue to the gates of the White House, demanding audience with the President. She was placed thereupon, by the police, in a government mental hospital until it was ascertained that she had eloped from the Lodge; she was then returned there. Her name was placed by the F.B.I. upon the list of those persons known to be a threat to Presidents of the United States.

[She made a number of frighteningly serious, intendedly homicidal attacks upon various persons in the sanitarium, and I often felt threatened in this regard. But her murderousness was expressed mainly in her largely unconscious use of verbal communication as a means of doing violence to one's sense of reality, including one's sense of personal identity. There were times, particularly in unusually stormy sessions during the early years, when I felt so threatened and enraged that I was seriously afraid lest I lost control of my own murderous feelings, and kill her.

[Over the more than 18 years of my work with her, a truly staggering multitude of staff personnel (as well as various fellow patients, in their fashions) have tried to help her become nonpsychotic, while presumably having largely to repress (as have I, myself) their tremendous investment in her remaining psychotic. These have included some ten psychiatric administrators of the various units (each housing about nine to twelve patients) in the sanitarium where she has dwelt. These administrative psychiatrists have served, in accordance with the routine of the sanitarium, from six months to several years—on the average, about two years. All of them have shown considerable devotion to her, and several have brought creative administrative approaches to bear in the treatment. A similar number of psychiatric social workers, a much larger number of nurses and occupational and recreational therapy personnel, and a far larger number still of attendants have contributed enormously to her treatment over the years. I wish here not merely to acknowledge their indispensable contributions, but to indicate what awesome demands the psychoanalytic treatment of a chronically schizophrenic patient can make upon the best efforts of a multitude of professionally trained persons. This long treatment effort could not have continued, of course, without the support, financial and psychological, of her relatives.

[Incidentally, as regards modifications of the psychoanalytic approach used in her treatment, on the one hand she has never been given any form of drug treatment (such as the phenothiazines), with the possible exception of occasional nighttime barbiturates prescribed by one or another of the psychiatric administrators in the early years of my work with her; on the other hand, she has yet to use the analytic couch.

[From the very beginning of our work, she manifested an awesome degree of ego dedifferentiation and ego fragmentation (or, to put the latter in Kleinian terms, splitting) as unconscious defenses against such emotions as guilt, grief, and love, and in an unconscious effort to realize her strivings for omnipotence. There were, she was utterly convinced, numerous "doubles" of everyone, including herself. When a male aide to whom she had been attached left the sanitarium, she did not miss him, for she knew there were 13 Mr. Mitchells, most or all of them still about, in various guises. She felt accused unfairly by all persons about her for her more destructive acts which, she was convinced, her malicious doubles had done. She once protested, "Well, there were nine hundred and ninety-seven tertiary skillion women [i.e., projected components, or "doubles," of herself] associated with Chestnut Lodge; so why should I be blamed for everything everybody did?" (The delusional experience here was, as usual, expressed as though it were the most obvious thing in the world.)

[She misidentified herself and others repeatedly and unpredictably. There were several Dr. Searles, and when she went on a shopping trip with an aide she experienced a succession of different aides with her, rather than being aware of changing emotions in herself toward a single aide. She had only "splashes of memory" of any experiences prior to her hospitalization, asserted that she had never had a mother or father or husband or children, and once when I started to ask something about her mother, protested, "Whenever you use the word 'mother,' I see a whole parade of women, each one representing a different point of view." More often than not, she reacted to me with the utter conviction that she had never seen me before, and very often expressed the conviction that I was the such-and-such person who had done malevolent things to her in her childhood—raped her, murdered her, and so on.

[She was unable to differentiate, in her experiencing and perceiving and thinking, between (a) figurative (metaphorical) and concrete modes of thought and communication, (b) animate and inanimate elements of reality, (c) human and nonhuman forms of life, (d) male and female persons, (e) adults and children, (f) fantasies (or nighttime dreams) and real events, or even (g) ideas and persons. Trees, walls of buildings, and so on were imbued with persons. Everything, in fact, had once existed in the form of a person who had been turned, by the malevolent, omnipotent, Circe-like outer forces such as myself, into a tree or a plant, or the wall of a building, or a rug, or whatever, and she strove anguishedly to find some means of liberating him or her into a human form again. She did not experience mental images of persons, from her current or past life, as such, but was convinced that the image was the flesh-and-blood person who somehow had been shrunk and imprisoned in her head.

[For the first year or two of our work she continued in the delusional conviction that a number of actual surgical operations she had undergone, in earlier years, had consisted in "their" having placed a chain upon her heart, installed machinery in her abdomen, and bored a hole through her skull, through which "they" ran her brain. For many subsequent years, she often spoke chillingly of "this head" (her own) or "that head" (mine); heads were unpredictably replaced by the omnipotent "them." She did not experience, for example, a collection of thoughts newly come into her head, but rather that she clearly now had a different head, literally, from the one she had worn a moment before.

[The content, although not the basic underlying themes, of her delusions has been ever-changing, throughout the years. For several years I used privately and wearily to feel that nearly every week she lived in some new, highly preoccupying main delusion, whose origin and possible links to reality were hopelessly unknown to me. At such times, it was utterly obvious to her that we—and, of course, all of her perceived reality—were comprised within "the giant frog," or "the sapphire," or "the duck," or whatever.

[Only after several years did she begin to be conscious, for brief times, of feeling murderous, and with that development became, of course, an appreciably less dangerous person. She has improved vastly, in many regards. No longer is she convinced that she is being moved geographically all over the world, among 48,000 Chestnut Lodges. Now she knows that she is moved emotionally by various of her fellow human beings whom she encounters in her daily life. She knows that there is only one Chestnut Lodge, and she feels realistically bored and discouraged and often despairing about her constricted life there. Her memory span has lengthened from, say, one or two days (her remembered continuity of experience never used to extend farther back than that, for she was "blocked" incessantly) to, gradually, weeks, months, and, on occasion, years. She is much better able to remember, with me, events of our preceding sessions. In recent years she has become far more genuinely human, experiencing her body much more as her own—although far from fully and consistently, even yet—and now relatively seldom looks at me as being a total stranger. Bit by bit, we are able increasingly to face the enormous grief-work which must be accomplished if she is ever to become enduringly nonpsychotic.

[*The problem of psychoanalytic technique, and the increasingly evident connections between her delusions and realistic components of myself.* As the years went on, she came into a more and more terribly isolated social position in the sanitarium, as personnel members and fellow patients who briefly had found her "crazy talk" (as it came to be known among them) enchanting and her rare moments of highly trenchant "straight talk" refreshing, became thoroughly alienated by reason of their helplessness to feel at all predictably related to her in any meaningful way. Over all these years I myself have found that about 98 percent of all that she says has no functionally usable meaning to me. Whether she has been expressing her "crazy talk" in a playfully teasing fashion or in a spirit of physical or emotional anguish, or of paranoid accusation, I literally have never found her capable of setting it aside *in toto* and functioning in a different, more rational mode of experience and interpersonal communication—no matter whether upon gentle encouragement or harsh demand from me.

[The most difficult aspect of the work, therefore, is the enduring of a quite terrible feeling of unrelatedness between us. A year or so ago I happened to see a portion of a science-fiction movie on TV, in which the central theme was the effort to communicate from earth with a being on a planet many millions of miles away—an endeavor both fascinating and eerie, during which the extraterrestrial being gradually became manifest, on the earthmen's radar screen, as an electrical pattern of vaguely human body-outline. I was immediately struck with the realization that Joan's and my task of trying to communicate with one another, despite the fact that we both speak English and are human in appearance and are geographically close to one another, is no less difficult, no less eerie, than that.]

*Langs:* Do you want to say anything to introduce this particular session?

*Searles:* Yes, very briefly. This session was on Thursday, September 22, 1977 [about two and a half months prior to this dialogue]. This woman comes in here for a fifty-minute session on Tuesday—comes by cab, without any attendant.

*Langs:* Still from the Lodge?

*Searles:* That's right; and she has a fifty-minute session on Thursday and a nearly two-hour session on Saturday. The reason for that schedule is that all patients at the Lodge get four hours of sessions per week. The reason for condensing her four hours into three visits to my office is to save the cab fare. There is a concern about finances, a realistic concern, and the cab is expensive, coming as it does from Rockville, about eight miles away. So this session I'm going to play back is one of the one-hour sessions[2]. I should mention also that in the most recent previous session, on Tuesday of that week, she had made the most explicit expression of suicidal inclination ever, from her, that I could recall. Now, that had been a concern of mine for years—that she might suicide—and I had described (Searles, 1972) my own despair in the context of the work with her as involving at times suicidal preoccupations and impulses on my own part, as was the case once again in that Tuesday session. But in that Tuesday session there was, as I say, the most explicit reference to it on her part, and expressed with enough despondent affect to leave me quite concerned. Now, I was not sufficiently concerned to have called her unit

2. The reader is referred to the Appendix to this chapter, which includes the uninterrupted transcript of the session presented here, as well as Searles's further comments on the material.

and asked them to keep her under suicidal observation. I did not; but short of that, I was quite concerned.

She had asked me, specifically, toward the end of that Tuesday session whether she was supposed to go back to Chestnut Lodge and hang herself with a necktie. She evidently inferred that communication from my somber demeanor, you see. That is, there was a lot of projection on her part, in addition to my—genuinely, no doubt—rather somber demeanor, and I had pointed out to her at the time that I was the one who was wearing a necktie. That is, I thought the question as to what suicidal feelings *she* might have, as distinguished from what ones *I* may have, you see, was an issue. But I did want to mention to you, by way of introduction to the session you'll hear, that I had been concerned about the possibility of suicide on her part—not on my own part, but on hers, on that occasion.

*Langs:* Yes. And was that the only intervention that you made in that particular session?

*Searles:* No, no, no; I made many verbal responses. The session you'll hear will give you a sample of how much verbal interaction there is. But that was the main thing about that Tuesday session, and I had thought it an excellent session. I rate each session afterward, in filing it away, according to three different categories of quality as regards both therapeutic and research value. I thought it was one of the more collaborative ones.

*Langs:* Would you say then that you tend to be more active with this woman than with your other patients?

*Searles:* Than I do with neurotic patients—far more, far more.

*Langs:* That's reflected in your '72 paper.

*Searles:* Yes. She sits up in the chair, in the same place where you are presently sitting, about three feet diagonally in front of mine. I always dictate the date of the session and an addendum of about five minutes immediately after it, before I see my next patient. I will begin the tape.

[The descriptions of vocal tones, throughout, are mine. There proved to be no silences of more than a minute or so in duration during this session; parenthetically, there has been no lack of pre-dominantly silent sessions in my work with this woman over the years.

[The very odd-seeming phenomenon of my making asides to the microphone, during the session, is something which I took to doing, at first quite gingerly, some few years ago. I started doing this for a number of reasons. First, I had grown tired, after several years of recording the sessions, of also making notes during each as to whether she was nonverbally confirming, or not confirming, my vocalized surmises to her; it was much easier simply to mention this to the recorder. Secondly, I had grown so annoyed with her attune-ment to what the introjects were saying, while largely ignoring me, that I took to talking to my recorder, in revenge, while she conversed with her introjects. Thirdly, I found that, in actual practice, my vocalized asides to the recorder proved to be far less distracting, or otherwise offensive, to her than one might suppose.

[Lastly, the timing of Dr. Langs's and my comments, while we were listening to the playback of this session between Mrs. Douglas and myself, is not precisely as reproduced here, for the reason that his secretary typed up only fragments of the session itself. This was due, I understand, to impairments in the recording itself.]

DR. SEARLES: Testing—testing: one-two-three-four-five-six-seven-eight-nine-ten. This is the one-hour session with Mrs. Joan Douglas on Thursday, September 22, 1977, in my office. I am of course, having in mind how—uh—suicidal she sounded in the last few minutes of the session on Tuesday, so I'm gonna be particularly—uh—I *intend* to be particularly to trying to—uh—help her.—Now, *here* I notice I have to be careful—not to say, "Help her to—uh—become more suicidal," or "Help her to commit suicide." Anyhow, it's—obvious, my ambivalence about all that. I did *not* call Little Lodge; I didn't even come close to—well, I came *rather* close to, but not *very* close to calling Little Lodge, to—suggest they keep an eye on her, against the possibility of suicide. But I did *not* call them. And it hasn't preyed on my mind, since last time—*much;* it has a *little.* I have had some thought—about—if she were to kill herself, what that would do to—well, the *research,* I guess, has been my main thought, what it would do to—the way the papers would be received—past ones and in the future, any I might write about her. I can't imagine writing anything about her if she were to suicide, I can't write—imagine writing any more. But I think I'm *clearly playing down* my—what it would *do* to me *personally* if she killed herself.

*Langs:* This is your dictation before the session?

*Searles:* Yes, I do a bit of that when there is something that I intend to be particularly alert to, to try and help her. Now here I notice I have to be careful not to say "help her to become more suicidal" or even "help her to commit suicide." Did you hear that? I want to make sure you hear that. I had to be careful to say that I was concerned to help her *not* suicide. You see it was my ambivalence toward her, you see. For many years I have felt that, in working with suicidally inclined patients, one of the most difficult tasks for the therapist is to become and remain aware of his own wishes—so highly unacceptable to his superego, of course—that the patient *will* suicide. It seems to me so important for the therapist to be aware of these, because otherwise he will act in, during the sessions (with, for example, reaction-formation behavior, being unduly overprotective, alarmedly and alarmingly overprotective) in such a fashion as to increase the risk of the patient's suiciding.

*Langs:* That's the countertransference issue that you are confronted with?

*Searles:* Yes.

*Langs:* Let me say something. It brings up a point that I find very interesting. I refrained from saying this when you just introduced the material, but one of the things I'm most interested in is that this is a really excellent opportunity to hear something of how you work with a patient.

*Searles:* It is—short of seeing a video tape—the best kind of opportunity.

*Langs:* This is excellent. Secondly, this is taking place in a modified frame. And of course you know my great interest in that subject.

*Searles:* I know; that's why I thought it would interest you.

*Langs:* I'm very interested in the functions of tape recording these sessions. I must say that it is only in a dialogue such as you develop that we can really get to these issues—because of your frankness about your subjective feelings, which most analysts either try to shut out or tend to ignore in their writings. And one of the things that occurs to me about the taping was that in reading your 1972 paper, I experienced at times a great sense of confusion—and you even referred to that yourself. I remember, for example, that when I first abstracted that paper I could identify a number of brilliant ideas about how a delusional patient is so unconsciously perceptive of aspects of yourself you were not conscious of. But then there were whole islands of material that you presented that I could not fathom at all.

*Searles:* I know, terribly confusing. She was confusing to me. Maybe two or three percent of the things that she says are somewhat understandable to me. Over the years, the handful of colleagues who have listened to one or another of the tapes have attributed to me far more understanding of her—because of my long experience with her—than I actually possess. It is a staggeringly confusing experience, working with her.

*Langs:* I found myself amazed when you would extract some meaning out of fragments that I could not comprehend.

*Searles:* I've got the tape of this session ready for you to hear. This session is one of the more relaxed ones where you will not feel overwhelmed as you would with a lot of them.

*Langs:* Okay, so this leads me to my point.

*Searles:* Now be sure we get to hear this hour or I will be very, very distressed.

*Langs:* I'll be very quick about it. I'm only saying this because I think it will be borne out in this material. It struck me that the despair that you must feel in working with a patient of this kind must be quite enormous. And that the tape recording and the creation of a research setting was—

*Searles:* Very great sport.

*Langs:* Very much a part of an effort to be able to tolerate the confusion—

*Searles:* Right.

*Langs:* —and the danger of just wanting to give up.

*Searles:* Oh, yes.

*Langs:* And here the tape recording may well become a kind of nonhuman way of trying to prevent yourself from being overwhelmed by her chaos or by thoughts of giving up on her—it is a type of framework cure. It is apparent, too, that the research interest and recording would have a tremendous impact on you personally. So it all serves in part as a third party or object designed also to absorb a great deal of her aggression and destructiveness.

*Searles:* Yes.

*Langs:* It's like a proxy that helps you deal with what would otherwise be too much to handle.

*Searles:* That's right, I spoke about it in the transitional objects paper (Searles, 1976). I spoke of the tape recorder in that paper. I was referring there to this patient.

*Langs:* As it also serves so many of the functions that you spoke of in terms of the nonhuman environment.

*Searles:* Yes.

*Langs:* So again that your first thought, which doesn't fool you for a second I'm sure, is that you're concerned about the research. But you must have known that you were concerned about the impact of her reactions upon yourself, and had a need to displace your anxieties, rather than their being unbearable for you.

*Searles:* That's right. There is a great deal I could say about the place of the tape recorder in the work with her; but we won't get to hear this session if I do.

*Langs:* Okay, we'll get to it later on.

*Searles:* Now as usual, the recorder is sitting on the floor on the other side of the desk, clearly visible, and the mike is on the near edge of my desk.

[Sound of double doors between office and waiting room opening and closing, as I look into waiting room and find that she has not yet arrived—a not infrequent occurrence.]

It's me opening the door to see if she's out there, she usually is sitting waiting. Incidentally, here is a snapshot of her, taken about nine years ago on the beach with some little boy who was no relation of hers. The patients had gone to the beach on a vacation.

So, to return to this session, I called at the building where she lived to see where she is. It happens every once in a while—it is not rare—that there is some delay, usually no more than a few minutes, in her getting there.

I called to see where she was. This is me calling to her unit [to, in actuality, my answering service].

DR. SEARLES: It's now 10:30. I'm gonna call—uh—[sound of phone being dialed as I call my answering service]. This is Dr. Searles. Any calls? [Lady at answering service, while looking to see if there's been a message, asks me how I've been.] Pretty good; how about you? [She replies that she's been fine, and that there are no messages.] Thank you [said with sincere relief]. [To tape recorder:] I called and asked if there were any calls. Another five minutes, I'll call Little Lodge [the particular building where she lives at Chestnut Lodge].

[Only a few seconds later, sound of door closing as Mrs. Douglas enters waiting room, looking grim but not angry.]

DR. SEARLES: Hi [relatively casual, noncommittal sounding. I am waiting in inner office, with double doors to waiting room open].

MRS. DOUGLAS [scarcely audible, but prompt, murmur in response to my greeting].

[Sounds of double doors between waiting room and office closing.]

[I sigh, and clear my throat politely.]

[Silence is broken by sound of siren going by.]

[Sound of my getting up, going into storeroom briefly—for what purpose, I don't recall, probably to equip myself with matches, as usual, in case she needs some. She routinely gets out her cigarettes at the beginning of each session, and often is in need of matches for them. It is my assumption that for her to equip herself with matches, at her sanitarium building where several very ill patients dwell, is not necessarily easy for her and the staff to accomplish consistently, as she starts out from there for each session.]

*Searles:* Yes. The door is open and she walks in. She is in the waiting room, standing there. I indicate for her to come in. Incidentally, I explain in a dictated note at the end of this tape about the way the session had begun.

*Langs:* At this point she is sitting silently with you?

*Searles:* Yes.

*Langs:* So there is an initial period of silence.

*Searles:* Yes.

*Langs:* Do you want to say anything about this silence?

*Searles:* No, at the end of the tape I dictate a few things.

*Langs:* All right, let's take it then as we hear it.

*Searles:* She doesn't look much at me, customarily. She is sitting there usually looking diagonally to the side some, usually looking as though she is listening to voices, or remaining alert in case any occur—making herself available in case any voices occur.

*Langs:* Is this an unusual silence, at the beginning of the session?

*Searles:* No, very usual. There have been many totally silent sessions. Very discouraging, often. The silent ones have often been very discouraging; but don't worry about this one. You see, I don't know at this point without hearing anything from her in the session.

*Langs:* Right. So here is a patient who is suicidal, comes a bit late.

*Searles:* She is chronically—severely, chronically psychotic, is the main thing she is, and I am concerned about how suicidal she may be.

*Langs:* Right, and she doesn't say anything, so you have no idea then for the moment where she's at?

*Searles:* Exactly.

*Langs:* Do you feel with her—I've been thinking about projective identification—do you feel a special sense of pressure in terms of what she is kind of having you experience?

*Searles:* Do you want to hear this session?

*Langs:* Okay.

*Searles:* Stay with this session. Then after you have heard all you can stand for like ten minutes or so we can take a break and discuss it.

*Langs:* All right.

*Searles:* This is a relatively relaxed session, much more so than various others around the same time I could have played.

*Langs:* Relaxed, you mean also for yourself?

DR. SEARLES: Um? [gently inquiring tone. Playback shows that the initial silence had lasted for four minutes.]
MRS. DOUGLAS: Mm, mm [softly, but tone of negation].
DR. SEARLES: Well, did you—just *hear* something—so—clearly that you—assumed I must have heard it, too, or —? [said in a tone of gentle insistence].

*Searles:* Let me explain something there. She much of the time looks as though she is listening to voices. She shows every sign that she is hearing them and nodding sometimes. In this case she looked as though she had heard something and looked at me in a way she often does, as though assuming I heard it too. There is a certain look that gives me to know that that's what she is assuming. So I said, "Did you hear something so clearly that you assumed that I must have heard it, too?" So although I start the actual talking here, she had murmured and looked at me in such a way as to initiate—

*Langs:* Let me say this because I could see something. I know something of my style of responding to clinical material, and I see you have many things you want to present and clarify. If we take two meetings to do this one session we may be better off. We'll play it by ear. I don't want to feel pressured to get so deeply into the material, to the point where we will miss chances for discussion.

*Searles:* All right. We'll never get through this session if you do this one the way you do with the residents who report a line of data and then you discuss it for a couple of pages. We'll never get through this session. I'll be terribly disappointed if you don't get through this session.

*Langs:* Well, we'll do it—I promise. But I'll tell why I want to speak: it occurs to me to ask you about your technique here. And I think it is so important for you to help us understand your technique.

*Searles:* Okay.

*Langs:* It's a chance for you to talk about it based on direct clinical data.

*Searles:* Well, I'm well aware of the usual disapproval of the therapist's initiating the conversation, breaking the silence, and in general I try to let the patient start to talk. But here was an instance where she had given me what I took as a very clear cue: she assumed that I, too, had heard this hallucinatory voice.

*Langs:* Now, do you also feel with this kind of psychotic patient that this approach enables you to begin to make some kind of contact—your verbalizing what you feel she is experiencing?

*Searles:* Yes; you'll find it's a beautiful session.

*Langs:* All right. So your attempt was to identify what you felt she was communicating to you?

*Searles:* Yes, right. Now I'll tell you this, that tantalization is a very big part of the work with her. She feels terribly tantalized by me. She once called me, for example, "God's receptionist"—that is, that I welcome her and tell her that God will be with her in a moment; she was clearly implying that God never shows up. She is a remarkably witty woman and I feel tantalized by her something awful. It occurs to me now that one of the more taboo forms of being tantalized is that I was being tantalized that she might kill herself. This touches upon a gratifying aspect of that possibility—namely, that I would then be free from this bondage; but I'm not going to be.

*Langs:* Which she is testing out all the time?

*Searles:* Yes; so it's no great coincidence that I feel excrutiatingly tantalized now, here, at the possibility that you may not get to hear the whole session today. It would be terribly disappointing.

*Langs:* Okay, let's get to it.

*Searles:* That's what I mean by the reflection process, as I called it in my two articles (Searles, 1955, 1962) on supervision—the process wherein difficulties in the patient-therapist relationship become reflected in the therapist-supervisor relationship.

*Langs:* Yes, the reflection process.

MRS. DOUGLAS [replies promptly, in a tone of explaining]: My mother says if this isn't my room, I shouldn't smoke in it. But [voice becomes softer] *I* think it's *mine.*
DR. SEARLES: So you don't see where she gets the impression that it's not yours.
MRS. DOUGLAS: *She* never thinks *any*thing is hers or mine [said in stronger tone, and one of feeling disgusted with her mother]; *I* don't know—
DR. SEARLES [interrupting, in tone of interest and mild surprise]: Really?—hers either, huh?
MRS. DOUGLAS [yawning]: I don't know why.

*Searles:* I should explain that oftentimes during our sessions, for many months, it has been clear that the voice that she most often hears is that of her "giant mother." That's a very largely delusional construct that doesn't have much consonance with her real, long-deceased mother. So when she talks about "she" says such and such, that's familiar to me.

*Langs:* My subjective experience may be interesting. I suspect that it is going to be very difficult to keep up with.

*Searles:* Oh yes, that's why I am playing a session where you won't feel too overwhelmed. There was one session, also in recent months, where I had loaned her several books, or got several at the beginning of the session, and there was a nice adaptive context for you, to see how she reacted to that. I was terribly hurt that she only selected one book, and that rather grudgingly. It very slowly dawned on me, almost entirely after the session, listening to a playback of it as I sometimes do, that she had reacted negatively to my offering her the books as being an attempt to dominate her; she is very sensitive to attempts to dominate her. But that was a session that was very verbose and would have been awfully difficult to listen to.

DR. SEARLES [tone of gentle persistence]: She seems very self-effacing? [After pause of a second or two, I say in an aside to the microphone nearby on my desk—it being scarcely necessary to turn my head to do so:] Joan nods.

MRS. DOUGLAS [makes some very brief, inaudible comment in the midst of big yawn].

DR. SEARLES: You want some—uh—Sprite? [For years, in our sessions, I have served one or another brand of soft drink to us. I asked her this question in a tone of gentle inquiry.]

*Searles:* Now that's a ritual; I got some Sprite for her and some for myself. That's a time-honored ritual that we have been doing for a few years. It used to be another kind of soft drink—one or another kind—but Sprite in recent months. Usually early in the session she sometimes will ask for it, not infrequently she will bring up a request for it, at some point in a session.

*Langs:* Would you say something about introducing these kinds of concrete gratifications then into the treatment?

*Searles:* I know you wouldn't like that at all, I know that.

*Langs:* I would like to hear your thinking on it though.

*Searles:* Well, working with somebody like this is so terribly bleak that I justify it on the basis that one is permitted some shred of human gratification, some bit of social nicety. Now she construes all kinds of things to it. She doesn't assume it's the soft drink that it actually is.

*Langs:* That's what I was going to say—

*Searles:* She assumes that it's a different substance each time, even though the can says Sprite. It's a different substance that I give to her with some deliberate intent, often benevolent, but in any case that I give to her specifically because of its chemical effect on her—is putting it too simply. Because it may be sometimes a person that she is called on to transform back into—a person, something like that. I don't pretend to know all the different delusional meanings.

*Langs:* We'll see what she does with it by looking at the material that's now going to follow. What I heard so far was a reference to yourself, that she brought into a delusion. The auditory hallucination seems to have something to do with an area she was working over in terms of herself and you.

*Searles:* Can't smoke in here because it's not her room.

*Langs:* Yes, and being in control of this space, of this place. So when you picked up the business about whose room it is, it may have sounded somewhat demeaning. Unconsciously, she may have felt that you were alluding to yourself. If she was alluding primarily to you unconsciously, she would then take your intervention as a self-commentary. I don't know if this hypothesis will be borne out in the subsequent material. But as I listen to her, I really try to identify what I call the *me/not-me interface* (Langs, 1978a), with which I think you are familiar. It implies that every communication, regardless of manifest content, is a reference to both herself and you. The adaptive context determines the primary focus, as well as the implications of the underlying meanings and genetic ties, and so forth. So she may be saying something mainly about herself, or about you—perhaps something related also to her suicidal threat. She may want you to assume better command of the therapeutic situation and space for some reason—the adaptive context is unclear as yet.

*Searles:* That's a very powerful motive of hers, the wishing I would assert myself in a masterful, commanding, taking-charge way.

*Langs:* Yes, then she could introject—

*Searles:* Over against tremendously castrative, penis-envy stuff on her part.

*Langs:* Right, or to undermine your capacity to do that, to threaten you, frighten you. Now, at this point you introduce the gratification. Let's see what follows.

*Searles:* I might add that she does smoke during sessions with rare exceptions; in more than nine-tenths of our sessions she smokes several cigarettes. I don't smoke—haven't for a few years now, myself. I go into the store room to get—

*Langs:* Incidentally, again the timing of the concrete gratification suggests a framework cure related to your struggle against being despairing, giving up, becoming too destructive toward her—the same functions we discussed a bit with the tape recorder. But I think that you are suggesting that in reality working with patients of this kind is so disorganizing for the analyst, so difficult that it may be unfeasible without these modicums of gratifications. It think that raises a very serious question that must be answered empirically—by listening to the communications from both patients and analysts in therapy sessions.

*Searles:* Right. I'm sure that this kind of giving her a soft drink would be commonplace at Chestnut Lodge, the way they work there at Chestnut Lodge.

*Langs:* I want to hear her direct and indirect comments on it now.

*Searles:* I opened it for her, that's more of the gratification for me as well as her. It is one of the few things that I do that I feel I can do capably. In the work with her, I can get the Sprite, open the can and pour it; so it's one place where I am quite professional. (Laughter.)

*Langs:* You know by the way that in principal the Kleinian's feel that schizophrenics can and should be analyzed in a basic frame without these kinds of modifications in the frame.

*Searles:* I know Bryce Boyer thinks so, yes.

*Langs:* Boyer and Rosenfeld.

*Searles:* That's to be taken with a big grain of salt, a lot of that stuff. They do a lot of gratifying, I'm sure, that they dissociate.

*Langs:* Yes. That's a great problem; it began with Freud. I can't get over this sequence: you make the comment about demeaning, then you go to something that you feel you can do, you can function with.

I'm always interested in the timing of a deviation, the antecedents that prompt its invocation, which are always very crucial in understanding it and how the patient will experience it. Modifications in the frame are a part of an adaptive sequence—of the spiraling communicative interaction.

*Searles:* Yes, A lot of times I don't like her well enough to give her any soft drink or to offer her any; I have feelings of sufficient hate or resentment, or alienation from her, that I don't want to.

*Langs:* You actually will not in fact offer it to her.

*Searles:* On occasion I refused.

MRS. DOUGLAS [promptly nods, and grunts affirmatively].
[I grunt in acknowledgment of her affirmative reply, and go to storeroom and bring back the Sprite cans, open them, and pour a glass for her, and one for myself. I provide a can for each of us. This wordless process takes about a minute or two. I have seated myself again by the time Mrs. Douglas asks:]
MRS. DOUGLAS [tone of astonishment, wondering, and much concern]: Should I bring my little *dog* to the *hour?* [Here she is referring to a cloth dog, a transitional object which she has possessed for some two or three years, and of which she has spoken many times in her sessions with me.]

*Searles:* Now she has a little stuffed dog I've never seen. She said, "Should I bring my little dog to the hour?"

*Langs:* That's beautiful.

*Searles:* This is her first transitional object that I am aware of, which she has started speaking of within the last three years, probably two years, and many kinds of delusional experiences emanate from that or center upon that. She keeps it in her room. I recently learned that it is about a foot long and I learned that in this hour and this was the first time she asked if she should bring this dog to the hour.

*Langs:* All right, so what is her unconscious interpretation to you, if I may put it as a question?

*Searles:* Well, you're being very annoying to me now. You've got a chance to learn how intensive psychotherapy with an enormously psychotic woman is done.

*Langs:* Right, but I want to take up the way—

*Searles:* So don't teach me too much.

*Langs:* I don't know how else to do it. Well, let me just say it positively then. I think that my question was too provocative.

*Searles:* All right.

*Langs:* She is saying then that you went for a transitional object— the Sprite—that you had a need for it. I see it not only as one deviation begetting another, but also as a highly condensed unconscious interpretation. The adaptive context is the key; her association is a remarkably valid commentary.

*Searles:* It makes a lot of sense—excellent, yes. But you must remember that that's part of the ritual, like a Japanese dance or something. Every session, practically, we have this goddamned Sprite.

*Langs:* But I would say also that it has a positive quality for her; it introduces the opportunity for something that she could then use for illusion and play. I am not implying that it is necessarily detrimental. Taking the deviation as the adaptive context enables me to organize the material as Type Two derivatives. What I thought might be quite disorganized begins to take definitive shape.

*Searles:* Yes, I can appreciate that because the material tends to be really overwhelming from her.

*Langs:* And when I hear her allude now to her transitional object, should she bring it to the hour—

*Searles:* This is a real landmark for her to be asking that, because she has referred dozens of times in recent years to that dog, and it has only gradually dawned on me that it is a transitional object for her, and that that's a big improvement for her to have developed a transitional object. And now, for the first time, she asks if she should bring it to the office. I happened to have been supervising for about two or three years an analytic candidate who is working with a patient who has transitional objects which are kept right there in the office and the candidate does very skillful work with these, and that was one of the things that affected the way I heard my patient asking if she should bring it to the office.

*Langs:* Right. But it demonstrates once again exactly what you wrote about in the '72 paper: your thesis that she is in touch with your unconscious needs. This communication really very clearly shows just that.

*Searles:* Okay, fair enough.

DR. SEARLES [after a pause of only a second or so, in matter-of-fact, businesslike tone]: How large is it?
MRS. DOUGLAS [explanatory, collaborative tone]: You know, those little cotton dogs [of which in actuality there is only one; for years she has experienced, more often than not, singular things or persons as plural] they have at the Lodge—about that big.
DR. SEARLES [matter-of-factly, for the benefit of the tape recorder]: About eight or ten inches. Well, you wonder if you should, huh?

*Searles:* Now my immediate reaction was that I didn't want the embarrassment of her bringing a great big stuffed dog through the lobby of this building, that's why I said, "How big is it?"—that was my conscious thought. I now get thinking about a penis, but anyhow—

MRS. DOUGLAS: Well, or take it to a hospital?
DR. SEARLES [in unchallenging tone]: Well, it does seem in *need* of some kind of treatment, does it?

MRS. DOUGLAS [softly, agreeing]: Yeah. Doesn't feel at all well once it's died, commit suicide.

DR. SEARLES [gently, noncommittally]: Hm.

MRS. DOUGLAS: I think it's been a men—[For many years, any *man* had been, in her experience, so consistently multiple a being that she had dropped the term "man" from her vocabulary. She invariably referred, therefore, to any man as a "men."]—uh—woman too long; it's a men—needs [voice much softer now, and seemingly repeating what an hallucinatory voice has just said to her] to become a men.

*Searles:* Now it's nothing as a man—that's plural; she says: a *men*—too long,—or a woman, I forget which.

*Langs:* She made a slip, she shifted from one to the other.

*Searles:* That's one thing about the improvement in her—I don't think I missed this slip but for the first time in recent months she made a slip of the tongue the way a neurotic patient does, and shows the same kind of disconcerted reaction, and it's a real sign of improvement.

*Langs:* Yes, and it's a sense of layering that you hadn't experienced.

*Searles:* Yes.

DR. SEARLES [very faintly]: Oh. [Tone as if to say, "I see." Then, after a couple of seconds' pause, I go on, in my usual voice.] That is, if a men is—uh kept as a—woman too long, he feels the way the little dog is feeling [tone is one of simply rephrasing what she has just said—not at all challenging the validity of her statement. Then I add, in a quiet aside to the microphone:] Joan nods. [Pause of a few seconds.] Well, some thought that maybe—bringing him to the hour—bringing the—dog—to the hour, maybe *I* can help—maybe *I* can take care of him, hm? [said in an unpressuring, matter-of-fact, unchallenging tone, in a spirit of making sure that I understand what she is saying, and of encouraging her to say more. Then,

after a pause of several seconds, I resume:] That is, *I* look to be
the kind of—person, or—doctor, who might—be able to help
a—very despondent—uh—men?—hm?

MRS. DOUGLAS [makes faint, affirmative murmur, which impels me to tell the mike, softly:] Joan nods.

*Searles:* I make this aside to the tape recorder. I talk to my microphone and I make these asides to it sometimes.

*Langs:* So next, she brings up the notion of the need for therapy.

*Searles:* Right. I immediately felt that her own suicidal
inclinations—and maybe *my* own, now that I think of it, but hers,
was my thought at the time—were being projected onto the toy dog,
the stuffed dog.

*Langs:* You see again I have to play it straight with you. You know
what I do with the residents. This is the way in which I listen: first, in
terms of introjects, and secondly, in terms of projections.

*Searles:* All right. You what?

*Langs:* Listen in terms of the introjects.

*Searles:* This stuff is absolutely filled with introjects and projects.
That's one thing that I thought would interest you—as so many of
the sessions with her are.

*Langs:* So, I would formulate this material in terms of your
introduction of the deviant gratification, her perceiving it as an
expression of your need for a transitional object, something to hold
on to, and now in terms of what she is taking in from you, at least this
is her communication. Well, she is now saying that she perceives the
modification as a communication of a need for help on your part.

*Searles:* Right, that makes sense; right.

*Langs:* And you are experiencing in our discussion today what we
talked about last time, what all of my residents experience. I'm so

tuned in on the patient's unconscious perceptions and valid introjections that I seldom get away from them. It is such a crucial part of what's going on in the therapeutic interaction. And as a general principle, her commentary is well taken: every deviation communicates a therapeutic need on the part of the therapist. I don't believe I stressed that sufficiently.

*Searles:* Oh, no; you have emphasized that. I think you have, quite fully.

*Langs:* The therapeutic need is clear?

*Searles:* Quite a lot. I think so, yes.

*Langs:* This is what she is saying for the moment.

*Searles:* Yes; oh, yes. You will like this, I'm sure—really.

*Langs:* What I like of course is that this is a schizophrenic woman because I've seen only a few such patients. It is striking to me how sensitive and communicative she is in respect to frame issues.

DR. SEARLES [after a pause of nearly a minute, I ask, in a firm tone, but one expressive of carefully thinking my way along]: Is *that* a *kind* of feeling—*you* have had some *experience* of?—that is, feeling—uh, despondent, and having been in—what? [tone of "How to put it?"]—such-and-such a person too long, and needing to—
MRS. DOUGLAS [interrupting]: Oh, *I* was *in* somebody, was I? [tone of surprise].
DR. SEARLES: *I* don't know [in tone of, "How in hell would *I* know?—I only *work* here"].—*I'm* trying to s-s-s-see if *you've* ever had any *experience* of what the—men in the—little cloth dog is feeling? [Tone becomes exasperated and ironic here.] Patient says simultaneously, "I don't know" [in tone as though to say, "I haven't the vaguest idea"].
DR. SEARLES [going on persistently, without pause]: That is, any—have *you* ever felt so your*self*, to some extent? [I trail off, mumbling, as if to soften any undue pressure I am putting upon her.]

MRS. DOUGLAS [dubiously, and barely audibly]: Umm.

DR. SEARLES [persistently]: In a simple—way—have *you* ever *felt despondent?*—hm?

MRS. DOUGLAS [faintly and in a childlike tone, negatingly]: Uh-uh. [Then, after a few seconds' pause, she says in rather harsh, strong, adult voice:] I've *been* a *rug* [tone as if to say, "If that's what you mean"].

DR. SEARLES [quickly]: You have—

MRS. DOUGLAS [interrupting him, in the same strong voice]: *Rugs* [she explains] make you feel sort of [and she adds a word which is inaudible].

DR. SEARLES: Rugs make you feel sort of what?

MRS. DOUGLAS: Dreadful.

DR. SEARLES: You've been *this* rug, for instance [referring to the wall-to-wall carpet in the office], for instance—you've been this rug [and in aside to microphone], Joan looks at this rug—confirmatory.

MRS. DOUGLAS [asks in rather loud, direct tone]: Do *you* have—all my passport, and all that?

DR. SEARLES: Your passport? [polite, careful tone]. Well, you—

MRS. DOUGLAS [interrupting him]: *One* doctor does; I don't know which one.

DR. SEARLES: You're not sure I'm the one who has.

MRS. DOUGLAS: No [confirmatorily].

DR. SEARLES: Passport—uh?—to enable you to—uh—leave for giant country?—or—what? [For many years, as my 1972 paper details, she has been concerned with trying to build a giant body for herself, to enable her to return to "giant country."]

MRS. DOUGLAS [explains, in rather soft voice]: Return to—giant country.

DR. SEARLES [brisk, direct tone]: Well, do *you* find you're becoming despondent here?—or what?—this—this country?

MRS. DOUGLAS: Well, I haven't been *conscious;* so I don't know where I've—I've *been* [said in a rather small voice].

DR. SEARLES [very faintly, by way of acknowledgment]: Hm. [Then, in my usual voice:] Are you—conscious of having been here—uh—a couple of sessions ago, and toward the *end* of the session, saying—"Then I'm—should go back to the Lodge and *hang* myself from the *ceiling* with a—necktie?" Do you recall that?—you don't recall that?

MRS. DOUGLAS [gives a light, brief chuckle of amusement after I have said "necktie"]: No; no [dismissing it without apparent difficulty].

DR. SEARLES [in aside to microphone]: Joan seems clearly amused. [Then I say to her, in persistent tone:] But *that's about* how—despondent the men in the—cloth dog seems to be feeling?—huh?

MRS. DOUGLAS: Well, she seems better today. I think she didn't have any sleep, or enough sleep. *Today* she seems all right. But—I—I had never heard that she was a *men* before.

DR. SEARLES: Well, are you—do you—do you feel that *I'm telling* you that she is?

MRS. DOUGLAS [tone of explaining]: Somebody in my *head* just said that. [Pause of a few seconds.] Well, they say it's—uh— *July* 27th.

DR. SEARLES: That's what someone in your head—just said?

MRS. DOUGLAS: "Today, July 27th."

DR. SEARLES [tone of deferential inquiry]: That's what *they* in your *head* say?

MRS. DOUGLAS: No; it came from outside.

DR. SEARLES: You—saw the morning newspaper today?

MRS. DOUGLAS: No. Well, *newspapers* have *never* been right.

DR. SEARLES [unchallenging tone]: You're *long since* disillusioned with the reliability of newspapers. [Then, in aside to microphone—in, as often, the same voice-volume:] Joan nods. [Then, after a pause of about one minute, I go on:] So it's *not Yom Kippur*, today—huh? No? Even though it's generally— *considered* to be; but they're—everyone else is—in error about that—hm? [said in ironic tone].

MRS. DOUGLAS: Oh, well, they've *always* said *that* was *Czechoslovakian*, but *I* think it's the *King* of *Egypt* [vigorous tone].

DR. SEARLES: Which one?—the one in my *right* eye?

MRS. DOUGLAS: *Left* eye.

[Relevant to this discussion of my eyes are two more portions of my previously mentioned 1972 paper concerning my work with Mrs. Douglas:]

"By late 1966 or early 1967 she had become able to sit with me, during the sessions in my office, with our chairs placed conventionally only a few feet apart, and to join me in a mutual effort to understand what was transpiring in the relationship. She looked often, without leaning forward, into my eyes, and in one of these sessions she was looking at my face in fascination as I was making some comment, and exclaimed, 'When you're talking about different people, your eyes become the eyes of whomever you're talking about. It's like a kaleidoscope. I've never seen anything like it before; it's fascinating'" (Searles, 1979a, p. 210). "I fell into assuming as the months went on that, from her way of speaking of such perceptions, she was seeing entire homunculi, as it were, in my eyes; but when I inquired into this in more detail on one of the later occasions she made clear that, as she had indicated earlier, what she was perceiving were the *eyes of* those persons in my eyes" (Searles, 1979a, p. 213).]

DR. SEARLES: I'm unclear what the *Czechoslovakian* has to do with *Yom Kippur.*

MRS. DOUGLAS: *I'm*—not familiar with what it is, either.

DR. SEARLES [persistently]: You've never heard that—phrase, "Yom Kippur," or "Yom Kippur" [stating it in the two usual pronunciations] before, huh?

MRS. DOUGLAS [rather faintly]: No.

DR. SEARLES: Never have, uh.

MRS. DOUGLAS: Uh-uh [she agrees].

DR. SEARLES [persistently]: You've never *read* anything of *Judaism?*—hm? [I know that, in actuality, although not Jewish herself, she is very familiar with many aspects of Judaism.]

MRS. DOUGLAS: Nope. [Then adds, very faintly:] Never have.

DR. SEARLES: July 23rd, they say, huh?

MRS. DOUGLAS [very faintly]: Yeah.

DR. SEARLES: You don't recall any *fireworks*—uh, say—two and a half weeks ago, huh? [Then, in barely audible aside to microphone:] Shakes her head.

DR. SEARLES [after pause of about two minutes, asks]: You're trying to *figure* your *age,* or what are you figuring?

MRS. DOUGLAS [confirmatorily]: Uh.

DR. SEARLES [in aside to microphone]: Joan nods; she's doing some figuring [with a pen and little notebook she carries in her purse].

MRS. DOUGLAS: Well, then you put five hundred billion into that?—five hundred billion—two, four, seven [pause of several seconds, while she goes on setting down numbers, not showing her work to me]. Not quite two [she concludes].

DR. SEARLES: You're not quite two years old? [She nods.] So you're—doing *supremely* well to—be able to *speak* as—capably as you—are; huh? [said with a degree of irony, but not unkindly. Then I add to microphone:] Joan shrugs.

MRS. DOUGLAS [tone of consulting me, though not showing me the figures in the notebook]: Well, four hundred—is it four hundred *average* years that they speak, or—uh—or four *medical days?* I think it's four hundred *average* years.

DR. SEARLES [interrupting and talking simultaneously]: Well, I suppose it *depends*—I suppose it *depends*—on—how *intensely* their *fond mother* longs to hear the sound of—their *voice*, so that she will have someone to *talk* to, to—help *dispel* her *loneliness*—some things like that. The time may *seem terribly* long.

MRS. DOUGLAS [in a soft voice]: Well, it does to me. [Then she adds, in a barely audible voice:] I think we've been—out on the water *too long*. I don't think the *water's* a healthy place to raise children. Think the *mountains* would be better.

DR. SEARLES: What, the *air's better?—or it's easier for a child to get oriented* as to where she or he is?—or—?

MRS. DOUGLAS: Well, *I* think the *air* is more pleasant.

DR. SEARLES: Too much humidity on the water? [unpressuring tone].

MRS. DOUGLAS: *Salt* [she explains emphatically. Then, after an only momentary pause, she says in reference to her pack of cigarettes:] I should think we'd be beyond using these things.

DR. SEARLES: Cigarettes?

MRS. DOUGLAS: Yes. [She adds a few inaudible words, among which is "building."]

DR. SEARLES: Beyond using those for—as material for a giant body? [Then I add in an aside to the microphone, in the same voice-volume:] Joan nods. [Then I say to her:] Should be—something what?—more substantial than that, or—?

MRS. DOUGLAS: Um [confirmatorily].

DR. SEARLES [to tape recorder]: More nods.

MRS. DOUGLAS: Twelve—Chestnut Lodges for the head, and twenty-seven for the body. [Pause of a few seconds.] Have to be picked up.

DR. SEARLES: Picked up, partly—picked up out of *despondency?*

MRS. DOUGLAS: No, from around—*wherever* they *are*. And *then* given to *me*. I thought *that's* what we came to a *psychiatrist for.*

DR. SEARLES: To construct—to get his help in constructing a giant body—

MRS. DOUGLAS [interrupts]: No, to have him *pick up* the things.

DR. SEARLES: Oh. [As if saying, "I see."]

MRS. DOUGLAS: And give them to me.

DR. SEARLES: Give them to you.

MRS. DOUGLAS [in defensively assertive tone]: They're all *built.* They're *there.*

DR. SEARLES: They only need picking up, huh? [unchallenging and relatively soft tone].

MRS. DOUGLAS: Uh-huh

DR. SEARLES [starting in businesslike, louder tone]: Now, the *person* in the *cloth dog*—needs—her, or his—*spirits* picked up, this—do they not?—hm? [ending in note of gentle inquiry].

MRS. DOUGLAS: Uhm [uncertain tone].

DR. SEARLES [after she has been silent for several seconds, I suggest, gently but persistently]: Maybe *you* don't care to use that—*phrase*, "picked up" in a sense—picked up *out* of despondency?—or—?

MRS. DOUGLAS: Well—*gathered together*—for—in order to be *returned* to 'em [she is speaking in a very cooperative tone here]. But *our* trouble has been that it's too difficult to—to *give* anything *back* to anybody [very decisive tone]. So *I* don't understand why they keep *taking* it *away* from us. 'Cause [i.e., because] they *know* that's been the experience: when you try to give something back to somebody—explosions, and all *kinds* of things like that.

DR. SEARLES [very faint, interested tone]: Hm.

MRS. DOUGLAS: I wouldn't want—the bàby—moved away if

she came there to *rest* for a day or so [said in tone of making a concession—of not wishing to be unreasonably demanding].

DR. SEARLES [tone of polite inquiry]: Came *where*—in the *chair?*

MRS. DOUGLAS [tone of correcting him, setting him straight]: At the Lodge.

DR. SEARLES: Oh [as if to say, "I see"; said quietly, un-challengingly. Then, after several seconds of silence, I suggest, in a gentle, polite, unchallenging tone:] She—may *need* a rest, huh?

MRS. DOUGLAS [softly]: Yeah. [Then, after several seconds of silence, she says, in voice of normal volume:] Well, I—imagine she—before she could have any *surgery* to—be turned *back* into a *men*, she'd have to be *able* to *eat*—

DR. SEARLES [interrupting in a polite but firm and relatively loud voice]: *I'm* unclear what brought the *baby* into this. I—who—were we *talking* about the *baby?*

MRS. DOUGLAS [explains, in a very collaborative tone]: Well, we were talking about—I *asked* you if I should *bring* the *cloth dog*—

DR. SEARLES: Yes, yes.

MRS. DOUGLAS: And *then you* talked about gathering her *spirits.*

DR. SEARLES: Picking up her spirits, or—uh—this—you *said* she's *despondent,* didn't you?—that—in the cloth dog, that—

MRS. DOUGLAS: I—guess I *did* [uncertain tone]—I don't—I don't remember [relatively faint tone].

DR. SEARLES: But that—that—the *baby*—*is* the cloth dog?—or is *in* the cloth dog?—that is—[tone of polite inquiry].

MRS. DOUGLAS: Yes.

DR. SEARLES: Hm.

MRS. DOUGLAS: *It's* her—part of her *mind. But* they said that *she* was a *he,* and *that's why* she's so *depressed.* [Said in strongly assertive, decisive voice; then she explains to me:] That's what the university [whence have come, for years, some of the halluci-natory voices she experiences] said.

DR. SEARLES: *They* say that—that—uh—*she's* a *he,* who has been—a *he* too long—and needs to become a woman, hm? [tone of unchallenging resumé, to be sure I understand the meaning of what she is saying].

MRS. DOUGLAS [correcting me in a friendly tone]: No, it's been—the other way around: it's been a—a *she* too long, and needs to become a men.

DR. SEARLES: Needs to become a men [said in comfortable tone of "I see; I've got it now"].

MRS. DOUGLAS: But *I* don't think *your left eye,* and the *one* that's in my *cloth dog* are *related* [tone of protest].

DR. SEARLES: You don't [rather amused, ironic tone].

RS. DOUGLAS: No.

DR. SEARLES: I seem—[tone of inquiry]

MRS. DOUGLAS [interrupting me]: *One* time the *left* eye was her *doctor.* But—uh—

DR. SEARLES [interrupting, but in an unchallenging way]: *Related* in *that* sense, huh?

MRS. DOUGLAS: Uh-huh [agreeing softly].

DR. SEARLES [quietly, in aside to microphone]: Joan nods. [Then I say, in normal tone of voice, to Mrs. Douglas:] But *not* related by family?—uh—[speaking in an unpressuring, unchallenging tone] No?

MRS. DOUGLAS [makes a very soft sound of negation].

DR. SEARLES [I report, quietly, to the microphone]: Shakes her head. [Then, after several seconds' silence, I say to her inquiringly:] You see—again, *I* was momentarily—wondered *what* had brought my *left eye* into this?—huh?

MRS. DOUGLAS [explains, emphatically, but her first couple of words are inaudible]: . . . so *sick!*

DR. SEARLES: What? It *does* look so sick?

MRS. DOUGLAS [agrees in soft murmur].

DR. SEARLES [quietly reporting to microphone]: Joan nods.

MRS. DOUGLAS [explains further]: Looks as though it really can't see anymore.

DR. SEARLES: Oh [tone as if saying, "I see"].

MRS. DOUGLAS: As though it isn't seeing out.

DR. SEARLES: Well it *does look*—somewhat as sick—as the — baby, or person, in the cloth dog—is—is, huh?

MRS. DOUGLAS: Well, no—it looks *sicker.*

DR. SEARLES: This—my left eye looks sicker.

MRS. DOUGLAS [soft murmur of confirmation].

DR. SEARLES: Oh. [Said quietly, as though saying, "I see."

Then, after a few seconds, I say:] Well *I* get some—sense of *how burdened you* may *feel*—that—uh—that—seems as though there are so *many* persons, round about, who are in *urgent* need of—*care.* Hm?

MRS. DOUGLAS [faint murmur of confirmation].

DR. SEARLES [quietly reporting to microphone]: Joan nods. [Then, after a pause of a couple of seconds, I say to her:] And *here I* sit, what—uh—apprently not even—*aware* that the person in my left eye is *very sick.* [I say this kindly, patiently, un-challengingly.]

MRS. DOUGLAS: Um [confirmatorily].

DR. SEARLES [quietly reporting to microphone]: More nods. [Then, after pause of several seconds, I say, thoughtfully, in inquiring tone:] Sick and unable to see?—hm?

MRS. DOUGLAS: Um [confirmatorily].

DR. SEARLES [quietly reporting to microphone]: Joan nods again.

MRS. DOUGLAS [after several seconds' silence]: Well, *maybe* he moved the—uh [tired sigh] French Mediterranean Seas *west,* and that's how he looked after he'd been—after he was taken out of them. They *do*—they *did sky* everybody [i.e., turn everybody into sky]. They *were strong* enough to do *that.* [She is speaking in a collaborative tone here, as though she is not sure, herself, about some of these things, and is trying to help clarify them.]

DR. SEARLES: That is, they turned everybody into sky. [Quiet aside to microphone:] Joan nods. [Then I say to her:] Well, that's a—what—a *relatively simple* task for a giant?—is it? [speaking, as usual, in persistent but casual, unchallenging tone].

MRS. DOUGLAS: I guess *so,* I don't know [rather vaguely, as though saying, "You can't prove it by me"].

DR. SEARLES [interrupting, and talking at same time as her last few words above]: —I mean, it would seem like a—rather *considerable feat,* by ordinary—any *ordinary earth* standards [speaking ironically and challengingly].

MRS. DOUGLAS [murmurs confirmatorily].

DR. SEARLES: But *you* don't—seem to think it—

MRS. DOUGLAS [interrupting me]: *I* think that when they—when they're skies, they're *dead.* They say [evidently having just now heard hallucinatory voices] they're not! [tone of surprise and wonderment]. Well, they *look* sort of—

DR. SEARLES [interrupting]: *They* say it's a form of *treatment*, do they? [tone of firm but polite inquiry].

MRS. DOUGLAS: *Gloppy* [finishing the comment I had interrupted]. Yes [in confirmation of my statement].

DR. SEARLES [rather faintly]: They do? [Quiet aside to microphone:] Joan nods.

MRS. DOUGLAS: "For *money*" [evidently quoting hallucinatory voice]. *I* don't think that's necessary—

DR. SEARLES [interrupting]: *Money*. Reminds me of your having put several coins on the desk [referring to her having done so in the most recent session—in an attempt to pay, from her very modest weekly allowance, for a session]—d'you recall? [She makes a barely audible confirmatory murmur, and I say quietly to microphone:] Joan nods.

MRS. DOUGLAS: But you gave them back to me [casual tone, by way of reminding me].

DR. SEARLES [in, similarly, casual tone]: That's right. You— in case I had forgotten?

MRS DOUGLAS: Yeah.

*Searles:* Isn't that beautiful; isn't that nice? That woman is really getting well, I'm telling you.

*Langs:* Here she corrects you quite consciously: you refer to her putting the coins on the desk, but didn't allude to your not accepting them. And what does she do? She immediately adds that very crucial point: your not accepting them.

*Searles:* I'm glad she did.

*Langs:* Yes. What's fascinating to me—and I've had this experience in hearing a few presentations of this kind—is that the unconscious communications from this woman are quite decipherable once the adaptive context has been identified. I'm not having as much difficulty as I had anticipated. I'm seeing far more than I imagined I would, by following the thread of the therapeutic interaction; without it, this would be sheer gibberish to me. But here, I had just had the very thought that she just produced consciously. And though I am perhaps more directly aware of its implication, this shows the positive qualities of her functioning on one level.

*Searles:* Yes, well I—you do register, I hope, how pleased I am that she is able to do this. She couldn't have done this two years ago, even if I had read your book five years ago. If I had known your views very well, I don't think she could have done this. She's really developing a sense of continuity and of being able to recall what she did and I did, and I've come to see my part in it a lot more than I used to, ten years ago.

*Langs:* This is what she has been teaching you, I suspect.

DR. SEARLES: Yes; I remember. [Then, after several seconds' pause:] That is, I *seemed* quite *unmindful* that that was— perhaps the *first* time in your *life* you had—felt moved to pay— some money for psychiatric treatment?—huh? [She starts laughing softly in amusement, and I start chuckling more loudly. We both are laughing together for a few moments.]

MRS. DOUGLAS: Shouldn't have *done* it; I didn't *know* that [but said lightly]. If you *offer* money to someone, it *means* they—they're *murderers*. I guess that's—

DR. SEARLES [interrupting her]: I *reacted* as—as though—you had, uh—

*Searles:* Can't you listen to it? You can't listen to it. You can't listen very long.

*Langs:* I've got to say something. It's so marvelous to see how she picks it up, and understands your unconscious communication to her. Her unconscious perception and introjection of your refusal of her money is twofold: first, that you responded as if there was something destructive in her, and second, you were being destructive toward her. It is such a striking commentary, with meaning along both sides of the me/not-me interface. In addition, you have written about the investment of the therapist in the patient's symptoms.

*Searles:* Well, I failed to see that, even until now. Until you pointed it out, I had not seen that; I had not. I felt that I had probably been more insulted than I had realized by the few little coins; I did notice that although she took a dollar bill, also, out of her purse, she didn't put that on the desk—only the coins. But I didn't realize how I was reacting against a healthy move on her part.

*Langs:* Yes, you see I wasn't sure that that was it, but I had the feeling it was so from what you said. This is the first time in twenty-five years she offered to pay her own money, which is where she should be.

*Searles:* That's right.

*Langs:* So this is a step toward differentiation and autonomy which you repudiated.

*Searles:* But don't forget that the patient will do such a thing in a manner that makes it very hard to see the positive motive in it.

*Langs:* Yes, of course. There is always intense ambivalance, and a mixture of growth and regression. To put it another way, the loving, constructive part is really predominant, but how difficult it is for us to keep remembering that—and the patient adds to that difficulty.

*Searles:* Okay, isn't that interesting?

*Langs:* Yes. That interlude has to be a major adaptive context for this session.

*Searles:* It's no coincidence, and I think I did see those things put together, when she said, "So I should go back to the Lodge and hang myself from the ceiling with a necktie"?

*Langs:* She said that after you refused the coins?

*Searles:* Yes, and I think that I did see that at the time. I don't want to play myself down too much in this. I think I did see that.

*Langs:* So that comment followed your refusal.

*Searles:* She inferred from my handing the coins back that there was no hope for her. [See Searles's commentary concerning this session, which provides an accurate picture of the interaction, concerning the coins, in that preceding session.]

*Langs:* So it was there already; that was her response at the end of that last session?

*Searles:* I think so, although I wasn't sure of that, I wasn't sure that she was—I wasn't sure enough—

*Langs:* And now she's coming back to it.

*Searles:* But it occurred to me at the time that she had reacted that badly to my handing the money back, because this is an aspect of myself that I'm conscious of—not needing anybody for anything, you know, that kind of stuff.

*Langs:* Let me put it to you another way. I think that this session really has to do with her wanting to get back to that issue.

*Searles:* This session?

*Langs:* Yes, and your interventions took her away from that. You see, that's inevitable when you intervene without identifying the intrapsychically significant adaptive context. And typically, that context is related to the unconscious transactions between you and the patient—actualities filled with meaning, present and past.

*Searles:* Well, she brings in money.

*Langs:* And then when she brought in the money, you picked it up, and she now does some very constructive therapeutic work.

*Searles:* I know.

*Langs:* She lets you know its meanings, and she does this in a very healthy kind of way.

*Searles:* You've got a style of giving supervision that is maximally engendering of jealousy on the recipient's part toward the patient, because you almost perfectly split your unfavorable comments, which are directed toward the poor bastardly therapist, and your glowingly favorable, solicitous, helpful, kind feelings, which are almost completely directed toward the patient.

*Langs:* That is really because of the nature of the data. I hope you can see that. It is a moment of countertransference expression on your part and efforts at cure on hers; I would respond differently at times when transference expressions predominate on her part and curative efforts on yours—I assure you. Still, I did make some kind comments to you here, because you got back to the essential issue. The session becomes very exciting at this point.

*Searles:* Oh, it's been exciting to me all the way along. I'm glad you are finding it so, too.

DR. SEARLES [interrupting her]: I *reacted* as—as though—you had, uh—

MRS. DOUGLAS [murmurs confirmatorily]: Addressed you as a murderer. I didn't—

DR. SEARLES [interrupting]: Hadn't *intended* to, had you?

MRS. DOUGLAS: Uh-uh [meaning "No"]. The *university* had me do it.

DR. SEARLES: Oh, was it *after* that?—I wonder if *you* recall— whether it was *after* my—I had—uh—*given* the money *back* to you, that you—*then wondered* if you should go back to the Lodge and hang yourself from the ceiling with a necktie?—Do *you* remember?—if that was the sequence?

MRS. DOUGLAS: N-n-no; *I* don't *remember* that, about hanging, and necktie.

DR. SEARLES: You don't?

MRS. DOUGLAS: I remember *thinking*—that I'm *in more ties* than—anyone else in *civilization*. And I *wondered if* the medical profession was ever going to get around to—*utilizing* them *intelligently*. But when giants are built—out of bodies, you wonder *where* they're going to use the *tie* [she ends this statement in a kind of helpless-wondering tone]. I guess, just in the *mind*—probably to build a mind—or eyesight.

*Searles:* It's starting to get a little clear to me now—that may be obvious to you, but I'm seeing it more clearly now—that I had reacted that if she becomes so well that she could start paying me for her psychotherapy, I will suicide.

*Langs:* You were the suicidal person, at the deepest level.

*Searles:* She introjected me.

*Langs:* And the tie represents her unconscious perception that you need the tie to her.

*Searles:* Right, I took up the ties in an emotional sense. I think that turned out to be a good thing.

> DR. SEARLES: Now, when *you* say "tie," could you *describe* what you're referring to? [firmly but not unkindly].
> MRS. DOUGLAS [in a tone as though this should be obvious]: Well, a *tie,* such as—
> DR. SEARLES [interrupts]: A necktie, such as this one? [Gesturing toward the one I'm wearing; then I report to the microphone:] Joan gestures toward this one. [Then, after a couple of seconds' pause, I say to her:] That is, they *could* be used *intelligently* by the medical profession, hm?
> MRS. DOUGLAS: They *say* so [she agrees]. They say that they're very *adpatable* for—*growth medicine.* [She is evidently reporting, here, what the hallucinatory voices are saying, and reporting this in a tone indicating that she is very skeptical that this is true.]
> DR. SEARLES: Hm [faintly and noncommittally].

*Langs:* I find her quite engaging in this session.

*Searles:* Very much so. Very witty person—very intelligent.

> MRS. DOUGLAS: But they haven't *explained* how they *use* them. [Said in casual tone; then, after several seconds of silence, she says "Hm!" in a tone clearly indicative of her having just heard the hallucinatory voices say something new and interesting.]
> DR. SEARLES [gently]: What did you hear then?
> MRS. DOUGLAS: They said you'd sew them all together and then you'd take them inside the head and—put the person in them and they *explode* [and she cackles briefly with amusement as she finished saying this]. *That* doesn't sound like the *proper treatment* for a *mind* [she comments, in protest and disbelief].

*Langs:* That's a representation of a pathologic symbiosis.

DR. SEARLES: Doesn't sound like very gentle treatment, does it? [I comment quietly].
MRS. DOUGLAS: Uh-uh [she agrees with my comment].

*Langs:* Here I stick with that same adaptive context: this is a further commentary on your refusal of the money.

*Searles:* I see.

*Langs:* I stay there because she stays there.

DR. SEARLES [I finish asking my question more rapidly now]: So that *instead* of thinking in terms of *emotional ties,* or *ties* of *affection,* your *head* has been *fixed* so that you think in terms of *neckties?* [speaking in the same firm but respectful tone as before].
MRS. DOUGLAS: Well I guess *so* [sounds accepting of my idea, but with the implication, "Although I never thought of it that way before"]—since I made—such a great *number* of them. But—when you *speak* of *concrete,* you *mean—food.*
DR. SEARLES: When you *say something* about—uh—having felt that you had more *ties* than anyone else in the world—huh?
MRS. DOUGLAS [gives murmur of agreement].
DR. SEARLES [I suggest quietly]: Might have meanings of *family ties?—bonds* of *affection?*
MRS. DOUGLAS: Well, *literally ties.* I *make ties* all the time [said with quiet firmness].
DR. SEARLES: Literally neckties, huh.
MRS. DOUGLAS: That's the way my *head* was fixed—to *do* that.
DR. SEARLES: Your *head* was *fixed* to—*turn figurative concepts into—concrete, literal* ones? [said firmly but respectfully].
MRS. DOUGLAS: Uh—[said faintly; sounds uncertain and therefore noncommittal].

*Searles:* She used to actually make ties, knit them. I tried for several years to persuade her to knit a tie for me but then I realized that our relationship couldn't permit, as yet, so tangible an expression of the positive feelings in it.

DR. SEARLES: Oh, I do? [said ironically]. I *mean that,* but for some reason don't say—"food"?

MRS. DOUGLAS [gives murmur of agreement].

DR. SEARLES: You were speaking about having made ties, huh? [Patient murmurs agreement.] Reminds me of my having—uh—entreated you, or asked you—urged you—for several years, to—make a necktie for me. [After a few seconds' pause, during which she makes no sign of remembering that, I go on, in a kindly but rather matter-of-fact tone.] And I—assume you *don't* remember that, because I've—mentioned it many times. [My comment ends, however, on a note of restrained impatience, exasperation, and probable bitterness.]

MRS. DOUGLAS [in a louder tone than usual]: Well, *I* remember *Ralph Mueller* [the name of a fellow patient, from that earlier era, with whom she had been relatively friendly; a pseudonym is used here]—Mr.—Von *Hindenberg's* ["Mr. Von Hindenberg"—her customary way of referring to one of her grand*mothers*—as I learned after some years] *eldest son—asking* me to make him a yellow tie.

DR. SEARLES [quietly]: I see.

*Searles:* He was a patient many years ago.

*Langs:* She said something about—

*Searles:* Ralph Mueller; she said he's Von Hindenburg's son. Ralph Mueller is, indeed, of German descent.

MRS. DOUGLAS: And I said I didn't—see how—*my*—yellow would do *him* any *good* [tone of helpless protest]. And he said, "Oh, yes, *you're* a source of *electricity,* and *your yellow* is your *blue,* and *I* need—more blue" [Mueller's words are quoted in a teasingly cynical tone], and I said, "But—if you mixed *my* blue with *your* blue, you'd get *black*" [tone of this quote is one of protest, but coquettish protest]. So [dejected tone] we didn't do anything about it. [Then, after several seconds of silence, she says in a more energetic way, apparently quoting something she has just heard the voices say:] Or *become a nymph.*

*Langs:* It seems to me that in several ways she is—despite the

evidence for a thought disorder—representing now your mutual
needs for a pathological symbiosis.

*Searles:* Black is the meaning of depression for her.

DR. SEARLES: Uh—*black*—*may* have some meaning of *depression?*—doesn't it?

MRS. DOUGLAS: Um [confirmatory tone].

DR. SEARLES [quietly, to microphone]: Joan nods. [I then say,
in much the same quiet tone, to her:] So that—*your* blue and *his*
blue—is—mixing *your* feeling blue with his feeling blue
might—cause—uh—*severe depression?*—is that the idea?

MRS. DOUGLAS [murmurs confirmatorily].

DR. SEARLES [quietly—but, as usual, easily audible to the
nearby patient—to the microphone]: Joan nods.

MRS. DOUGLAS [speaking with energetic interest]: *He* looks
*better* now [a couple of additional words are inaudible].

DR. SEARLES [interrupting]:—The *one* in the *left* eye *seems* to
be *perking up,* huh? [said in ironic, teasing tone].

MRS. DOUGLAS: Yes—has better *expression* [casually].

DR. SEARLES: Um. So—maybe—perhaps the *person* in your—
*cloth dog* would *also* benefit—from—being in the sessions?
[said in light, bantering tone].

MRS. DOUGLAS: Well, *you're* another *person!* [says this in tone
of strong objection].

DR. SEARLES: Mm—I *am* [tone of relatively little challenge in
this, mainly of trying to follow the way she is experiencing
things; then I say, in aside to microphone:] Joan gestures toward
*all* of my head [a note of awe comes through in this last
statement of mine].

*Searles:* Isn't that interesting? Do you want me to go back over this
part?

*Langs:* No, that's fine.

*Searles:* That's relatively unusual these days, for her to experience
me as having changed completely. So that person went out of the
room and this is a different one now in the chair—my chair. It's not

rare, but it's nearly rare now. It used to be very frequent—several times a session.

*Langs:* I believe that she's correctly saying that she's experiencing your interventions now as having a different quality, and as coming closer to understanding what she is struggling with.

*Searles:* Maybe so. I related it to the fact that, as you've heard, my first stance about the cloth dog had been not at all encouraging of her bringing it to the session, and now this time I was suggesting that perhaps if the cloth dog were here, he or she could benefit from my help.

*Langs:* Well, let's see where she takes it.

Mrs. Douglas: Someone went out of the room [said in a tone of speaking to herself, and of implying, "This must be what happened"].

Dr. Searles [speaking in an attemptedly firm, brisk manner]: I—I've *taken* an *entirely different stand* about the *cloth dog?*—is that it?

Mrs. Douglas: No.

Dr. Searles: The person who was here *before* wasn't encouraging you at all to *bring* the cloth dog to the session.

Mrs. Douglas: No.

Dr. Searles: No?—They weren't? [Here I sound clearly uncertain as to what her "No" means.]

Mrs. Douglas: Uh-uh [meaning "No"]. See [she explains], *you two* are the *twins* of the two who went out.

Dr. Searles: "Twins"—*you* know what "twins" always remind me of [light tone; then, when she looks uncomprehending, I explain]: Ralph and Louise [said in tone as though this should be obvious; these are the names of younger siblings of hers, who were twins, and one of whom died in infancy].

Mrs. Douglas [gives an artificial-sounding cackle, then says, barely audibly and in an absent-minded manner]: I don't know about them.

Dr. Searles: You don't know them? You never heard of them—huh? [speaking in a quiet, unpressuring way].

Mrs. Douglas [very faintly]: No.

Dr. Searles: Of course, when you mentioned *Ralph Mueller,*
I was—I *remember* Ralph Mueller. I also remember that one of
your brothers is named Ralph. [All this was said in the tone of an
efficient pedagogue.]

Mrs. Douglas: *I* don't *have* any brothers [said defiantly and
rather nastily].

Dr. Searles: You don't [said with the kind of patience with
which one might speak to an imbecile].

Mrs. Douglas: Uh—at least, *not* that I've *met* up to date
[becoming somewhat less sure of herself].

Dr. Searles: Well, I'm *aware* that Ralph hasn't *put in an
appearance* since you—came to Chestnut Lodge; I—I *am conscious* of that [tone of starting off in patronizingly "helpful"
vein, but ending in a kind one]. But I—do recall, when you were
in touch with your Joan—Mitchell [her maiden name]—Douglas [her married name] identity—part of your identity, you
spoke about having one time raised rabbits with Ralph [said
gently but firmly].

Mrs. Douglas: No [very faintly].

Dr. Searles: When you were children.

Mrs. Douglas: No [sounding surer that I am in error].

Dr. Searles: Now, Ralph Mueller [starting off in a pedagogical tone again]—

Mrs. Douglas [interrupting me]: Not *me; I* don't *have* any
brothers, anyway.

*Langs:* To me, I hear her say that that's not relevant in this session,
that you are introducing something that has no dynamic meaning
inside her head at this time. Following an intervention, I always
listen to the patient's associations as a commentary on what I've
done—and I hope to first find the kernel of truth to it, and then the
distortions.

*Searles:* Do you want to elaborate more on what you feel I should
have addressed myself to?

*Langs:* Well, here again I think what you are doing is shifting
away from the prevailing adaptive context and outside of the rela-

tionship with yourself—and the way in which she was working that over.

*Searles:* That is, by bringing the cloth dog into it I was changing away from our interaction.

*Langs:* Yes, the cloth dog, and then shifting back to the genetics in terms of her brother and all the rest. For me, the central issue is still the unfinished business about the coins, which you initially picked up when she began to work it over with you, and now you have gotten sidetracked.

*Searles:* Right.

*Langs:* I must say I have discovered—and I hadn't realized this, but I would state it now—that I don't make an intervention without some connection to the therapeutic interaction, and most often center on it. Even when there is a major outside life experience, I would be clear as to the link to the therapeutic interaction—whether I say it to the patient or not. I take everything the patient says as a commentary, valid and distorted, on what I am doing and on the therapeutic interaction. But I believe I have consistently validated that that's where the patient is at.

*Searles:* That makes a lot of sense. I think that it is particularly interesting, then, that her sense of identity is so dependent on such things.

*Langs:* Oh, it would, exactly.

*Searles:* That is, if I am trying to help her to know that she is Joan Douglas, it sure isn't going to work if I'm trying to do so when she is finding the interaction not relevant to what's in her head.

*Langs:* Right. It's all a question of timing, and when she brings it up meaningfully—when it comes up as an issue for her.

DR. SEARLES: You don't; I see [said in tone of having decided not to press the matter at all further for the time being]. Uh—so

*you*—wouldn't have *any* reason, then, to feel *hurt*—if—*brothers*
don't *visit* you, because *you* don't *have* any, anyway—right?
[Quiet aside to microphone:] Joan nods.

*Langs:* There again, you've taken her disappointment and now
displaced it onto the brother, but she is insisting she won't let you do
it.

*Searles:* Right.

*Langs:* Which I think is marvelous. Plenty of neurotics would go
along with it manifestly, she won't even do that. And we will see: if
my thesis is right, she is going to come back to you and the money
issue, and to the autonomy issue.

*Searles:* Very interesting.

Dr. Searles: Ralph Mueller, incidentally, I recall, used to be
a good tennis player?—hm?
Mrs. Douglas: No [decisively].
Dr. Searles: He didn't? [in tone of genuine surprise].
Mrs. Douglas: *I* don't think he's ever *played* tennis. *He*
wouldn't think that playing tennis was *appropriate* [said in tone
implying that he is a very aloof, formal person; I am not sure
enough of my own recollections, of this fellow patient of hers
from twenty-five years ago, to recall whether she is remembering
accurately].
Dr. Searles: Really? He's too—concerned about—uh—
what?—his dignity?—or what?
Mrs. Douglas [confirmatory murmur; then, in tone of much
livelier interest, says]: Well, *I* played tennis when I *first* came to
the Lodge, because I didn't *know* any better. No [in tone of
starting to say that "No one warned me not to"]—I came from a
*hospital,* and I hadn't met my *parents* yet, or my *family,* and—
the *hospital* said to go play tennis, so I played tennis, and every
time I went out—on the tennis court, I got *shot!*
Dr. Searles: Really? [tone of mild interest].
Mrs. Douglas [laughs briefly in amused-sounding way]: Uh-
huh. Being a stupid little baby, running around playing tennis,
it *never entered my mind* that it was *wrong.*

*Langs:* What's beautiful about this is the image of the play space, the treatment as a play space and the feeling of its creation and then its destruction. So it just adds to my hypothesis that for the moment, she feels she can't play in that space, that she's lost it now. The play space has been destroyed by the refusal of her money and by your recent interventions that address outside relationships rather than the therapeutic interaction. The reference to the need for a safe play space is very interesting in a schizophrenic woman, as is her comment: "It never entered my mind that it was wrong"—an allusion to an unrecognized error.

*Searles:* I found this material gratifying in that she so rarely speaks of a fellow patient, and a real one, and here is a reference to one, from twenty-five years ago, whom I remembered, whom it happened I admitted to Chestnut Lodge, the man she speaks of, and I remembered how she used to play tennis.

*Langs:* I'm experiencing her in a way that you're not because you are addressing the manifest content, while I am organizing the latent content as Type Two derivatives around your spiraling communicative interaction with her.

MRS. DOUGLAS: I just thought they were mean things to keep *shooting* at me. But at the end they explained that I had to *save* the *doctors, save* the *nurses, save* practically *every*body; but—
DR. SEARLES: So that you mustn't *take time* to—enjoy a game of tennis?—Is that what they implied?
MRS. DOUGLAS: Well, *that* was—that was the *easiest place* to *shoot* me, was on the tennis court.
DR. SEARLES: Oh!—they were *shooting* you *with patients* that you were to take care of?—Is that—? [said in a tone of genuine surprise, and of awe].
MRS. DOUGLAS [confirmatory murmur].

*Searles:* That's what I call brilliant intuition. I really was pleased that I understood that.

*Langs:* I didn't see that at all.

*Searles:* So that she probably reacts to my many, as you will find them, intrusions: she has more patients for her to take care of.

*Langs:* Right, exactly: the need to cure the doctor. She seems to confirm my hypothesis through indirect means. That's true psycho-analytic validation via Type Two derivatives (Langs, 1978a).

DR. SEARLES [aside to microphone]: Joan nods. [Then, after several seconds' pause, I say to her:] I get the *general* sense of— what a *hell* of a *welcome* to a *new—environment*, huh?

MRS. DOUGLAS [confirmatory murmur].

DR. SEARLES [very quietly to microphone]: Joan nods. [Then to her, in tone of a kind, patient pedagogue:] You had come *from a hospital.* Do you *recall—what hospital,* or anything of—?

MRS. DOUGLAS: St. Stephen's Hospital [not the name of any actual hospital where she had been].

DR. SEARLES [ironically]: Oh; is that in—uh, Padua?—or Odessa? [One of her delusions was that she was a graduate of various foreign medical schools.]

MRS. DOUGLAS: London [tiredly].

DR. SEARLES: Oh [faintly].

MRS. DOUGLAS: It was—well, it might *not* have been Lon-don—maybe it's Czechoslovakia; I'm not very—*certain* about *anything,* about myself.

DR. SEARLES: Well, is it—*remotely* possible that it may have been—[ironic tone]

MRS. DOUGLAS [interrupting me]: —Probably was London.

DR. SEARLES: You guess London. Couldn't have been any-thing as *mundane* as The Institute of Living in Hartford, Connecticut [ironic tone—referring here to the sanitarium from which she had been transferred to Chestnut Lodge].

MRS. DOUGLAS [murmurs negatively].

DR. SEARLES [aside to microphone]: Joan shakes her head, confidently [ironic tone].

MRS. DOUGLAS: No; no I haven't been there.

DR. SEARLES [interrupting her]: St. Stephen's—St. Stephen's is—uh—that's not St. Vincent's, either—huh? [Ironically, refer-ring here to a hospital where she had been hospitalized more than once in childhood. Then I add, in aside to microphone:]

Joan shakes her head. [To her, I explain, as I get up and go to the storeroom:] Gonna get some cough drops [for myself].

*Searles:* She went to St. Vincent's as a child in New York and had a mastoidectomy. She was eight years of age.

MRS. DOUGLAS [speaking in normal tone of voice, as usual, although I am momentarily not present]: Oh!—St. *Vincent's—your wife* worked at St. Vincent's.

DR. SEARLES [I have returned to my chair, and happen to have heard what she said]: She *did;* I see [not at all questioning this].

MRS. DOUGLAS [murmurs agreement]: In the East; but—uh—

DR. SEARLES [interrupting]: What was—what *name* did she— go by, then?—Do you recall?

MRS. DOUGLAS: John Lawlor [explains to me as though this should be obvious; this is the name of a surgeon who had operated upon her on one or more occasions during her childhood].

DR. SEARLES [ironic, patient-pedagogue tone]: My wife, John Lawlor, huh? That's par [starting to say "That's par for the course"]—do you feel that a *great many*—uh, women are married to—or, men are married to women named—uh—John?— huh?—John—quite—

MRS. DOUGLAS: *Seems* so.

DR. SEARLES [ironically]: Well, my *wife John Lawlor* worked at St. uh, *Vincent's* Hospital, huh?

MRS. DOUGLAS [says after several seconds' pause]: I *think* it's your wife; it—uh—*might* be your *son's* wife.

DR. SEARLES: Dr. John Lawlor?—hm?

*Searles:* I knew he'd been one of her early physicians at the time.

MRS. DOUGLAS: I don't know if he's—or if she—actually was *given* a *license* [uncertainly], or if she *posed* as John Lawlor; *he* was a very good doctor—and licensed—but she—just went in—I think she murdered him and took over the job. Like, rough stuff.

DR. SEARLES: She had—she, uh—had some *rivalrous feeling* toward him? [Tone of polite inquiry; then after a couple of seconds' pause, in aside to microphone:] Joan nods. [Then I say to her:] She evidently *felt* convinced she could do the job *better* than he was doing it. [Then, after a moment's silence, I say quietly to microphone:] More nods.

*Langs:* When I get the feeling that you are coming back closer to the issue, she brings up a more positive image again.

*Searles:* About the good doctor? I thought that, by your own standards, you couldn't completely condemn this work, because she is talking about a good doctor, see? (Laughter.)

*Langs:* I like to believe it is the patient's evaluation, not mine.

MRS. DOUGLAS: What, does that turn you off, or on—changing my—knees?

DR. SEARLES: Changing your knees? [evenly, and without apparent surprise that she had asked].

MRS. DOUGLAS [explaining]: You *look* better when I—do *this.*

DR. SEARLES [aside to microphone]: Joan—puts her—left over—one or another knee—crossing the leg.

MRS. DOUGLAS: Right—

DR. SEARLES: I *look* better when you—have your—right leg crossed over your left leg—the *left* eye looks better?—*my* left eye? [saying this in unchallenging manner; she makes some inaudible murmur in response]. Well, in general, do you *wonder* if it *turns me on,* at all—*sexually*—when you—shift your legs about?—or cross your legs?

MRS DOUGLAS: No [in tone of genuine negation, and implying that she had never had any such thought].

DR. SEARLES: Ya hadn't wondered that, huh? [relatively unpressuring, accepting tone].

MRS. DOUGLAS: Uh-uh [confirming her previous response, casually].

*Langs:* She says, No, that's not me. Well, we'll see what she does.

MRS. DOUGLAS [After a few moments of silence, she gives an amused belly-laugh, and says]: The *right* eye, maybe, wondered it, but—

DR. SEARLES [interrupting, in amused-sounding tone]: *My right* eye, huh?

MRS. DOUGLAS: Yeah. *I* thought the *right* eye was *suffering* from my—*now* it looks *pained,* so it's keeping the leg *that* way, so then I put it—

DR. SEARLES [interrupting, to comment for the benefit of the microphone]: Putting your left—Joan had the left leg over the right leg that time. [I am sounding rather amused. Then, after a few moments of silence, I ask:] Well—uh—what?—there's *some*-one in *one* or *both* these eyes who is—*terribly* concerned about propriety?—appropriateness?—or—?

MRS. DOUGLAS: Thinks so [in tone of "I think so."].

DR. SEARLES: Something as Ralph Mueller is? [Then, in quiet aside to microphone:] Vigorous nods.

MRS. DOUGLAS [brief but unamused-sounding laugh]: Well, *she's a very* good *fixed doctor.*

DR. SEARLES: The one in the *right* eye?

MRS. DOUGLAS: Yes. She's—she's *not conscious.* [Then, after a few seconds' pause, she says uncertainly, as if to herself:] Well, *maybe* she is *now,* though. *Hope* so.

DR. SEARLES: You *hope* she *is* conscious?

MRS. DOUGLAS [affirmative murmur].

DR. SEARLES: You don't think her being—

MRS. DOUGLAS [interrupting]: Well, *I* prefer *conscious* doctors to—*mechanical* ones [ironic and somewhat caustic tone].

DR. SEARLES: Although you *sound* as though you *think* the *consciousness may*—be somewhat *distracting*—hm?—to the—doctor [said in firm but polite, rather patronizing, pedagogical tone].

MRS. DOUGLAS [faintly]: Yeah.

DR. SEARLES [very quietly, to microphone]: Nods.

MRS. DOUGLAS: Well, *she's* the *electric*—doctor.

DR. SEARLES: That is, it *may* be better—

MRS. DOUGLAS [interrupting]: She *seems* to be *completely stripped* of *all electricity now* [speaking considerably more loudly than I had just been speaking].

DR. SEARLES: This is—still the—one in my *right eye* [said casually, unpressuringly].

MRS. DOUGLAS: Yeah. [Then, after a few seconds' silence:] It *is* a *men.*

DR. SEARLES: That's what *they* just said, in your *head?*

MRS. DOUGLAS [confirmatory murmur].

DR. SEARLES [barely audibly, to microphone]: Nods.

MRS. DOUGLAS: But the *right* eye's a *woman;* but she's a *men specialist.* She's not much of a—I guess she's a *mother whale.*

DR. SEARLES: Well—well, *I'm* reminded that *Joan* once told me that she—had to *rely* upon her *dog* to—*tell* her whether this or that person—were a *friend* or an *enemy* [said with a kind of casual interest].

MRS. DOUGLAS [noncommittal murmur].

DR. SEARLES: And *you*—have to *rely* upon—someone, or ones, in your *head*—to—tell you whether—the one in my right eye is a *men* or a *woman*—huh?

MRS. DOUGLAS: Well, it's a *woman.*

DR. SEARLES: It is a woman [unchallengingly].

MRS. DOUGLAS: The right eye's a woman, and the left eye's a men.

DR. SEARLES: Hm. Now [ironic tone, referring here to rare occasions in the past when she has perceived the two persons in my eyes as being married], whether they're *married* is another *question?*—huh? [Then, after a moment's silence, I say to microphone:] Joan nods. [Then I press her a bit.] Huh?

*Searles:* On occasion, she did—at least once—perceive them as married.

MRS. DOUGLAS: Well, I—think she's—she's a very good doctor; she wouldn't *hurt* anyone [rather subdued voice].

DR. SEARLES [relatively loudly]: The *one* in the *right* eye? [Patient nodded.] So that *if* she married, she wouldn't—*isn't* the *type* who would *murder* her *husband?*

MRS. DOUGLAS: Uh-uh [faintly, in agreement with what I have just suggested].

DR. SEARLES: She isn't. [Quietly; then in same quiet voice, to microphone:] Joan confirms that.

MRS. DOUGLAS [after several seconds of silence, in a strong voice]: It *must* be what we have in the *box* down there—that—

*Searles:* She is referring to the tape recorder.

*Langs:* I've been waiting for that. Let's pause a minute.

*Searles:* She's used to the damned recorder. In many sessions she doesn't make any reference to it at all.

*Langs:* Not directly, perhaps. I've been listening for indirect references to the tape recorder throughout, and haven't really been able to find clear-cut derivatives. But now when she comes back to it manifestly, I'll expect them. I'm trying to understand why it comes up at this point. I think all of these interventions have mixed qualities, of being very helpful and yet in some way hurtful. So that they have both positive and negative implications.

I also was going to say that the experience of playing back one's own interventions and having to reexperience them is one of the most difficult things for any therapist to do. I admire your courage—but it is one of the few ways an analyst can really learn. You yourself would, I feel certain, raise many questions about your own work. Let's see where she goes now. I felt that things were getting diffused and kind of lost. And I find that we are now coming back to a frame issue, because I think that's very much what concerns her.

*Searles:* The question of whether the wife would murder her husband may tie in with that.

*Langs:* Or at a time when you get to the issue of murder and so forth. So, now she is going to try and get back to you to—

DR. SEARLES [interrupting]: The—recorder?
MRS. DOUGLAS [nods]: —that *thinks—against* the patients, or *about* the patients.

*Langs:* It's the box that thinks against the patient, is that it?

*Searles:* Yes.

*Langs:* So now, she comes to the destructiveness of the deviation; now you can see it.

*Searles:* It's coming from the box.

*Langs:* Right. And you can see a closer reference to her unconscious perception of you at this point. She attributes it not to you but to the box. We are back to something I said in the very beginning of our discussion: the division between yourself and the recorder, and how she can use this to divide her fantasies and feelings, and to express them in a way that has less of an impact on you—and herself. I would expect eventually to find the other side too: that the hope for cure is in the box at times. Still, I would hypothesize that the destructive functions of the tape recorder will, in the long run, outweigh its positive contributions.

*Searles:* Maybe so, but I do not believe so. For one thing, its detrimental impact can be lessened by my attentiveness to the negative meanings, for her, of my use of the recorder. For example, I was startled one time, several years ago, when she referred to the tape recorder as "your daughter," and I was completely baffled, until it occurred to me that I was showing toward it the kind of tender solicitude—intimacy—that she associates with a father's showing toward his daughter. She used to ask me to listen to it, too, incidentally. We used to listen to it briefly, a couple of minutes or so at a time, dozens of different times over the years.

*Langs:* So that she could be jealous and envious of your relationship with the tape recorder too.

*Searles:* Oh, yes, yes—very much so.

DR. SEARLES: "The patients"—what are you referring to?— *we're* the patients, you and I? or what?
MRS. DOUGLAS: I *think so* [and laughs in apparent amusement].
DR. SEARLES [in tone of trying to sound amused]: And *some*body is thinking *against us*, huh?

*Langs:* Could we go back? I just want to hear this again.

DR. SEARLES: "The patients"—what are you referring to?— *we're* the patients, you and I? or what?
MRS. DOUGLAS: I *think so* [and laughs in apparent amusement].

DR. SEARLES [in tone of trying to sound amused]: And *some-*
body is thinking *against us,* huh?
MRS. DOUGLAS: Yeah [trying to sound amused].
DR. SEARLES: In the box?
MRS. DOUGLAS [nods]: Making us gasp for breath.

*Searles:* I hadn't been aware of gasping myself—maybe I had—nor
had she.

MRS. DOUGLAS: *That's* very *different* looking today—that—
machine [comments in a chatting kind of fashion].

*Searles:* She is referring to the tape recorder.

DR. SEARLES [faintly]: It *is?*
MRS. DOUGLAS: Those *discs* are so *black.* [Pause of a few
seconds.] They don't have any little thing sticking up on them,
either. [She is referring to the spools—"discs"—on which the
tape is wound, and to the fact that there is no loose end of the
tape—as there often is—sticking up in the air, near the center of
the spool. She has not left her chair in making these observations. The tape recorder is clearly visible underneath my desk,
over on the other side of it, on the floor.] Is *that* what *I* am?—that
*machine?*—the *head* is *that?* [She sounds seriously concerned.]
DR. SEARLES: You wonder if—*your head* is *that machine?*
[calm, unchallenging tone.]
MRS. DOUGLAS: Um [tone of agreement].
DR. SEARLES: I don't understand *why* you *ask.* [My tone here is
more personal and informal, less pedagogical, patronizing, or
ironic]. You have some—say something of what—that—what
*brings* that question—to your—mind?
MRS. DOUGLAS: I don't know, I just *got* the *thought*—that
maybe that's what this head is [tone of talking in an informal,
intimately-collaborative spirit about a very bizarre subject].
DR. SEARLES: Oh; that would explain—some—of the phenomena?—that are going on in your—in that head? [Then after
a moment, I add, to microphone:] Joan nods.
MRS. DOUGLAS: Well, then—then *I* have to be more *careful*
about what I *do* in here. I—I—didn't *know* I was a *machine, or*

that I could—you know—*change* the *course* of the machine by—
what I'm *doing* in here: just trying to pick up everything and
straighten everything around.

DR. SEARLES: Well, d'you *suppose* you may—st—*still* be
*smarting* a bit, from my having—uh—asked if—your *head* had
been fixed so that—*figurative* concepts, like emotional bonds,
get—*experienced* by you in terms of *literal*—ties, like neckties?
D'you suppose you may be kinda—ss—uh—*offended* by my
*saying* that, hm?

MRS. DOUGLAS [confirmatory murmur]: It looks *better* now;
it's just like *yours*.

DR. SEARLES [aside to microphone]: Joan did confirm that.
[Then I ask her:] *Which* looks better?

MRS. DOUGLAS [interrupts me while I'm asking the above
question]: That's *another* one.

DR. SEARLES: The *left* eye?

MRS. DOUGLAS: Um [confirmatorily].

*Langs:* I think here again that you are taking her away from her
commentary about the tape recorder. I thought you were going to
bring up the tape recorder more directly, but of course you shifted
away from that in your intervention. You sensed that she was
reacting to something that you had done, but shifted away from the
more immediate adaptive context of the recorder. She had experienced inappropriate destruction, depression. She represents this
interactionally.

*Searles:* Yes, the discs look black. I noticed that this time, the
meaning of depression.

*Langs:* She is saying that there is an interactional depression. She
feels that both of you are trying to solve a depression in the things
that you are doing. And tape recording the sessions, capturing a piece
of her, not losing her and so forth, is one means of undoing loss and
depression. I think that this is what she is saying.

*Searles:* Good point. That's what we've never been able to get
through, is the depressive phase of her treatment.

*Langs:* Well, you see, in my opinion the tape recording would preclude that. So long as you are solving your depression by possessing her and using a noninterpretative means to do so, and as long as she is possessed by you in that way, there would not be sufficient actual loss and separation to permit its working through. The recording also alters the communicative properties of the bipersonal field, depriving her of the play space she also needs to resolve her—and your—depression.

*Searles:* Maybe so. I think you greatly underestimate how far she has come over the years during which the sessions have been recorded, and I think you underestimate the positive values of the recordings; they have made possible, for example, this present discussion we are having, a discussion potentially very useful to my further work with her. But what you say is very thought-provoking.

*Langs:* Go back a bit. Let's pick it up. So you take her away from the tape recorder. You protect the tape recorder. You protect your recording of the sessions by going to another topic. You sense something in the session is disturbing her, but you move it away from that deviation. Remember, the tape recorder is a frame issue. Anytime one frame issue comes up, other frame issues will be addressed. They come up together; also, one represents the other.

*Searles:* Okay.

DR. SEARLES: Looks just like what?

MRS. DOUGLAS: *Right* eye.

DR. SEARLES: Oh, it *does*? [Both the patient and I sound, as innumerable times before in this session and in many others in recent years, something as though we are comparing impressions of a movie we are both watching.]

MRS. DOUGLAS [qualifying a bit what she has just said]: Not *quite* as *large.*

DR. SEARLES: Hm [tone of mild interest].

MRS. DOUGLAS: But—it has more of the *expression* of the right eye. Is that what you *want* to *accomplish*? [She asks in wondering tone of a naive child.]

DR. SEARLES: Well, I *do seem* to you *totally preoccupied* with the *people in my eyes*, do I not? [asking this in the tone of a polite pedagogue].

MRS. DOUGLAS [laughs in obvious amusement]: Yes.

DR. SEARLES: Is that right? [I say in amused aside to microphone:] Joan nods. [Then, I say to her:] So that—do—you don't
*ever* feel that I'm actually aware of *you?*—is that right? [I begin
this question in a semi-amused tone, but end it in one of nascent
alarm, and of being close to feeling appalled.]

*Langs:* You see, "don't ever"—you generalize, rather than stating
it as referring to right now.

MRS. DOUGLAS: Well-ll—[uncertain tone. Then she adds
quite decisively:] Well, you're *more interested* in the *phenomena*
of *yourself.*

*Langs:* Still, she is saying that she feels you are more preoccupied
with your own interests than hers, and you are picking that up.

*Searles:* Yes, I thought of her as conveying an image of me as
maximally narcissistic, literally, yes.

*Langs:* Including through the tape recording?

*Searles:* Yes. I'll play that last comment of hers again.

MRS. DOUGLAS: Well-ll—[uncertain tone; then she adds quite
decisively:] Well, you're *more interested* in the *phenomena* of
*yourself.*

*Langs:* That's as straightforward as you can say that. To me, that's
marvelous. You're more interested in the phenomena of yourself
than her.

*Searles:* Yes. I felt there was, of course, a great deal of projection
involved in that, in addition to my actual narcissism. That last part
again: "So that you don't *ever* feel that I am actually aware of *you?* Is
that right?"

*Langs:* There I think you do yourself a disservice.

*Searles:* I know. I feel that we've reached a point with this issue so that I could start calling her on it, because I think that she does feel that I am talking to her a great deal.

*Langs:* Yes, of course.

*Searles:* But I've heard this kind of thing from her so many times that I'm trying to confront her with it because I think it is not true. It has some truth in it; but I'm trying, in a sense, to break through this defense.

> DR. SEARLES: I am. [Said calmly and unchallengingly. I am not trying, here, to indicate that I fully concur with the validity of what she has just said—for I do not; but I have learned that it goes better when I do not challenge her or argue with her at such junctures.]
> MRS. DOUGLAS: *I* don't think that's *right* to *do*—if one's a *woman*, and the other's a *men*—to have them look *alike* [said in tone of protest and wonderment].
> DR. SEARLES: Not right to *either* of them—huh?
> MRS. DOUGLAS: Uh-uh [confirmatorily].

*Langs:* She's experiencing pressure from you to conform to something within yourself. She says, "It's not right to make the man and the woman become the same."

*Searles:* Oh, yes; that's right. I attach so much significance to her confirming of impressions of mine—it's obvious—and I tell my tape recorder like a miser hoarding his gold, as if I were saying, "Here is another twenty bucks, tape recorder: she confirmed that one."

*Langs:* Right. But I go beyond recognizing that she has confirmed my hypothesis, which she does rather nicely. I then look for the elaboration of her response in the metaphorical content, what I call Type Two derivatives.

> DR. SEARLES [barely audibly, to microphone]: Joan nods— confirms that. [Then, after several seconds, I suggest to her:] Not right that they be made to look like *twins*, huh?
> MRS. DOUGLAS [replies in strongly assertive tone]: *Well,* if

they're the *same person,* it's all right; but if they're *two different* persons—they *still look* like *two different* persons now.

DR. SEARLES: They do? [quietly, calmly].

MRS. DOUGLAS [quietly]: Yeah.

DR. SEARLES: You say that as though it's something of a *relief*—to see that.

MRS. DOUGLAS: No.

DR. SEARLES: No?—*you* don't care if they look exactly—

MRS. DOUGLAS [interrupts me in a very loud voice]: Well, *I* don't know if you can *put two people back together* again. I mean [voice softens again], in *my experience* of putting—someone back together is that they always *explode.*

DR. SEARLES: Are *you* referring, for *one* thing—among *many, many other* things, maybe—referring to *divorces?*—that people who've been *divorced* can't be—put back together again?—is that one of the things—

MRS. DOUGLAS: Oh, no [as if to say, "Not at all"].

DR. SEARLES: That's *not* what you're referring to [in tone of accepting that it is not].

MRS. DOUGLAS: Uh-uh [agreeing that it is not]. Just [she explains] about building a head.

DR. SEARLES [grunt in acknowledgment of her explanation].

MRS. DOUGLAS: And taking pages out of a book, and then trying to return them to the book is always disastrous, too. Once they *come* out they should *stay* out and be a *person,* and go on their way—develop *themselves,* instead of trying to go *back.* [She says this in a tone of describing a grim prospect for them.]

DR. SEARLES [after having tried a couple of times, relatively mildly, to interrupt her as she was finishing the above remarks]: *Back* into the *confinement* of being in a *book?* [tone of unpressuring inquiry].

MRS. DOUGLAS: Yeah [softly]—or being with the same group of persons again.

DR. SEARLES: Oh [very softly, indicating, "I see"]—whom they've *outgrown,* is that the idea?

MRS. DOUGLAS: Um [affirmatively]; I guess *so* [indicating, "Although I hadn't thought of it that way before"]—or the *air,* maybe, does something to them, so they're not—they can't go back [said in tone of having thought of an interesting new possibility to speculate about; then, after a pause of about fifteen seconds, she goes on:]—*but* ya—I—I think—I mean, we *return* to our *homes,* and we *return* to our own *countries,* and everything. That's all right [tone of reassuring herself].

DR. SEARLES: Ah, I *still*—ya see, *my* memory was that— toward the end of—the previous session, you said [clearing my throat], "So I should go *back* to the *Lodge* and—uh—tie my—tie the necktie to the ceiling, and *hang* myself?" *Something* like that, you said. [I make this statement in a fatigued, but tenaciously assertive tone.]

MRS. DOUGLAS [promptly]: I don't recall that.

DR. SEARLES: I—I—I understand; you *said* you didn't recall that. But—I wondered if going *back* to the *Lodge*—uh—*involves* that, uh—something of what you're *speaking* of?—that is, like going *back* into a book, once you've—[all this said in a thoughtful, tentative, undemanding tone].

MRS. DOUGLAS: Uh [confirmatorily].

DR. SEARLES: It *does.* [Then adding, to microphone:] Joan nods.

MRS. DOUGLAS [hastily taking it back]: *Oh,* no; I wasn't in a *book.* I was a *newborn baby* when I came over.

DR. SEARLES: Came over—?

MRS. DOUGLAS [tone of explanation]: Giant baby when I came out to sea; I was only—three and a half months old. [Pause of a few seconds.] No; I must've been older than that—if I was born in *1919.* [She was born several years before that, in actuality.]

DR. SEARLES: 1919? [polite tone].

MRS. DOUGLAS: No—I came—out to sea in *1920.*

DR. SEARLES: You did? [polite tone, not at all argumentatively].

MRS. DOUGLAS: Um [confirmatorily]; I was born—which *month?*—*"April"* [in tone of having just been given the answer from within her head].

DR. SEARLES: If *you* were born in *1920*—uh, you were born, then, when—*Joan* was, uh, about—*seven* years old [said in firm, matter-of-fact tone].

MRS. DOUGLAS: *I* was born in—nine—teen *nineteen* [tone of having to search her mind to come up with this answer].

DR. SEARLES: Well, that was when *Joan* was about *six* years old [matter-of-fact, unargumentative tone].

MRS. DOUGLAS: Um [faintly and in noncommittal tone. Then, after a few seconds of silence, she asks, in relatively loud and astonished tone:] Is *that*—is *that* that *name*?

DR. SEARLES: You *wonder* if this *left eye* [referring to my own, at which she has just been looking] is Joan? [asked in ironically polite, pedagogical tone, which becomes gentle at the end of the question]—Huh?

MRS. DOUGLAS: Well—[uncertainly].

DR. SEARLES [interrupting]: The left eye.

MRS. DOUGLAS [strong tone of assurance now]: I was told that the name—J-o-a-n—is a *Western* name. I thought [tone uncertain again] the right eye was an Easterner. [Her long-held delusional distinctions between "Westerners" and "Easterners" are very complex and still largely unfathomable to me. These are not referable to the actual geography of the planet Earth. I have sometimes thought that "Westerners" are dead people—those who have "gone west," so to speak; but it is not nearly that simple.]

DR. SEARLES: Are you asking if the *right eye* is that name? [Then, softly, to microphone:] Joan nods; it's the right eye.

MRS. DOUGLAS: Well, the right—*I* thought the *right* eye was—named—uh, *Giuseppe—Giacopolo* [a name I'd never heard before; she said this in a light, teasing tone].

DR. SEARLES: Hm [noncommittal tone]. *Look* very *Italian?*—the right eye?

MRS. DOUGLAS: No; it doesn't—it looks Swedish [again in light, teasing tone].

DR. SEARLES: Well, it's an unusual name for a Swede, isn't it? [in half-serious tone].

MRS. DOUGLAS: Mm [affirmatively].

DR. SEARLES [to microphone]: Joan nods [and I laugh in amusement].

MRS. DOUGLAS: Well, it was just *named* by *Italy* [she also sounds amused], maybe. Thought it was *murdered* by Italy. [She does not sound amused.] It looks *Swedish.* [She sounds puzzled, and wondering.]

DR. SEARLES: Well [tone of offering a possible explanation], do *I* speak of *Joan* as though she were the *apple* of my *eye?*—is that—is—is that *one*—huh?. [She shakes her head.] No?—I don't?

MRS. DOUGLAS [decisively]: No; I wouldn't think that would do you any good at all. [Pause of a few seconds; a few words are inaudible here.] Being a *giant doctor,* you're not allowed to go *in* anywhere.

DR. SEARLES: Hm. Well, you're *referring* to your*self* as a giant doctor, is that right? [polite tone].

MRS. DOUGLAS: No.

DR. SEARLES: To *me* as a giant doctor? [same tone].

MRS. DOUGLAS: Um [affirmative tone].

DR. SEARLES [quietly, to microphone]: Joan nods. [Then, to her:] "Not allowed to go in anywhere" [saying this in inquiring tone].

MRS. DOUGLAS: Well, you're *in* the *head* [she explains loudly]; but I mean, when you speak to a—a patient in there, I don't think you're allowed to go *into* the patient [describing, here, what she gathers to be the situation in my head].

DR. SEARLES: *Too* apt to *explode* the patient?—or? [tone of relatively mild interest].

MRS. DOUGLAS: Mm [affirmative tone].

DR. SEARLES [quietly and in rather bored tone, to microphone]: Joan nods vigorously.

MRS. DOUGLAS: And East and West together would be—uh—*total power,* and so probably would be quite an explosion. It *looks* as though it *needs* to be exploded.

DR. SEARLES: "It"—what's "it" [rather bored tone, but one of trying tenaciously to understand what she is experiencing and saying].

MRS. DOUGLAS: Left eye [she replies]; need to be *opened up.*

DR. SEARLES: Oh; so an *explosion*—can be—*therapeutic?*—or, uh—[tone of mild, nonargumentative interest].

MRS. DOUGLAS: *No* [scoffing tone], because you always *die.* Well [tone of conceding a point], it makes you *grow*—

DR. SEARLES [interrupting, to press a momentary advantage]: Beneficial [offering this as a synonym for "therapeutic"]. Well, you *say* it *needs* to be, as though it might be—*well for* it.

MRS. DOUGLAS [talking argumentatively at the same time]: Well, it maybe isn't old enough.

DR. SEARLES: Oh [as though to say, "Oh, I see"].

MRS. DOUGLAS: I don't know *what* the age for explosions is.

[Pause of a couple of seconds.] "'Bout seven" [apparently having just been told this by a voice in her head. Then goes on in a quieter tone, saying to herself:] That's not that old; that's only about three.

DR. SEARLES: The right eye? [firm, pedagogical tone].

MRS. DOUGLAS: The left eye.

DR. SEARLES: Left eye [tone of accepting her correction].

MRS. DOUGLAS: Three or four, it still has a long time to go before it needs to explode [relaxed tone. Then she asks:] Can you feel that?

DR. SEARLES: Feel what?—What you're doing to your ear?

MRS. DOUGLAS: My scratching—yeah.

DR. SEARLES: Well, *I* was *touching* my *face*, was I, when you were just doing that?

MRS. DOUGLAS: No; you—you—you made a sort of *grimace* while I scratched behind my ear.

DR. SEARLES: Oh, while you were scratching behind your ear.

MRS. DOUGLAS: I decided you were made out of that bone in there. [Patient had a mastoidectomy in childhood, leaving a depression in the mastoid bone behind the ear.]

DR. SEARLES: Mastoid bone?

MRS. DOUGLAS: Yeah; they scratched you out.

DR. SEARLES: Is that the bone where you have a—uh—indentation in it?

MRS. DOUGLAS: Mm [affirmatively].

DR. SEARLES: The *left* one; yes. You decided that they scratched me out of—your—left mastoid bone? [tone of mild interest, but not astonishment, and not opposing this idea].

MRS. DOUGLAS: No—that they *built* your *head* out of it—out of what they scratched; they *scraped* the bone in there.

DR. SEARLES: Oh [in tone of saying mildly, "Oh, I see"].

MRS. DOUGLAS: *This* head doesn't *run* any more; it's not— *attached* to anything [speaking of her head with a startling concreteness and objectivity—very unusual on her part]. I mean, it *used* to—uh—be *very enlightened,* and *intelligent,* and—*full* of *ideas* [laughs in amused-sounding way], and *I* would just *say,* you know, what *it gave* me to say.

DR. SEARLES [saying in aside to microphone, as she is saying the last few words above]: Radio-head gesture. Radio-head gesture [referring here to a certain gesture she had made many times, for years, in explaining that her head is a radio-head, and that what she is saying consists simply in messages received by it from afar, rather than her expressing thoughts of her own].

MRS. DOUGLAS: But it isn't a radio any more [she says, in tone of objecting to what I've just said to the microphone].

DR. SEARLES: Hm [tone of noncommittal interest]. *I'm unclear*, and maybe *you* are, whether you—feel it more as a *loss*, or a *relief*, huh?

MRS. DOUGLAS: Mm [uncertainly].

DR. SEARLES: That change [explanatory tone].

MRS. DOUGLAS: Well, I feel a *little* loss; but—I'd—I'd *prefer* to be *conscious*.

DR. SEARLES: You would? [unchallengingly].

MRS. DOUGLAS: Sure—to do my *own* thinking. I—I—of course, I'll have to go to *school*. I mean, it's *difficult* for—one to *pretend* to be a *great doctor* [tone of protest] when ya haven't had any—the only *experience* I have *about* medicine was when I was a *fixed* doctor [again, her so-frequent tone of a kind of nonhuman concreteness in saying this]—and they *fixed* me as a *baby*.

DR. SEARLES: Well, you *prefer* to do your *own* thinking—not to have a radio-head?—hm?

MRS. DOUGLAS [affirmatively]: Mm.

DR. SEARLES [to microphone]: Joan nods. [Then, to her, indicating the time is up, I say in a gentle tone:] Okay.

MRS. DOUGLAS [says loudly, while she is getting up and putting her ash tray back onto the desk, and I am helping her into her coat, and we are walking toward the door]: *Well*, I'd *like* to go to *school*—but I guess we—they say in Europe you can't go to school until you're *eight*. [Then she adds in softer tone, to herself:] That's a *long* time away, for *me*; I'm only just *two*. Five, six—six more years.

DR. SEARLES [asking, in pedagogical tone]: Well, isn't *this* a *form* of going to school for—both of us? [Then, in aside to microphone:] Joan nods.

MRS. DOUGLAS: But *still*, see, when you have a *radio*-head— [she begins, in tone of making a strong protest or objection]

DR. SEARLES: As *I* do? You mean I *do* have a radio-head? [interrupting and talking over her, in rather ironic tone].

MRS. DOUGLAS: —you can actually—[then, in answer to my question, decisively]—I think you do.

DR. SEARLES: You *do;* I see [politely, not challengingly].

MRS. DOUGLAS: You—you—uh, *feel* more as though you're *in* school, and there *is* somebody directing your thinking; but when you're *not* [word or two inaudible].

DR. SEARLES [opening door to usher her out, as usual]: I'll see you.

MRS. DOUGLAS [says, as she goes out]: I'll have to have my head *fixed* again.

DR. SEARLES: So long [sounds of doors closing, as usual].

[Dr. Searles says to microphone, as soon as she has left:]

She said, as she started out, "I'll have to have my head fixed again," or "Do you think I'll have to have my head fixed again?" or, I think *probably* what she said was, "Maybe I'll have to have my head fixed again." It was said rather casually.

I [had] helped her on with her coat. *Beautiful* session—*lovely, lovely, lovely* session [in far more warmly enthusiastic tone than any in which I had spoken during the session itself]. I think of playing it for Bob Langs, although I hadn't thought much about that in the session. *Beautiful* session; I'm *very* relieved at the—uh—that this, uh, that she's alive, really, and—uh—

Now, I of *course* thought about—that [question,] should she bring the cloth dog to the sessions?—that's the first time she's ever asked that—and I hear in it a meaning of, should she bring her feelings of suicidal despondency to the session? And, uh, —————— [a current supervisee] has been doing a lot of very interesting work with a patient of hers who—has cloth dogs, and [other stuffed] animals in the sessions; I've heard from ——— ——— for a couple years about that patient. So I had some considerable urge to suggest to Joan to bring it here; but I think we can get along without—her needing to bring the cloth dog here. I think it's probably better not to; but—

She drank the can of Sprite, and I had a can of Sprite. She left three—cigarette butts in the ash tray. Uh, she walked in about two minutes late, into the waiting room. I said, "Hi." She murmured something, by way of acknowledgment, and walked in [i.e., into the office itself]. She was looking grim, as she often does, but not angry. She has a great deal to be grim about; I didn't take it personally, really.

She was wearing her—uh, Navy blue—summer top coat, with the horizontal, white, narrow stripes, and her six-inch-wide-brimmed, Navy blue, plaid, straw hat. And, uh, she put her coat and hat on the couch, and sat down [in the usual chair, diagonally placed a few feet away from mine]. She was wearing a dress I've seen only a few times—summer dress, tan and brown colors—mostly beige kind of tan. It's not a favorite dress of mine—I say it as though it were *my* dress [tone of mild interest but no great surprise]. But anyhow—it looks all right on her. She wore no stockings, heel—uh—shoes were leather, open-toed, leather sandals, medium heels. Her hair looked nice, parted on the left, as usual, and pulled back with a barrette. She wore no lipstick—hasn't worn any in *years*—and [again, noting with mild interest] I say it as though *that's* a good thing—I notice. She wore her glasses, as usual.

Now, uh, it's a, uh [opening blinds to look outside]—partly cloudy—day out, sunshiny, but it's partly cloudy, and it's been a bit cooler lately; it's a pleasant day. [I have routinely included, in my comments to the recorder at the end of each session, some word about the weather, with the thought that I may someday find, on further study of the tapes, that Mrs. Douglas's so-changeable moods are more affected by changes in the weather than one might think. My superficial impression is that there is no very marked positive correlation here.]—Uh—she lit her own cigarettes—uh—now, uh—*beautiful, beautiful* session—*beautiful* session—*lovely, lovely, lovely* session [said with heartfelt admiration for, and cherishing of, it]. *Fascinating* session. The explosions, I of course thought of her mother's innumerable explosions [of temper]. *Beautiful* session.

The tape recorder, as usual, is over on the other side of the desk, on the floor—on the rug. Now, I made one note in the session [namely, "1045—You put 500 billion into that figure—"]. The session started about 10:32. When she said, "You put 500 billion into that figure," she had her little spiral notebook and was writing in it. Now, *I* wasn't looking at it; I was sitting over in my chair. But she was speaking for all the world as though I were looking at it with her.

*Beautiful* session. The reference to the mastoidectomy—it happened that as she was feeling her mastoidectomy-fissure behind her left ear, *I* had just been touching my face somewhere up *near* my ear—not the same place, but—she was obviously pleased, and wondered if *I* felt it [i.e., felt her feeling the mastoidectomy-fissure].

Now, I'm aware that she projects upon me—onto my known [i.e., known to me], real narcissism—she projects upon that her own *enormous* absorption with her self—different parts of her self—uh—so that she reacts to me as being *almost completely* occupied with relationships between persons in my eyes.

*Beautiful, beautiful* session—the reference to Ralph Mueller—*lovely*— eeand the 1920 and—undoubtedly—or 1919— *undoubtedly* the birth of a sibling, maybe her brother Ralph— very possibly.

Today *is* Yom Kippur—uh, thinking of it in terms of—I don't know if she may need to *deny* that it's Yom Kippur; I'm not sure *why* she would need to—because of its connotations of the past, Day of Atonement for past, uh, sins, things like that.

This—I helped her on with her coat—this is all of my notes on this session with Joan—uh—see, I wondered how much she might feel, in the sessions, a sense of having *greatly outgrown* her existence at Chestnut Lodge, so that to go *back into* it is— uh—very despondent—despondency-engendering. This is all of my notes on the session with Joan on Thursday, September 22, 1977.

*Langs:* This schizophrenic patient is really never totally self-invested; there is always some form of object-relatedness, unconscious perception and introjection, and all.

*Searles:* I would certainly agree, yes.

*Langs:* I noticed a reference to a book—another deviation you had mentioned. Some of it became confusing for me. There is something else that I want to mention, because I think you are so sensitive to it and I plan to write about it. I think another thing you are saying about this session is that you felt that she held you very well—you know, the holding of the therapist by the patient. I think that there are qualities in this session that stress your need to be held and that heighten her capacity to hold you. She maintains you in many appropriate senses of the term. She sort of sets you straight from time to time, as when she wouldn't accept some of your interventions that really weren't pertinent. So perhaps you felt, not only a sense of gratification, but also a kind of therapeutic symbiotic hold and tie that would foster growth in both of you. I think that this session has some of those qualities.

*Searles:* Yes.

*Langs:* It's also exhausting; it really is. I'm sure it has been so for you. Anything that you would want to add at this point?

*Searles:* Well, my enthusiasm is undoubtedly defensive. I mean that when anyone enthuses as much as I did at the end of that session, that I'm denying loss. That is, the more she manifests such improvement in ego functioning as she was manifesting in this session, the more I would tend to feel not only gratification concerning this improvement, but also loss of the gratifications involved in her former, even more deeply ill modes of relating with me.

*Langs:* You are also denying loss and pessimism. You are picking up islands of good sessions and of promising functioning. And yet the background is a history of twenty-five years of hospitalization and psychosis. So, for you to feel optimistic under these conditions must have its defensive aspects.

*Searles:* It makes you feel crazy, you know, to hope. I noticed in listening back to this session—I have had experience, maybe a half a dozen times in past years, maybe ten times at the very most, of one or another colleague (usually himself an expert in psychoanalytic therapy with schizophrenic patients) listening to a recording of my session with her, one or another session, and heretofore the colleague has let the session be played, you see, with few interruptions, and has felt fascinated with it. They seem genuinely fascinated with her and they usually make some kind of enthusiastic comments about the worth of the work; but they don't make anything like as many comments as you have, and of course not the kind of comments you've made, and my feeling is that you inevitably responded as you did—in a way, had to—but you very usefully did.

*Langs:* I'm glad you said that.

*Searles:* But you miss a lot in terms of the flow of the session; you're bound to. I think one thing you miss is something of the pressure and the anxiety one feels in the session with such a person as this; you miss that.

*Langs:* Perhaps so.

*Searles:* You miss that. But—I'm trying to be brief—but I felt a sense of despondency that had to have a lot of countertransference in it.

*Langs:* Despondency in terms of what?

*Searles:* Despondency, and on my part I felt terribly disappointed.

*Langs:* As to what I said, or to the session?

*Searles:* Well, I felt terribly disappointed that, in the main, you chose to teach me—which you can, and I've learned a lot from what you said, and I shall no doubt go on learning, thinking, about what you said—but I felt terribly disappointed that you didn't simply let me teach you what it's like to work with a very, very ill woman. You've got a lot to teach me. But I still think that the despondency had some very specific kind of meanings that I kept feeling, a sense of something approaching despair that it was obvious that you were going to keep telling me and wanting to interrupt and stop, and the flow of the sessions all gone and I at one point, or at some time I was feeling very murderous toward you; I guess it was obvious to you. And I was thinking ironically that "Well, it's clear what I'm going to do: I'm going to hang myself in this suite of offices. The only thing I haven't decided, and I will leave that up to you, whether I'm to hang myself from the ceiling of this room or the store room." You see, I'm trying to tell you that what's happening here is so relevant to what's going on in the patient—that damned reflection process again, you see—that with the fragmentation I felt it as a fragmentation of the experience of listening to the tape.
The fragmentation and the attendant despondency, and surely

there has been a lot of that in her life and that's been so hard to deal with, so that the crazy sessions where an awful lot is said and even if I don't get two cents in, in the session, she carries on a whole dialogue. That's the way it used to be years ago. That was so much easier to stand then her coming in silent, being silent the whole session, looking very despondent.

So when I'm enthusing what a wonderful session it is, then we are listening back to it and I'm feeling this despondency and murderous feeling and despair, I'm sure it's all part of the same package.

*Langs:* Right. Would you take it further? Because in part you seem to be responding to my imposing an awareness in you of the extent to which she was working you over therapeutically in the session. Do you think that that was part of it?

*Searles:* Well, yes.

*Langs:* Because that's what happens.

*Searles:* That you've imposed an awareness in me of what?

*Langs:* Well, what you are saying is that I focused on that thread to the virtual exclusion of all other threads. What you wanted instead really was for me to share with you the interest in the psychotic contents and things of that sort.

*Searles:* Right, right.

*Langs:* I don't listen that way. This happens with all of my supervision. Much teaching by others is done in terms of the fascination of dynamics, while I'm always shifting back into the therapeutic interaction. I believe that that fascination is often a distraction from the immediacy of the unconscious communicative interaction. I myself never lost the sense of the flow; I felt the session flowed beautifully. I really did. You felt it otherwise I think because again you wanted me to experience something quite different from what I experienced. And this is what I come up against again and again. For me, dynamics and genetics have meaning only when appended to the immediate therapeutic interaction.

*Searles:* Well, in a sense—and this is a great oversimplification—I felt that you were doing to me what you kept telling me I was doing to her.

*Langs:* Which was?

*Searles:* Namely, intruding.

*Langs:* Intruding upon you, yes.

*Searles:* Stopping me, the same thing.

*Langs:* Now, my contention is that as a supervisor, my first responsibility is to the patient (Langs 1978b, 1979). Your comments last time about the way I supervise helped me think further about it. I do my supervision, and this is what you are saying, primarily through an identification with the patient and only secondarily with the therapist.

*Searles:* Yes. I do a lot of mine that way, also.

*Langs:* I feel that that's my responsibility: to know where the patient is at. It means again that I may seem to neglect how anxious, frightened, and all the rest, the therapist is, but I have to let him know where the patient is. In other words, my main function as a supervisor is to say consciously what I feel the patient is experiencing and conveying unconsciously, and have the patient indirectly confirm it.

*Searles:* Yes, I do quite a bit of that.

*Langs:* That imposes a great burden on the therapist. I'm well aware of it, but again that's where the difference in the supervisory bipersonal and therapeutic bipersonal fields come in. I really am a silent therapist, but I'm a damned active, intrusive, rough—though, when necessary, supportive—supervisor. I do it in response to the therapeutic needs of the patient as they are expressed in the material. There were some major frame issues here. It doesn't always have to be the frame, but it will be when there is a tape recorder. And there was—

*Searles:* The pay, the previous session.

*Langs:* Yes, the offer of money, which was such a beautiful issue, and the serving of the Sprite. I truly believe now—I am totally convinced—that the frame is an essential component to a truly therapeutic symbiosis. I think the patient responds intensely to any disruption in the frame, even a schizophrenic patient.

*Searles:* It makes a lot of sense.

*Langs:* And the other side of it is the therapist's own, for whatever reasons, investment in a deviant frame. I disturb that need, that effort directed toward pathological symbiosis. Because after all, as I said about the literature (Langs 1976b), there have been very few analysts who have advocated adherence to the frame. I could count them on one hand.

*Searles:* I remember seeing your long article (Langs, 1975c), that one you referred me to; yes, I found that very interesting, how few of them there were.

*Langs:* Let me just say a final word. To me this was an extremely meaningful experience. I have to apologize if I seemed unappreciative. I am well aware of the strength it takes to make a presentation of this kind—and of the attendant anxiety it generates.

*Searles:* You mean referring to the recording?

*Langs:* Oh, today especially. Today was the most meaningful session we had, without a question.

*Searles:* I'm glad. Good, good; I'm glad. I thought you would find it interesting. I never really expected you to have as much useful to point out to me about it. I never suspected that.

*Langs:* That always comes up, because I'm listening differently than everybody else.

*Searles:* Very interesting.

*Langs:* So if I have to apologize for it, I do. But it's where I'm at and it's where I feel the patient is at. And it's what analysts have neglected, so it needs discussing.

*Searles:* Well, I'm sure I've learned a lot today about it.

*Langs:* I really appreciate your presentation and your candidness. I too have learned a great deal. Thank you very much.

# APPENDIX TO CHAPTER 4

# I. UNINTERRUPTED TRANSCRIPT OF SESSION WITH MRS. JOAN DOUGLAS

Testing—testing: one-two-three-four-five-six-seven-eight-nine-ten. This is the one-hour session with Mrs. Joan Douglas on Thursday, September 22, 1977, in my office. I am, of course, having in mind how—uh—suicidal she sounded in the last few minutes of the session on Tuesday, so I'm gonna be particularly—uh—I *intend* to be particularly to trying to—uh—help her.—Now, *here* I notice I have to be careful—not to say, "Help her to—uh—become more suicidal," or "Help her to commit suicide." Anyhow, it's—obvious, my ambivalence about all that. I did *not* call Little Lodge; I didn't even come close to—well, I came *rather* close to but not *very* close to calling Little Lodge, to—suggest they keep an eye on her, against the possibility of suicide. But I did *not* call them. And it hasn't preyed on my mind, since last time—*much;* it has a *little*. I have had some thought—about—if she were to kill herself, what that would do to—well, the *research*, I guess, has been my main thought, what it would do to—the way the papers would be received—past ones and in the future, any I might write about her. I can't imagine writing anything

about her if she were to suicide, I can't write—imagine writing any
more. But I think I'm *clearly playing down* my—what it would *do* to
me *personally* if she killed herself.

[Sound of double doors between office and waiting room opening
and closing, as I look into waiting room and find that she has not yet
arrived—a not-infrequent occurrence.] It's now 10:30. I'm gonna
call—uh—[sound of phone being dialed as I call my answering
service]. This is Dr. Searles. Any calls? [Lady at answering service,
while looking to see if there's been a message, asks me how I've been.]
Pretty good; how about you? [She replies that she's been fine, and
that there are no messages.] Thank you [said with sincere relief]. [To
tape recorder:] I called and asked if there were any calls. Another five
minutes, I'll call Little Lodge [the particular building where she
lives at Chestnut Lodge].

[Only a few seconds later, sound of door closing as Mrs. Douglas
enters waiting room, looking grim but not angry.]

DR. SEARLES: Hi [relatively casual, noncommittal sounding. I am
waiting in inner office, with double doors to waiting room open].

MRS. DOUGLAS [scarcely audible, but prompt, murmur in response
to my greeting].

[Sounds of double doors between waiting room and office closing.]

[I sigh, and clear my throat politely.]

[Silence is broken by sound of siren going by.]

[Sound of my getting up, going into storeroom briefly—for what
purpose, I don't recall, probably to equip myself with matches, as
usual, in case she needs some. She routinely gets out her cigarettes at
the beginning of each session, and often is in need of matches for
them. It is my assumption that for her to equip herself with matches,
at her sanitarium building where several very ill patients dwell, is not
necessarily easy for her and the staff to accomplish consistently, as
she starts out from there for each session.]

DR. SEARLES: Um? [gently inquiring tone. Playback shows that the
initial silence had lasted for four minutes.]

MRS. DOUGLAS: Mm, mm [softly, but tone of negation].

DR. SEARLES: Well, did you—just *hear* something—so—clearly
that you—assumed I must have heard it, too, or—? [said in a tone of
gentle insistence].

MRS. DOUGLAS [replies promptly, in a tone of explaining]: My mother says if this isn't my room, I shouldn't smoke in it. But [voice becomes softer] *I* think it's *mine.*

DR. SEARLES: So you don't see where she gets the impression that it's not yours.

MRS. DOUGLAS: *She* never thinks *any*thing is hers or mine [said in stronger tone, and one of feeling disgusted with her mother]; *I* don't know—

DR. SEARLES [interrupting, in tone of interest and mild surprise]: Really?—hers either, huh?

MRS. DOUGLAS [yawning]: I don't know why.

DR. SEARLES [tone of gentle persistence]: She seems very self-effacing? [After pause of a second or two, I say in an aside to the microphone nearby on my desk—it being scarcely necessary to turn my head to do so:] Joan nods.

MRS. DOUGLAS [makes some very brief, inaudible comment in the midst of a big yawn].

DR. SEARLES: You want some—uh—Sprite? [For years, in our sessions, I have served one or another brand of soft drink to us. I asked her this question in a tone of gentle inquiry.]

MRS. DOUGLAS [promptly nods, and grunts affirmatively].

[I grunt in acknowledgment of her affirmative reply, and go to storeroom and bring back the Sprite cans, open them, and pour a glass for her, and one for myself. I provide a can for each of us. This wordless process takes about a minute or two. I have seated myself again by the time Mrs. Douglas asks:]

MRS. DOUGLAS [tone of astonishment, wondering, and much concern]: Should I bring my little *dog* to the *hour?* [Here she is referring to a cloth dog, a transitional object which she has possessed for some two or three years, and of which she has spoken many times in her sessions with me.]

DR. SEARLES [after a pause of only a second or so, in matter-of-fact, businesslike tone]: How large is it?

MRS. DOUGLAS [explanatory, collaborative tone]: You know, those little cotton dogs [of which in actuality there is only one; for years she has experienced, more often than not, singular things or persons as plural] they have at the Lodge—about that big.

DR. SEARLES [matter-of-factly, for the benefit of the tape recorder]: About eight or ten inches. Well, you wonder if you should, huh?

MRS. DOUGLAS: Well, or take it to a hospital?

DR. SEARLES [in unchallenging tone]: Well, it does seem in *need* of some kind of treatment, does it?

MRS. DOUGLAS [softly, agreeing]: Yeah. Doesn't feel at all well once it's died, commit suicide.

DR. SEARLES [gently, noncommittally]: Hm.

MRS. DOUGLAS: I think it's been a men—[For many years, any *man* had been, in her experience, so consistently multiple a being that she had dropped the term "man" from her vocabulary. She invariably referred, therefore, to any man as a "men."]—uh—woman too long; it's a men—needs [voice much softer now, and seemingly repeating what an hallucinatory voice has just said to her] to become a men.

DR. SEARLES [very faintly]: Oh. [Tone as if to say, "I see." Then, after a couple of seconds' pause, I go on, in my usual voice:] That is, if a men is—uh kept as a—woman too long, he feels the way the little dog is feeling [tone is one of simply rephrasing what she has just said—not at all challenging the validity of her statement. Then I add, in a quiet aside to the microphone:] Joan nods. [Pause of a few seconds.] Well, some thought that maybe—bringing him to the hour—bringing the—dog—to the hour, maybe *I* can help—maybe *I* can take care of him, hm? [said in an unpressuring, matter-of-fact, unchallenging tone, in a spirit of making sure that I understand what she is saying, and of encouraging her to say more. Then, after a pause of several seconds, I resume:] That is, *I* look to be the kind of— person, or—doctor, who might—be able to help a—very despondent—uh—men?—hm?

MRS. DOUGLAS [makes faint, affirmative murmur, which impels me to tell the mike, softly:] Joan nods.

DR. SEARLES [after a pause of nearly a minute, I ask, in a firm tone, but one expressive of carefully thinking my way along]: Is *that* a *kind* of feeling—*you* have had some *experience* of?—that is, feeling—uh, despondent, and having been in—what? [tone of "How to put it?"]— such-and-such a person too long, and needing to—

MRS. DOUGLAS [interrupting]: Oh, *I* was *in* somebody, was I?" [tone of surprise].

DR. SEARLES: *I* don't know [in tone of, "How in hell would *I* know?—I only *work* here"]—*I'm* trying to s-s-s-see if *you've* ever had any *experience* of what the—men in the—little cloth dog is feeling? [Tone becomes exasperated and ironic here.] Patient says simultaneously, "I don't know" [in tone as though to say, "I haven't the vaguest idea"].

DR. SEARLES [going on persistently, without pause]: That is, any—have *you* ever felt so your*self*, to some extent? [I trail off, mumbling, as if to soften any undue pressure I am putting upon her.]

MRS. DOUGLAS [dubiously, and barely audibly]: Umm.

DR. SEARLES [persistently]: In a simple—way—have *you* ever *felt despondent?*—hm?

MRS. DOUGLAS [faintly and in a childlike tone, negatingly]: Uh-uh. [Then, after a few seconds' pause, she says in rather harsh, strong, adult voice:] I've *been* a *rug* [tone as if to say, "If that's what you mean"].

DR. SEARLES [quickly]: You have—

MRS. DOUGLAS [interrupting him, in the same strong voice]: *Rugs* [she explains] make you feel sort of [and she adds a word which is inaudible].

DR. SEARLES: Rugs make you feel sort of what?

MRS. DOUGLAS: Dreadful.

DR. SEARLES: You've been *this* rug, for instance [referring to the wall-to-wall carpet in the office], for instance—you've been this rug [and in aside to microphone:] Joan looks at this rug—confirmatory.

MRS. DOUGLAS [asks in rather loud, direct tone]: Do *you* have—all my passport, and all that?

DR. SEARLES: Your passport? [polite, careful tone]. Well, you—

MRS. DOUGLAS [interrupting him]: *One* doctor does; I don't know which one.

DR. SEARLES: You're not sure I'm the one who has.

MRS. DOUGLAS: No [confirmatorily].

DR. SEARLES: Passport—uh?—to enable you to—uh—leave for giant country?—or—what? [For many years, as my 1972 paper details, she has been concerned with trying to build a giant body for herself, to enable her to return to "giant country."]

MRS. DOUGLAS [explains, in rather soft voice]: Return to—giant country.

DR. SEARLES [brisk, direct tone]: Well, do *you* find you're becoming despondent here?—or what?—this—this country?

MRS. DOUGLAS: Well, I haven't been *conscious;* so I don't know where I've—I've *been* [said in a rather small voice].

DR. SEARLES [very faintly, by way of acknowledgment]: Hm.

[Then, in my usual voice:] Are you—conscious of having been here—uh—a couple of sessions ago, and toward the *end* of the session, saying—"Then I'm—should go back to the Lodge and *hang* myself from the *ceiling* with a—necktie?" Do you recall that?—you don't recall that?

MRS. DOUGLAS [gives a light, brief chuckle of amusement after I have said "necktie"]: No; no [dismissing it without apparent difficulty].

DR. SEARLES [in aside to microphone]: Joan seems clearly amused. [Then I say to her, in persistent tone:] But *that's about* how—despondent the men in the—cloth dog seems to be feeling?—huh?

MRS. DOUGLAS: Well, she seems better today. I think she didn't have any sleep, or enough sleep. *Today* she seems all right. But—I—I had never heard that she was a *men* before.

DR. SEARLES: Well, are you—do you—do you feel that *I'm telling* you that she is?

MRS. DOUGLAS [tone of explaining]: Somebody in my *head* just said that. [Pause of a few seconds.] Well, they say it's—uh—*July* 27th.

DR. SEARLES: That's what someone in your head—just said?

MRS. DOUGLAS: "Today, July 27th."

DR. SEARLES [tone of deferential inquiry]: That's what *they* in your *head* say?

MRS. DOUGLAS: No; it came from outside.

DR. SEARLES: You—saw the morning newspaper today?

MRS. DOUGLAS: No. Well, *newspapers* have *never* been right.

DR. SEARLES [unchallenging tone]: You're *long since* disillusioned with the reliability of newspapers. [Then, in aside to microphone—in, as often, the same voice-volume:] Joan nods. [Then, after a pause of about one minute, I go on:] So it's *not Yom Kippur*, today—huh? No? Even though it's generally—*considered* to be; but they're—everyone else is—in error about that—hm? [said in ironic tone].

MRS. DOUGLAS: Oh, well, they've *always* said *that* was *Czechoslovakian*, but *I* think it's the *King* of *Egypt* [vigorous tone].

DR. SEARLES: Which one?—the one in my *right* eye?

MRS. DOUGLAS: *Left* eye.

[Relevant to this discussion of my eyes are two more portions of my previously mentioned 1972 paper concerning my work with Mrs.

Douglas: "By late 1966 or early 1967 she had become able to sit with me, during the sessions in my office, with our chairs placed conventionally only a few feet apart, and to join me in a mutual effort to understand what was transpiring in the relationship. She looked often, without leaning forward, into my eyes, and in one of these sessions she was looking at my face in fascination as I was making some comment, and exclaimed, 'When you're talking about different people, your eyes become the eyes of whomever you're talking about. It's like a kaleidoscope. I've never seen anything like it before; it's fascinating'" (Searles, 1979a, p. 210). "I feel into assuming as the months went on that, from her way of speaking of such perceptions, she was seeing entire homunculi, as it were, in my eyes; but when I inquired into this in more detail on one of the later occasions she made clear that, as she had indicated earlier, what she was perceiving were the *eyes of* those persons in my eyes" (Searles, 1979a, p. 213).]

DR. SEARLES: I'm unclear what the *Czechoslovakian* has to do with *Yom Kippur*.

MRS. DOUGLAS: *I'm*—not familiar with what it is, either.

DR. SEARLES [persistently]: You've never heard that—phrase, "Yom Kippur," or "Yom Kippur" [stating it in the two usual pronunciations] before, huh?

MRS. DOUGLAS [rather faintly]: No.

DR. SEARLES: Never have, uh.

MRS. DOUGLAS: Uh-uh [she agrees].

DR. SEARLES [persistently]: You've never *read* anything of *Judaism?*—hm? [I know that, in actuality, although not Jewish herself, she is very familiar with many aspects of Judaism.]

MRS. DOUGLAS: Nope. [Then adds, very faintly:] Never have.

DR. SEARLES: July 23rd, they say, huh?

MRS. DOUGLAS [very faintly]: Yeah.

DR. SEARLES: You don't recall any *fireworks*—uh, say—two and a half weeks ago, huh? [Then, in barely audible aside to microphone:] Shakes her head.

DR. SEARLES [after pause of about two minutes, asks]: You're trying to *figure* your *age*, or what are you figuring?

MRS. DOUGLAS [confirmatorily]: Uh.

DR. SEARLES [in aside to microphone]: Joan nods; she's doing some figuring [with a pen and little notebook she carries in her purse].

Mrs. Douglas: Well, then you put five hundred billion into that?—five hundred billion—two, four, seven [pause of several seconds, while she goes on setting down numbers, not showing her work to me]. Not quite two [she concludes].

Dr. Searles: You're not quite two years old? [She nods.] So you're—doing *supremely* well to—be able to *speak* as—capably as you—are; huh? [said with a degree of irony, but not unkindly. Then I add to microphone:] Joan shrugs.

Mrs. Douglas [tone of consulting me, though not showing me the figures in the notebook]: Well, four hundred—is it four hundred *average* years that they speak, or—uh—or four *medical days*? I think it's four hundred *average* years.

Dr. Searles [interrupting and talking simultaneously]: Well, I suppose it *depends*—I suppose it *depends*—on—how *intensely* their *fond mother* longs to hear the sound of—their *voice,* so that she will have someone to *talk* to, to—help *dispel* her *loneliness*—some things like that. The time may *seem terribly* long.

Mrs. Douglas [in a soft voice]: Well, it does to me. [Then she adds, in a barely audible voice:] I think we've been—out on the water *too long. I* don't think the *water's* a healthy place to raise children. Think the *mountains* would be better.

Dr. Searles: What, the *air's* better?—or it's easier for a child to get *oriented* as to where she or he is?—or—?

Mrs. Douglas: Well, *I* think the *air* is more pleasant.

Dr. Searles: Too much humidity on the water? [unpressuring tone].

Mrs. Douglas: *Salt* [she explains emphatically. Then, after an only momentary pause, she says in reference to her pack of cigarettes:] I should think we'd be beyond using these things.

Dr. Searles: Cigarettes?

Mrs. Douglas: Yes. [She adds a few inaudible words, among which is "building."]

Dr. Searles: Beyond using those for—as material for a giant body? [Then I add in an aside to the microphone, in the same voice-volume:] Joan nods. [Then I say to her:] Should be—something what?—more substantial than that, or—?

Mrs. Douglas: Um [confirmatorily].

Dr. Searles [to tape recorder]: More nods.

Mrs. Douglas: Twelve—Chestnut Lodges for the head, and twenty-seven for the body. [Pause of a few seconds.] Have to be picked up.

Dr. Searles: Picked up, partly—picked up out of *despondency?*

Mrs. Douglas: No, from around—*wherever* they *are.* And *then* given to *me.* I thought *that's* what we came to a *psychiatrist for.*

Dr. Searles: To construct—to get his help in constructing a giant body—

Mrs. Douglas [interrupts]: No, to have him *pick up* the things.

Dr. Searles: Oh. [As if saying, "I see."]

Mrs. Douglas: And give them to me.

Dr. Searles: Give them to you.

Mrs. Douglas [in defensively assertive tone]: They're all *built.* They're *there.*

Dr. Searles: They only need picking up, huh? [unchallenging and relatively soft tone].

Mrs. Douglas: Uh-huh.

Dr. Searles [starting in businesslike, louder tone]: Now, the *person* in the *cloth dog*—needs—her, or his—*spirits* picked up, this—do they not?—hm? [ending in note of gentle inquiry].

Mrs. Douglas: Uhm [uncertain tone].

Dr. Searles [after she has been silent for several seconds, I suggest, gently but persistently]: Maybe *you* don't care to use that—*phrase,* "picked up" in a sense—picked up *out* of *despondency?*—or—?

Mrs. Douglas: Well—*gathered together*—for—in order to be *returned* to 'em, [she is speaking in a very cooperative tone here]. But *our* trouble has been that it's too difficult to—to *give* anything *back* to anybody [very decisive tone]. So I don't understand why they keep *taking* it *away* from us. 'Cause [i.e., because] they *know* that's been the experience: when you try to give something back to somebody— explosions, and all *kinds* of things like that.

Dr. Searles [very faint, interested tone]: Hm.

Mrs. Douglas: I wouldn't want—the baby—moved away if she came there to *rest* for a day or so [said in tone of making a concession—of not wishing to be unreasonably demanding].

Dr. Searles [tone of polite inquiry]: Came *where*—in the *chair?*

Mrs. Douglas [tone of correcting him, setting him straight]: At the Lodge.

Dr. Searles: Oh [as if to say, "I see"; said quietly, unchallengingly. Then, after several seconds of silence, I suggest, in a gentle, polite, unchallenging tone:] She—may *need* a rest, huh?

Mrs. Douglas [softly]: Yeah. [Then, after several seconds of silence, she says in voice of normal volume:] Well, I—imagine she—before she could have any *surgery* to—be turned *back* into a *men*, she'd have to be *able* to *eat*—

DR. SEARLES [interrupting in a polite but firm and relatively loud voice]: *I'm* unclear what brought the *baby* into this. I—who—were we *talking* about the *baby*?

MRS. DOUGLAS [explains, in a very collaborative tone]: Well, we were talking about—I *asked* you if I should *bring* the *cloth dog*—

DR. SEARLES: Yes, yes.

MRS. DOUGLAS: And *then you* talked about gathering her *spirits*.

DR. SEARLES: Picking up her spirits, or—uh—this—you *said* she's *despondent*, didn't you?—that—in the cloth dog, that—

MRS. DOUGLAS: I—guess I *did* [uncertain tone]—I don't—I don't remember [relatively faint tone].

DR. SEARLES: But that—that—the *baby*—*is* the cloth dog?—or is *in* the cloth dog?—that is—[tone of polite inquiry].

MRS. DOUGLAS: Yes.

DR. SEARLES: Hm.

MRS. DOUGLAS: *It's* her—part of her *mind. But* they said that *she* was a *he*, and *that's why* she's so *depressed* [said in strongly assertive, decisive voice; then she explains to me:] That's what the university [whence have come, for years, some of the hallucinatory voices she experiences] said.

DR. SEARLES: *They* say that—that—uh—*she's* a *he*, who has been—a *he* too long—and needs to become a woman, hm? [tone of unchallenging resume, to be sure I understand the meaning of what she is saying].

MRS. DOUGLAS [correcting me in a friendly tone]: No, it's been—the other way around: it's been a—a *she* too long, and needs to become a men.

DR. SEARLES: Needs to become a men [said in comfortable tone of "I see; I've got it now"].

MRS. DOUGLAS: But *I* don't think *your left eye*, and the *one* that's in my *cloth dog* are *related* [tone of protest].

DR. SEARLES: You don't [rather amused, ironic tone].

MRS. DOUGLAS: No.

DR. SEARLES: I seem—[tone of inquiry].

MRS. DOUGLAS [interrupting me]: *One* time the *left* eye was her *doctor*. But—uh—

Dr. Searles [interrupting, but in an unchallenging way]: *Related* in *that* sense, huh?

Mrs. Douglas: Uh-huh [agreeing softly].

Dr. Searles [quietly, in aside to microphone]: Joan nods. [Then I say, in normal tone of voice, to Mrs. Douglas:] But *not* related by family?—uh—[speaking in an unpressuring, unchallenging tone] No?

Mrs. Douglas [makes a very soft sound of negation].

Dr. Searles [I report, quietly, to the microphone]: Shakes her head. [Then, after several seconds' silence, I say to her inquiringly:] You see—again, *I* was momentarily—wondered *what* had brought my *left eye* into this?—huh?

Mrs. Douglas [explains, emphatically, but her first couple of words are inaudible]: . . . so *sick!*

Dr. Searles: What? It *does* look so sick?

Mrs. Douglas [agrees in soft murmur].

Dr. Searles [quietly reporting to microphone]: Joan nods.

Mrs. Douglas [explains further]: Looks as though it really can't see anymore.

Dr. Searles: Oh [tone as if saying, "I see"].

Mrs. Douglas: As though it isn't seeing out.

Dr. Searles: Well it *does look*—somewhat as sick—as the—baby, or person, in the cloth dog—is—is, huh?

Mrs. Douglas: Well, no—it looks *sicker.*

Dr. Searles: This—my left eye looks sicker.

Mrs. Douglas [soft murmur of confirmation].

Dr. Searles: Oh. [Said quietly, as though saying, "I see." Then, after a few seconds, I say:] Well *I* get some—sense of *how burdened you* may *feel*—that—uh—that—seems as though there are so *many* persons, round about, who are in *urgent* need of—care. Hm?

Mrs. Douglas [faint murmur of confirmation].

Dr. Searles [quietly reporting to microphone]: Joan nods. [Then, after a pause of a couple of seconds, I say to her:] And *here I* sit, what—uh—apparently not even—*aware* that the person in my left eye is *very sick*. [I say this kindly, patiently, unchallengingly.]

Mrs. Douglas: Um [confirmatorily].

Dr. Searles [quietly reporting to microphone]: More nods. [Then, after pause of several seconds, I say, thoughtfully, in inquiring tone:] Sick and unable to see?—hm?

MRS. DOUGLAS: Um [confirmatorily].

DR. SEARLES [quietly reporting to microphone]: Joan nods again.

MRS. DOUGLAS [after several seconds' silence]: Well, *maybe* he moved the—uh [tired sigh] French Mediterranean Seas *west*, and that's how he looked after he'd been—after he was taken out of them. They *do*—they *did sky* everybody [i.e., turn everybody into sky]. They *were strong* enough to do *that*. [She is speaking in a collaborative tone here, as though she is not sure, herself, about some of these things, and is trying to help clarify them.]

DR. SEARLES: That is, they turned everybody into sky. [Quiet aside to microphone:] Joan nods. [Then I say to her:] Well, that's a—what—a *relatively simple* task for a giant?—is it? [speaking, as usual, in persistent but casual, unchallenging tone].

MRS. DOUGLAS: I guess *so;* I don't know [rather vaguely, as though saying, "You can't prove it by me"].

DR. SEARLES [interrupting, and talking at same time as her last few words above]: —I mean, it would seem like a—rather *considerable feat*, by ordinary—any *ordinary earth* standards [speaking ironically and challengingly].

MRS. DOUGLAS [murmurs confirmatorily].

DR. SEARLES: But *you* don't—seem to think it—

MRS. DOUGLAS [interrupting me]: *I* think that when they—when they're skies, they're *dead*. They say [evidently having just now heard hallucinatory voices] they're not! [tone of surprise and wonderment]. Well, they *look* sort of—

DR. SEARLES [interrupting]: *They* say it's a form of *treatment*, do they? [tone of firm but polite inquiry].

MRS. DOUGLAS: *Gloppy* [finishing the comment I had interrupted]. Yes [in confirmation of my statement].

DR. Searles [rather faintly]: They do? [quiet aside to microphone:] Joan nods.

MRS. DOUGLAS: "For *money*" [evidently quoting hallucinatory voice]. *I* don't think that's necessary—

DR. SEARLES [interrupting]: *Money*. Reminds me of your having put several coins on the desk [referring to her having done so in the most recent session—in an attempt to pay, from her very modest weekly allowance, for a session]—d'you recall? [She makes a barely audible confirmatory murmur, and I say quietly to microphone:] Joan nods.

Mrs. Douglas: But you gave them back to me [casual tone, by way of reminding me].

Dr. Searles [in similarly casual tone]: That's right. You—in case I had forgotten?

Mrs. Douglas: Yeah.

Dr. Searles: Yes; I remember. [Then, after several seconds' pause:] That is, I *seemed* quite *unmindful* that that was—perhaps the *first* time in your *life* you had—felt moved to pay—some money for psychiatric treatment?—huh? [She starts laughing softly in amusement, and I start chuckling more loudly. We both are laughing together for a few moments.]

Mrs. Douglas: Shouldn't have *done* it; I didn't *know* that [but said lightly]. If you *offer* money to someone, it *means* they—they're *murderers*. I guess that's—

Dr. Searles [interrupting her]: I *reacted* as—as though—you had, uh—

Mrs. Douglas [murmurs confirmatorily]: Addressed you as a murderer. I didn't—

Dr. Searles [interrupting]: Hadn't *intended* to, had you?

Mrs. Douglas: Uh-uh [meaning "No"]. The *university* had me do it.

Dr. Searles: Oh, was it *after* that?—I wonder if *you* recall— whether it was *after* my—I had—uh—*given* the money *back* to you, that you—*then wondered* if you should go back to the Lodge and hang yourself from the ceiling with a necktie?—Do *you* remember?— if that was the sequence?

Mrs. Douglas: N-n-no; *I* don't *remember* that, about hanging, and necktie.

Dr. Searles: You don't?

Mrs. Douglas: I remember thinking—that I'm *in more ties* than—anyone else in *civilization*. And I *wondered if* the medical profession was ever going to get around to—*utilizing* them *intelligently*. But when giants are built—out of bodies, you wonder *where* they're going to use the *tie* [she ends this statement in a kind of helpless-wondering tone]. I guess, just in the *mind*—probably to build a mind—or eyesight.

Dr. Searles: Now, when *you* say "tie," could you *describe* what you're referring to? [firmly but not unkindly].

Mrs. Douglas [in a tone as though this should be obvious]: Well, a *tie*, such as—

DR. SEARLES [interrupts]: A necktie, such as this one? [Gesturing toward the one I'm wearing; then I report to the microphone:] Joan gestures toward this one. [Then, after a couple of seconds' pause, I say to her:] That is, they *could* be used *intelligently* by the medical profession, hm?

MRS. DOUGLAS: They *say* so [she agrees]. They say that they're very *adaptable* for—*growth medicine.* [She is evidently reporting, here, what the hallucinatory voices are saying, and reporting this in a tone indicating that she is very skeptical that this is true.]

DR. SEARLES: Hm [faintly and noncommittally].

MRS. DOUGLAS: But they haven't *explained* how they *use* them. [Said in casual tone; then, after several seconds of silence, she says "Hm!" in a tone clearly indicative of her having just heard the hallucinatory voices say something new and interesting.]

DR. SEARLES [gently]: What did you hear then?

MRS. DOUGLAS: They said you'd sew them all together and then you'd take them inside the head and—put the person in them and they *explode* [and she cackles briefly with amusement as she finished saying this]. *That* doesn't sound like the *proper treatment* for a *mind* [she comments, in protest and disbelief].

DR. SEARLES: Doesn't sound like very gentle treatment, does it? [I comment quietly].

MRS. DOUGLAS: Uh-uh [she agrees with my comment].

DR. SEARLES: When you *say something* about—uh—having felt that you had more *ties* than anyone else in the world—huh?

MRS. DOUGLAS [gives murmur of agreement].

DR. SEARLES [I suggest quietly]: Might have meanings of *family ties?*—bonds of *affection?*

MRS. DOUGLAS: Well, *literally ties.* I *make ties* all the time [said with quiet firmness].

DR. SEARLES: Literally neckties, huh?

MRS. DOUGLAS: That's the way my *head* was fixed—to *do* that.

DR. SEARLES: Your *head* was *fixed* to—*turn figurative concepts into—concrete, literal* ones? [said firmly but respectfully].

MRS. DOUGLAS: Uh—[said faintly; sounds uncertain and therefore noncommital].

DR. SEARLES [I finish asking my question more rapidly now]: So that *instead* of thinking in terms of *emotional ties,* or *ties* of *affection,* your *head* has been *fixed* so that you think in terms of *neckties?* [speaking in the same firm but respectful tone as before].

MRS. DOUGLAS: Well I guess *so* [sounds accepting of his idea, but with the implication, "Although I never thought of it that way before"]—since I made—such a great *number* of them. But—when you *speak* of *concrete,* you *mean—food.*

DR. SEARLES: Oh, I do? [said ironically]: I *mean that,* but for some reason don't say—"food"?

MRS. DOUGLAS [gives murmur of agreement].

DR. SEARLES: You were speaking about having made ties, huh? [Patient murmurs agreement.] Reminds me of my having—uh— entreated you, or asked you—urged you—for several years, to—make a necktie for me. [After a few seconds' pause, during which she makes no sign of remembering that, I go on, in a kindly but rather matter-of-fact tone.] And I—assume you *don't* remember that, because I've— mentioned it many times. [My comment ends, however, on a note of restrained impatience, exasperation, and probable bitterness.]

MRS. DOUGLAS [in a louder tone than usual]: Well, *I* remember *Ralph Mueller* [the name of a fellow patient, from that earlier era, with whom she had been relatively friendly; a pseudonym is used here]—Mr.—Von *Hindenberg's* ["Mr. Von Hindenberg"—her customary way of referring to one of her grand*mothers*—as I learned after some years] *eldest son—asking* me to make him a yellow tie.

DR. SEARLES [quietly]: I see.

MRS. DOUGLAS: And I said I didn't—see how—*my*—yellow would do *him* any *good* [tone of helpless protest]. And he said, "Oh, yes, *you're* a source of *electricity,* and *your yellow* is your *blue,* and *I* need—more blue" [Mueller's words are quoted in a teasingly cynical tone], and I said, "But—if you mixed *my* blue with *your* blue, you'd get *black*" [tone of this quote is one of protest, but coquettish protest]. So [dejected tone] we didn't do anything about it. [Then, after several seconds of silence, she says in a more energetic way, apparently quoting something she has just head the voices say:] Or *become* a *nymph.*

DR. SEARLES: Uh—*black—may* have some meaning of *depression?*—doesn't it?

MRS. DOUGLAS: Um [confirmatory tone].

DR. SEARLES [quietly, to microphone]: Joan nods. [I then say, in much the same quiet tone, to her:] So that—*your* blue and *his* blue— is—mixing your feeling blue with his feeling blue might—cause— uh—*severe depression?*—is that the idea?

MRS. DOUGLAS [murmurs confirmatorily].

DR. SEARLES [quietly—but, as usual, easily audible to the nearby patient—to the microphone:] Joan nods.

MRS. DOUGLAS [speaking with energetic interest]: *He* looks *better* now [a couple of additional words are inaudible].

DR. SEARLES [interrupting]: —The *one* in the *left* eye *seems* to be *perking up,* huh? [said in ironic, teasing tone].

MRS. DOUGLAS: Yes—has better *expression* [casually].

DR. SEARLES: Um. So—maybe—perhaps the *person* in your— *cloth dog* would *also* benefit—from—being in the sessions? [said in light bantering tone].

MRS. DOUGLAS: Well, *you're* another *person!* [says this in tone of strong objection].

DR. SEARLES: Mm—I *am* [tone of relatively little challenge in this, mainly of trying to follow the way she is experiencing things; then I say, in aside to microphone:] Joan gestures toward *all* of my head [a note of awe comes through in this last statement of mine].

MRS. DOUGLAS: Someone went out of the room [said in a tone of speaking to herself, and of implying, "This must be what happened"].

DR. SEARLES [speaking in an attemptedly firm, brisk manner]: I— I've *taken* an *entirely different stand* about the *cloth dog?*—is that it?

MRS. DOUGLAS: No.

DR. SEARLES: The person who was here *before* wasn't encouraging you at all to *bring* the cloth dog to the session.

MRS. DOUGLAS: No.

DR. SEARLES: No?—They weren't? [Here I sound clearly uncertain as to what her "No" means.]

MRS. DOUGLAS: Uh-uh [meaning "No"]. See [she explains], *you two* are the *twins* of the two who went out.

DR. SEARLES: "Twins—*you* know what "twins" always reminds me of [light tone; then, when she looks uncomprehending, I explain]: Ralph and Louise [said in tone as though this should be obvious; these are the names of younger siblings of hers, who were twins, and one of whom died in infancy].

MRS. DOUGLAS [gives an artificial-sounding cackle, then says, barely audibly and in an absent-minded manner]: I don't know about them.

DR. SEARLES: You don't know them? You never heard of them— huh? [speaking in a quiet, unpressuring way].

MRS. DOUGLAS [very faintly]: No.

DR. SEARLES: Of course, when you mentioned *Ralph Mueller,* I was—I *remember* Ralph Mueller. I also remember that one of your brothers is named Ralph. [All this was said in the tone of an efficient pedagogue.]

MRS. DOUGLAS: *I* don't *have* any brothers [said defiantly and rather nastily].

DR. SEARLES: You don't [said with the kind of patience with which one might speak to an imbecile].

MRS. DOUGLAS: Uh—at least, *not* that I've *met* up to date [becoming somewhat less sure of herself].

DR. SEARLES: Well, I'm *aware* that Ralph hasn't *put in an appearance* since you—came to Chestnut Lodge; I—I *am conscious* of that [tone of starting off in patronizingly "helpful" vein, but ending in a kind one]. But I—do recall, when you were in touch with your Joan—Mitchell [her maiden name]—Douglas [her married name] identity—part of your identity, you spoke about having one time raised rabbits with Ralph [said gently but firmly].

MRS. DOUGLAS: No [very faintly].

DR. Searles: When you were children.

MRS. DOUGLAS: No [sounding surer that I am in error].

DR. SEARLES: Now, Ralph Mueller [starting off in a pedagogical tone again]—

MRS. DOUGLAS [interrupting me]: Not *me; I* don't *have* any brothers, anyway.

DR. SEARLES: You don't; I see [said in tone of having decided not to press the matter at all further for the time being]. Uh—so *you*— wouldn't have *any* reason, then, to feel *hurt*—if—*brothers* don't *visit* you, because *you* don't *have* any, anyway—right? [Quiet aside to microphone:] Joan nods. [Then, to her:] Ralph Mueller, incidentally, I recall, used to be a good tennis player?—hm?

MRS. DOUGLAS: No [decisively].

DR. SEARLES: He didn't? [in tone of genuine surprise].

MRS. DOUGLAS: *I* don't think he's ever *played* tennis. *He* wouldn't think that playing tennis was *appropriate* [said in tone implying that he is a very aloof, formal person; I am not sure enough of my own recollections, of this fellow patient of hers from twenty-five years ago, to recall whether she is remembering accurately].

DR. SEARLES: Really? He's too—concerned about—uh—what?— his dignity?—or what?

Mrs. Douglas [confirmatory murmur; then, in tone of much livelier interest, says]: Well, *I* played tennis when I *first* came to the Lodge, because I didn't *know* any better. No [in tone of starting to say that "No one warned me not to"]—I came from a *hospital,* and I hadn't met my *parents* yet, or my *family* and—the *hospital* said to go play tennis, so I played tennis, and every time I went out—on the tennis court, I got *shot!*

Dr. Searles: Really? [tone of mild interest].

Mrs. Douglas [laughs briefly in amused-souding way]: Uh-huh. Being a stupid little baby, running around playing tennis, it *never entered my mind* that it was *wrong.* I just thought they were mean things to keep *shooting* at me. But at the end they explained that I had to *save* the *doctors, save* the *nurses, save* practically *every*body; but—

Dr. Searles: So that you mustn't *take time* to—enjoy a game of tennis?—Is that what they implied?

Mrs. Douglas: Well, *that* was—that was the *easiest place* to *shoot* me, was on the tennis court.

Dr. Searles: Oh!—they were *shooting* you *with patients* that you were to take care of?—Is that—? [said in a tone of genuine surprise, and of awe].

Mrs. Douglas [confirmatory murmur].

Dr. Searles [aside to microphone]: Joan nods. [Then, after several seconds' pause, I say to her:] I get the *general* sense of—what a *hell* of a *welcome* to a *new—environment,* huh?

Mrs. Douglas [confirmatory murmur].

Dr. Searles [very quietly to microphone]: Joan nods. [Then to her, in tone of a kind, patient pedagogue:] You had come *from a hospital.* Do you *recall—what hospital,* or anything of—?

Mrs. Douglas: St. Stephen's Hospital [not the name of any actual hospital where she had been].

Dr. Searles [ironically]: Oh; is that in—uh, Padua?—or Odessa? [One of her delusions was that she was a graduate of various foreign medical schools.]

Mrs. Douglas: London [tiredly].

Dr. Searles: Oh [faintly].

Mrs. Douglas: It was—well, it might *not* have been London— maybe it's Czechoslovakia; I'm not very—*certain* about *anything,* about myself.

DR. SEARLES: Well, is it—*remotely* possible that it may have been—[ironic tone]

MRS. DOUGLAS [interrupting me]: —Probably was London.

DR. SEARLES: You guess London. Couldn't have been anything as *mundane* as The Institute of Living in Hartford, Connecticut [ironic tone—referring here to the sanitarium from which she had been transferred to Chestnut Lodge].

MRS. DOUGLAS [murmurs negatively].

DR. SEARLES [aside to microphone]: Joan shakes her head, confidently [ironic tone].

MRS. DOUGLAS: No; no I haven't been there.

DR. SEARLES [interrupting her]: St. Stephen's—St. Stephen's is— uh—that's not St. Vincent's either—huh? [Ironically, referring here to a hospital where she had been hospitalized more than once in childhood. Then I add, in aside to microphone:] Joan shakes her head. [To her, I explain, as I get up and go to the storeroom:] Gonna get some cough drops [for myself].

MRS. DOUGLAS [speaking in normal tone of voice, as usual, although I am momentarily not present]: Oh!—St. *Vincent's—your wife* worked at St. Vincent's.

DR. SEARLES [I have returned to my chair, and happen to have heard what she said]: She *did;* I see [not at all questioning this].

MRS. DOUGLAS [murmurs agreement]: In the East; but—uh—

DR. SEARLES [interrupting]: What was—what *name* did she—go by, then?—Do you recall?

MRS. DOUGLAS: John Lawlor [explains to me as though this should be obvious; this is the name of a surgeon who had operated upon her on one or more occasions during her childhood].

DR. SEARLES [ironic, patient-pedagogue tone]: My wife, John Lawlor, huh? That's par [starting to say "That's par for the course"]—do you feel that a *great many*—uh, women are married to—or, men are married to women named—uh—John?—huh?— John—quite—

MRS. DOUGLAS: *Seems* so.

DR. SEARLES [ironically]: Well, my *wife John Lawlor* worked at St. uh, *Vincent's* Hospital, huh?

MRS. DOUGLAS [says after several seconds' pause]: I *think* it's your wife; it—uh—*might* be your *son's* wife.

DR. SEARLES: Dr. John Lawlor?—hm?

MRS. DOUGLAS: I don't know if he's—or if she—acutally was *given* a *license* [uncertainly], or if she *posed* as John Lawlor; *he* was a very good doctor—and licensed—but she—just went in—I think she murdered him and took over the job. Like, rough stuff.

DR. SEARLES: She had—she, uh—had some *rivalrous feeling* toward him? [Tone of polite inquiry; then after a couple of seconds' pause, in aside to microphone:] Joan nods. [Then I say to her:] She evidently *felt* convinced she could do the job *better* than he was doing it. [Then, after a moment's silence, I say quietly to microphone:] More nods.

MRS. DOUGLAS: What, does that turn you off, or on—changing my—knees?

DR. SEARLES: Changing your knees? [evenly, and without apparent surprise that she had asked].

MRS. DOUGLAS [explaining]: You *look* better when I—do *this*.

DR. SEARLES [aside to microphone]: Joan—puts her—left over—one or another knee—crossing the leg.

MRS. DOUGLAS: Right—

DR. SEARLES: I *look* better when you—have your—right leg crossed over your left leg—the *left* eye looks better?—*my* left eye? [saying this in unchallenging manner; she makes some inaudible murmur in response]. Well, in general, do you *wonder* if it *turns me on,* at all—*sexually*—when you—shift your legs about?—or cross your legs?

MRS. DOUGLAS: No [in tone of genuine negation, and implying that she had never had any such thought].

DR. SEARLES: Ya hadn't wondered that, huh? [relatively unpressuring, accepting tone].

MRS. DOUGLAS: Uh-uh [confirming her previous response, casually. Then, after a few moments of silence, she gives an amused belly-laugh, and says:] The *right* eye, maybe, wondered it, but—

DR. SEARLES [interrupting, in amused-sounding tone]: *My right* eye, huh?

MRS. DOUGLAS: Yeah. *I* thought the *right* eye was *suffering* from my—*now* it looks *pained,* so it's keeping the leg *that* way, so then I put it—

DR. SEARLES [interrupting, to comment for the benefit of the microphone]: Putting your left—Joan had the left leg over the right leg that time. [I am sounding rather amused. Then, after a few moments of silence, I ask:] Well—uh—what?—there's *some*one in *one* or *both* these eyes who is—*terribly* concerned about propriety?—appropriateness?—or—?

MRS. DOUGLAS: Thinks so [in tone of "I think so."].

DR. SEARLES: Something as Ralph Mueller is? [Then, in quiet aside to microphone:] Vigorous nods.

MRS. DOUGLAS [brief but unamused-sounding laugh]: Well, *she's* a *very* good *fixed doctor*.

DR. SEARLES: The one in the *right* eye?

MRS. DOUGLAS: Yes. She's—she's *not conscious*. [Then, after a few seconds' pause, she says uncertainly, as if to herself:] Well, *maybe* she is *now*, though. *Hope* so.

DR. SEARLES: You *hope* she *is* conscious?

MRS. DOUGLAS [affirmative murmur].

DR. SEARLES: You don't think her being—

MRS. DOUGLAS [interrupting]: Well, *I* prefer *conscious* doctors to—*mechanical* ones [ironic and somewhat caustic tone].

DR. SEARLES: Although you *sound* as though you *think* the consciousness *may*—be somewhat *distracting*—hm?—to the—doctor [said in firm but polite, rather patronizing, pedagogical tone].

MRS. DOUGLAS [faintly]: Yeah.

DR. SEARLES [very quietly, to microphone]: Nods.

MRS. DOUGLAS: Well, *she's* the *electric*—doctor.

DR. SEARLES: That is, it *may* be better—

MRS. DOUGLAS [interrupting]: She *seems* to be *completely stripped* of *all electricity now* [speaking considerably more loudly than I had just been speaking].

DR. SEARLES: This is—still the—one in my *right eye* [said casually, unpressuringly].

MRS. DOUGLAS: Yeah. [Then, after a few seconds' silence:] It *is* a *men*.

DR. SEARLES: That's what *they* just said, in your *head*?

MRS. DOUGLAS [confirmatory murmur].

DR. SEARLES [barely audibly, to microphone]: Nods.

MRS. DOUGLAS: But the *right* eye's a *woman;* but she's a *men specialist*. She's not much of a—I guess she's a *mother whale*.

DR. SEARLES: Well—well, *I'm* reminded that *Joan* once told me that she—had to *rely* upon her *dog* to—*tell* her whether this or that person—were a *friend* or an *enemy* [said with a kind of casual interest].

MRS. DOUGLAS [noncommittal murmur].

DR. SEARLES: And *you*—have to *rely* upon—someone, or ones, in your *head*—to—tell you whether—the one in my right eye is a *men* or a *woman*—huh?

MRS. DOUGLAS: Well, it's a *woman*.

DR. SEARLES: It is a woman [unchallengingly].

MRS. DOUGLAS: The right eye's a woman, and the left eye's a men.

DR. SEARLES: Hm. Now [ironic tone, referring here to rare occasions in the past when she has perceived the two persons in my eyes as being married], whether they're *married* is another *question?*—huh? [Then, after a moment's silence, I say to microphone:] Joan nods. [Then I press her a bit.] Huh?

MRS. DOUGLAS: Well, I—I think she's—she's a very good doctor; she wouldn't *hurt* anyone [rather subdued voice].

DR. SEARLES [relatively loudly]: The *one* in the *right* eye? [Patient nodded.] So that *if* she married, she wouldn't—*isn't* the *type* who would *murder* her *husband?*

MRS. DOUGLAS: Uh-uh [faintly, in agreement with what I have just suggested].

DR. SEARLES: She isn't. [Quietly; then in same quiet voice, to microphone:] Joan confirms that.

MRS. DOUGLAS [after several seconds of silence, in a strong voice]: It *must* be what we have in the *box* down there—that—

DR. SEARLES [interrupting]: The—recorder?

MRS. DOUGLAS [nods]: —that *thinks*—*against* the patients, or *about* the patients.

DR. SEARLES: "The patients"—what are you referring to?—*we're* the patients, you and I? or what?

MRS. DOUGLAS: I *think so* [and laughs in apparent amusement].

DR. SEARLES [in tone of trying to sound amused]: And *some*body is thinking *against us,* huh?

MRS. DOUGLAS: Yeah [trying to sound amused].

DR. SEARLES: In the box?

MRS. DOUGLAS [nods]: Making us gasp for breath. *That's* very *different* looking today—that—machine [comments in a chatting kind of fashion].

DR. SEARLES [faintly]: It *is?*

MRS. DOUGLAS: Those *discs* are so *black.* [Pause of a few seconds.] They don't have any little thing sticking up on them, either. [She is referring to the spools—"discs"—on which the tape is wound, and to the fact that there is no loose end of the tape—as there often is—sticking up in the air, near the center of the spool. She has not left her chair in making these observations. The tape recorder is clearly visible underneath my desk, over on the other side of it, on the floor.] Is *that* what *I* am?—that *machine?*—the *head* is *that?* [She sounds seriously concerned.]

DR. SEARLES: You wonder if—*your head* is *that machine?* [calm, unchallenging tone.]

MRS. DOUGLAS: Um [tone of agreement].

DR. SEARLES: I don't understand *why* you *ask.* [My tone here is more personal and informal, less pedagogical, patronizing, or ironic]. You have some—say something of what—that—what *brings* that question—to your—mind?

MRS. DOUGLAS: I don't know, I just *got* the *thought*—that maybe that's what this head is [tone of talking in an informal, intimately-collaborative spirit about a very bizarre subject].

DR. SEARLES: Oh; that would explain—some—of the phenomena?—that are going on in your—in that head? [Then after a moment, I add, to microphone:] Joan nods.

MRS. DOUGLAS: Well, then—then *I* have to be more *careful* about what I *do* in here. I—I—didn't *know* I was a *machine, or* that I could—you know—*change* the *course* of the machine by—what I'm *doing* in here: just trying to pick up everything and straighten everything around.

DR. SEARLES: Well, d'you *suppose* you may—st—*still* be *smarting* a bit, from my having—uh—asked if—your *head* had been fixed so that—*figurative* concepts, like emotional bonds, get—*experienced* by you in terms of *literal*—ties, like neckties? D'you suppose you may be kinda—ss—uh—*offended* by my *saying* that, hm?

MRS. DOUGLAS [confirmatory murmur]: It looks *better* now; it's just like *yours.*

DR. SEARLES [aside to microphone]: Joan did confirm that. [Then I ask her:] *Which* looks better?

MRS. DOUGLAS [interrupts me while I'm asking the above question]: That's *another* one.

DR. SEARLES: The *left* eye?

MRS. DOUGLAS: Um [confirmatorily].

DR. SEARLES: Looks just like what?

MRS. DOUGLAS: *Right* eye.

DR. SEARLES: Oh, it *does?* [Both the patient and I sound, as innumerable times before in this session and in many others in recent years, something as though we are comparing impressions of a movie we are both watching.]

MRS. DOUGLAS [qualifying a bit what she has just said]: Not *quite* as *large.*

DR. SEARLES: Hm [tone of mild interest].

MRS. DOUGLAS: But—it has more of the *expression* of the right eye. Is that what you *want* to *accomplish?* [She asks in wondering tone of a naive child.]

DR. SEARLES: Well, I *do seem* to you *totally preoccupied* with the *people in my eyes,* do I not? [asking this in the tone of a polite pedagogue].

MRS. DOUGLAS [laughs in obvious amusement]: Yes.

DR. SEARLES: Is that right? [I say in amused aside to microphone:] Joan nods. [Then, I say to her:] So that—do—you don't *ever* feel that I'm actually aware of *you?*—is that right? [I begin this question in a semi-amused tone, but end it in one of nascent alarm, and of being close to feeling appalled.]

MRS. DOUGLAS: Well-ll—[uncertain tone. Then she adds quite decisively:] Well, you're *more interested* in the *phenomena* of *your-self.*

DR. SEARLES: I am. [Said calmly and unchallengingly. I am not trying, here, to indicate that I fully concur with the validity of what she has just said—for I do not; but I have learned that it goes better when I do not challenge her or argue with her at such junctures.]

MRS. DOUGLAS: *I* don't think that's *right* to *do*—if one's a *woman,* and the other's a *men*—to have them look *alike* [said in tone of protest and wonderment].

DR. SEARLES: Not right to *either* of them—huh?

MRS. DOUGLAS: Uh-uh [confirmatorily].

DR. SEARLES [barely audibly, to microphone]: Joan nods—confirms that. [Then, after several seconds, I suggest to her:] Not right that they be made to look like *twins,* huh?

MRS. DOUGLAS [replies in strongly assertive tone]: *Well,* if they're the *same person,* it's all right; but if they're *two different* persons— they *still look* like *two different* persons now.

DR. SEARLES: They do? [quietly, calmly].

Mrs. Douglas [quietly]: Yeah.

Dr. Searles: You say that as though it's something of a *relief*—to see that.

Mrs. Douglas: No.

Dr. Searles: No?—*you* don't care if they look exactly—

Mrs. Douglas [interrupts me in a very loud voice]: Well, *I* don't know if you can *put two people back together* again. I mean [voice softens again], in my *experience* of putting—someone back together is that they always *explode*.

Dr. Searles: Are *you* referring, for *one* thing—among *many, many other* things, maybe—referring to *divorces?*—that people who've been *divorced* can't be—put back together again?—is that one of the things—

Mrs. Douglas: Oh, no [as if to say, "Not at all"].

Dr. Searles: That's *not* what you're referring to [in tone of accepting that it is not].

Mrs. Douglas: Uh-uh [agreeing that it is not]. Just [she explains] about building a head.

Dr. Searles [grunt in acknowledgment of her explanation].

Mrs. Douglas: And taking pages out of a book, and then trying to return them to the book is always disastrous, too. Once they *come* out they should *stay* out and be a *person*, and go on their way—develop *themselves*, instead of trying to go *back*. [She says this in a tone of describing a grim prospect for them.]

Dr. Searles [after having tried a couple of times, relatively mildly, to interrupt her as she was finishing the above remarks]: *Back* into the *confinement* of being in a *book?* [tone of unpressuring inquiry].

Mrs. Douglas: Yeah [softly]—or being with the same group of persons again.

Dr. Searles: Oh [very softly, indicating, "I see"]—whom they've *outgrown*, is that the idea?

Mrs. Douglas: Um [affirmatively]; I guess *so* [indicating, "Although I hadn't thought of it that way before"]—or the *air*, maybe, does something to them, so they're not—they can't go back [said in tone of having thought of an interesting new possibility to speculate about; then, after a pause of about fifteen seconds, she goes on:]—*but* ya—I—I think—I mean, we *return* to our *homes*, and we *return* to our own *countries*, and everything. That's all right [tone of reassuring herself].

DR. SEARLES: Ah, I *still*—ya see, *my* memory was that—toward the end of—the previous session, you said [clearing my throat], "So I should go *back* to the *Lodge* and—uh—tie my—tie the necktie to the ceiling, and *hang* myself?" *Something* like that, you said. [I make this statement in a fatigued, but tenaciously assertive tone.]

MRS. DOUGLAS [promptly]: I don't recall that.

DR. SEARLES: I—I—I understand; you *said* you didn't recall that. But—I wondered if going *back* to the *Lodge*—uh—*involves* that, uh—something of what you're *speaking* of?—that is, like going *back* into a book, once you've—[all this said in a thoughtful, tentative, undemanding tone].

MRS. DOUGLAS: Uh [confirmatorily].

DR. SEARLES: It *does*. [Then adding, to microphone:] Joan nods.

MRS. DOUGLAS [hastily taking it back]: *Oh*, no; I wasn't in a *book*. I was a *newborn baby* when I came over.

DR. SEARLES: Came over—?

MRS. DOUGLAS [tone of explanation]: Giant baby when I came out to sea; I was only—three and a half months old. [Pause of a few seconds.] No; I must've been older than that—if I was born in *1919*. [She was born several years before that, in actuality.]

DR. SEARLES: 1919? [polite tone].

MRS. DOAGLAS: No—I came—out to sea in *1920*.

DR. SEARLES: You did? [polite tone, not at all argumentatively].

MRS. DOUGLAS: Um [confirmatorily]; I was born—which *month?*—"April" [in tone of having just been given the answer from within her head].

DR. SEARLES: If *you* were born in *1920*—uh, you were born, then, when—*Joan* was, uh, about—*seven* years old [said in firm, matter-of-fact tone].

MRS. DOUGLAS: *I* was born in—nine—teen *nineteen* [tone of having to search her mind to come up with this answer].

DR. SEARLES: Well, that was when *Joan* was about *six* years old [matter-of-fact, unargumentative tone].

MRS. DOUGLAS: Um [faintly and in noncommittal tone. Then, after a few seconds of silence, she asks, in relatively loud and astonished tone:] Is *that*—is *that* that *name?*

DR. SEARLES: You *wonder* if this *left eye* [referring to my own, at which she has just been looking] is Joan? [asked in ironically polite, pedagogical tone, which becomes gentle at the end of the question]— Huh?

MRS. DOUGLAS: Well—[uncertainly].

DR. SEARLES [interrupting]: The left eye.

MRS. DOUGLAS [strong tone of assurance now]: I was told that that name—J-o-a-n—is a *Western* name. I thought [tone uncertain again] the right eye was an Easterner. [Her long-held delusional distinctions between "Westerners" and "Easterners" are very complex and still largely unfathomable to me. These are not referable to the actual geography of the planet Earth. I have sometimes thought that "Westerners" are dead people—those who have "gone west," so to speak; but it is not nearly that simple.]

DR. SEARLES: Are you asking if the *right eye* is that name? [Then, softly, to microphone:] Joan nods; it's the right eye.

MRS. DOUGLAS: Well, the right—*I* thought the *right* eye was— named—uh, *Giuseppe—Giacopolo* [a name I'd never heard before; she said this in a light, teasing tone].

DR. SEARLES: Hm [noncommittal tone]. *Look* very *Italian?*—the right eye?

MRS. DOUGLAS: No; it doesn't—it looks Swedish [again in light, teasing tone].

DR. SEARLES: Well, it's an unusual name for a Swede, isn't it? [in half-serious tone].

MRS. DOUGLAS: Mm [affirmatively].

DR. SEARLES [to microphone]: Joan nods [and I laugh in amusement].

MRS. DOUGLAS: Well, it was just *named* by *Italy.* [She also sounds amused], maybe. Thought it was *murdered* by Italy. [She does not sound amused.] It looks *Swedish.* [She sounds puzzled, and wondering.]

DR. SEARLES: Well [tone of offering a possible explanation], do *I* speak of *Joan* as though she were the *apple* of my *eye?*—is that—is— is that *one*—huh? [She shakes her head.] No?—I don't?

MRS. DOUGLAS [decisively]: No; I wouldn't think that would do you any good at all. [Pause of a few seconds; a few words are inaudible here.] Being a *giant doctor,* you're not allowed to go *in* anywhere.

DR. SEARLES: Hm. Well, you're *referring* to your*self* as a giant doctor, is that right? [polite tone].

MRS. DOUGLAS: No.

DR. SEARLES: To *me* as a giant doctor? [same tone].

MRS. DOUGLAS: Um [affirmative tone].

DR. SEARLES [quietly, to microphone]: Joan nods. [Then, to her:] "Not allowed to go in anywhere" [saying this in inquiring tone].

MRS. DOUGLAS: Well, you're *in* the *head* [she explains loudly]; but I mean, when you speak to a—a patient in there, I don't think you're allowed to go *into* the patient [describing, here, what she gathers to be the situation in my head].

DR. SEARLES: *Too* apt to *explode* the patient?—or? [tone of relatively mild interest].

MRS. DOUGLAS: Mm [affirmative tone].

DR. SEARLES [quietly and in rather bored tone, to microphone]: Joan nods vigorously.

MRS. DOUGLAS: And East and West together would be—uh—*total power,* and so probably would be quite an explosion. It *looks* as though it *needs* to be exploded.

DR. SEARLES: "It"—what's "it" [rather bored tone, but one of trying tenaciously to understand what she is experiencing and saying].

MRS. DOUGLAS: Left eye [she replies]; needs to be *opened up.*

DR. SEARLES: Oh; so an *explosion*—can be—*therapeutic?*—or, uh—[tone of mild, nonargumentative interest].

MRS. DOUGLAS: *No* [scoffing tone], because you always *die.* Well [tone of conceding a point], it makes you *grow*—

DR. SEARLES [interrupting, to press a momentary advantage]: Beneficial [offering this as a synonym for "therapeutic"]. Well, you *say* it *needs* to be, as though it might be—*well for* it.

MRS. DOUGLAS [talking argumentatively at the same time]: Well, it maybe isn't old enough.

DR. SEARLES: Oh [as though to say, "Oh, I see"].

MRS. DOUGLAS: I don't know *what* the age for explosions is. [Pause of a couple of seconds.] " 'Bout seven" [apparently having just been told this by a voice in her head. Then goes on in a quieter tone, saying to herself:] That's not that old; that's only about three.

DR. SEARLES: The right eye? [firm, pedagogical tone].

MRS. DOUGLAS: The left eye.

DR. SEARLES: Left eye [tone of accepting her correction].

MRS. DOUGLAS: Three or four, it still has a long time to go before it needs to explode [relaxed tone. Then she asks:] Can you feel that?

DR. SEARLES: Feel what?—What you're doing to your ear?

MRS. DOUGLAS: My scratching—yeah.

DR. SEARLES: Well, *I* was *touching* my *face*, was I, when you were just doing that?

MRS. DOUGLAS: No; you—you—you made a sort of *grimace* while I scratched behind my ear.

DR. SEARLES: Oh, while you were scratching behind your ear.

MRS. DOUGLAS: I decided you were made out of that bone in there. [Patient had a mastoidectomy in childhood, leaving a depression in the mastoid bone behind the ear.]

DR. SEARLES: Mastoid bone?

MRS. DOUGLAS: Yeah; they scratched you out.

DR. SEARLES: Is that the bone where you have a—uh—indentation in it?

MRS. DOUGLAS: Mm [affirmatively].

DR. SEARLES: The *left* one; yes. You decided that they scratched me out of—your—left mastoid bone? [tone of mild interest, but not astonishment, and not opposing this idea].

MRS. DOUGLAS: No—that they *built* your *head* out of it—out of what they scratched; they *scraped* the bone in there.

DR. SEARLES: Oh [in tone of saying mildly, "Oh, I see"].

MRS. DOUGLAS: *This* head doesn't *run* any more; it's not—*attached* to anything [speaking of her head with a startling concreteness and objectivity—very unusual on her part]. I mean, it *used* to—uh—be *very enlightened,* and *intelligent,* and—*full* of *ideas* [laughs in amused-sounding way], and *I* would just *say,* you know, what *it gave* me to say.

DR. SEARLES [saying in aside to microphone, as she is saying the last few words above]: Radio-head gesture. Radio-head gesture [referring here to a certain gesture she had made many times, for years, in explaining that her head is a radio-head, and that what she is saying consists simply in messages received by it from afar, rather than her expressing thoughts of her own].

MRS. DOUGLAS: But it isn't a radio any more [she says, in tone of objecting to what I've just said to the microphone].

DR. SEARLES: Hm [tone of noncommittal interest]. *I'm unclear,* and maybe *you* are, whether you—feel it more as a *loss,* or a *relief,* huh?

MRS. DOUGLAS: Mm [uncertainly].

DR. SEARLES: That change [explanatory tone].

MRS. DOUGLAS: Well, I feel a *little* loss; but—I'd—I'd *prefer* to be *conscious.*

DR. SEARLES: You would? [unchallengingly].

MRS. DOUGLAS: Sure—to do my *own* thinking. I—I—of course, I'll have to go to *school.* I mean, it's *difficult* for—one to *pretend* to be a *great doctor* [tone of protest] when ya haven't had any—the only *experience* I have *about* medicine was when I was a *fixed* doctor [again, her so-frequent tone of a kind of nonhuman concreteness in saying this]—and they *fixed* me as a baby.

DR. SEARLES: Well, you *prefer* to do your *own* thinking—not to have a radio-head?—hm?

MRS. DOUGLAS [affirmatively]: Mm.

DR. SEARLES [to microphone]: Joan nods. [Then, to her, indicating the time is up, I say in a gentle tone:] Okay.

MRS. DOUGLAS [says loudly, while she is getting up and putting her ash tray back onto the desk, and I am helping her into her coat, and we are walking toward the door]: *Well,* I'd *like* to go to *school*—but I guess we—they say in Europe you can't go to school until you're *eight.* [Then she adds in softer tone, to herself:] That's a *long* time away, for *me;* I'm only just *two.* Five, six—six more years.

DR. SEARLES [asking, in pedagogical tone]: Well, isn't *this* a *form* of going to school for—both of us? [Then, in aside to microphone:] Joan nods.

MRS. DOUGLAS: But *still,* see, when you have a *radio*-head—[she begins, in tone of making a strong protest or objection]

DR. SEARLES: As *I* do? You mean I *do* have a radio-head? [interrupting and talking over her, in rather ironic tone].

MRS. DOUGLAS: —you can actually—[then, in answer to my question, decisively]—I think you do.

DR. Searles: You *do;* I see [politely, not challengingly].

MRS. DOUGLAS: You—you—uh, *feel* more as though you're *in* school, and there *is* somebody directing your thinking; but when you're *not* [word or two inaudible].

DR. SEARLES [opening door to usher her out, as usual]: I'll see you.

MRS. DOUGLAS [says, as she goes out]: I'll have to have my head *fixed* again.

DR. SEARLES: so long [sounds of doors closing, as usual].

[Dr. Searles says to microphone, as soon as she has left:]

She said, as she started out, "I'll have to have my head fixed again," or "Do you think I'll have to have my head fixed again?" or, I think *probably* what she said was, "Maybe I'll have to have my head fixed again." It was said rather casually.

I [had] helped her on with her coat. *Beautiful* session—*lovely, lovely, lovely* session [in far more warmly enthusiastic tone than any in which I had spoken during the session itself]. I think of playing it for Bob Langs, although I hadn't thought much about that in the session. *Beautiful* session; I'm *very* relieved at the—uh—that this, uh, that she's alive, really, and—uh—

Now, I of *course* thought about—that [question,] should she bring the cloth dog to the sessions?—that's the first time she's ever asked that—and I hear in it a meaning of, should she bring her feelings of suicidal despondency to the session? And, uh, ——— ——— [a current supervisee] has been doing a lot of very interesting work with a patient of hers who—has cloth dogs, and [other stuffed] animals in the sessions; I've heard from ——— ——— for a couple years about that patient. So I had some considerable urge to suggest to Joan to bring it here; but I think we can get along without—her needing to bring the cloth dog here. I think it's probably better not to; but—

She drank the can of Sprite, and I had a can of Sprite. She left three—cigarette butts in the ash tray. Uh, she walked in about two minutes late, into the waiting room. I said, "Hi." She murmured something, by way of acknowledgment, and walked in [i.e., into the office itself]. She was looking grim, as she often does, but not angry. She has a great deal to be grim about; I didn't take it personally, really.

She was wearing her—uh, Navy blue—summer top coat, with the horizontal, white, narrow stripes, and her six-inch-wide-brimmed, Navy blue, plaid, straw hat. And, uh, she put her coat and hat on the couch, and sat down [in the usual chair, diagonally placed a few feet away from mine]. She was wearing a dress I've seen only a few times—summer dress, tan and brown colors—mostly beige kind of tan. It's not a favorite dress of mine—I say it as though it were *my* dress [tone of mild interest but no great surprise]. But anyhow—it looks all right on her. She wore no stockings, heel—uh—shoes were leather, open-toed, leather sandals, medium heels. Her hair looked nice, parted on the left, as usual, and pulled back with a barrette. She wore no lipstick—hasn't worn any in *years*—and [again, noting with mild interest] I say it as though *that's* a good thing—I notice. She wore her glasses, as usual.

Now, uh, it's a, uh [opening blinds to look outside]—partly cloudy—day out, sunshiny, but it's partly cloudy, and it's been a bit cooler lately; it's a pleasant day [I have routinely included, in my comments to the recorder at the end of each session, some word about the weather, with the thought that I may someday find, on further study of the tapes, that Mrs. Douglas's so-changeable moods are more affected by changes in the weather than one might think. My superficial impression is that there is no very marked positive correlation here.]—Uh—she lit her own cigarettes—uh-now, uh—*beautiful, beautiful* session—*beautiful* session—*lovely, lovely, lovely* session [said with heartfelt admiration for, and cherishing of, it]. *Fascinating* session. The explosions, I of course thought of her mother's innumerable explosions [of temper]. *Beautiful* session.

The tape recorder, as usual, is over on the other side of the desk, on the floor—on the rug. Now, I made one note in the session [namely, "1045—You put 500 billion into that figure—"]. The session started about 10:32. When she said, "You put 500 billion into that figure," she had her little spiral notebook and was writing in it. Now, *I* wasn't looking at it; I was sitting over in my chair. But she was speaking for all the world as though I were looking at it with her.

*Beautiful* session. The reference to the mastoidectomy—it happened that as she was feeling her mastoidectomy-fissure behind her left ear, *I* had just been touching my face somewhere up *near* my ear—not the same place, but—she was obviously pleased, and wondered if *I* felt it [i.e., felt her feeling the mastoidectomy-fissure].

Now, I'm aware that she projects upon me—onto my known [i.e., known to me], real narcissism—she projects upon that her own *enormous* absorption with her self—different parts of her self—uh— so that she reacts to me as being *almost completely* occupied with relationships between persons in my eyes.

*Beautiful, beautiful* session—the reference to Ralph Mueller— *lovely*—and the 1920 and—undoubtedly—or 1919—*undoubtedly* the birth of a sibling, maybe her brother Ralph—very possibly.

Today *is* Yom Kippur—uh, thinking of it in terms of—I don't know if she may need to *deny* that it's Yom Kippur; I'm not sure *why* she would need to—because of its connotations of the past, Day of Atonement for past, uh, sins, things like that.

This—I helped her on with her coat—this is all of my notes on this session with Joan—uh—see, I wondered how much she might feel, in the sessions, a sense of having *greatly outgrown* her existence at Chestnut Lodge, so that to go *back into* it is—uh—very despondent—despondency-engendering. This is all of my notes on the session with Joan on Thursday, September 22, 1977.

## II. FURTHER COMMENTS BY HAROLD F. SEARLES

The following comments were not made by me during the dialogue with Dr. Langs. I am setting them down here in order to acquaint the reader with some of the significances I saw in the session which has just been detailed. These remarks will be very sketchy, partly because of limitations of space here. For years, I have felt that a whole book could usefully be written concerning the meanings of any one of the richer of my sessions with this woman—a book which would trace, for example, the determinants of her responses and mine in the context of the history of her life, and in the context of the overall course of this long therapeutic endeavor.

As regards my note at the end of the session, the fact that I thought of this session as one which would be of interest to Dr. Langs introduces, of course, an additional motive to my functioning during the session, a motive and a possible element of artificiality about which one could speculate at length. But on the other hand, there are dozens, and probably even hundreds, of tapes in my files concerning this woman about which I have felt comparable enthusiasm.

Again as regards my dictated note, her having left the cigarette butts in the ash tray at the end of the session is something I found worthy of mention for the reason that this was a *relatively* recent development, and one which I found reason to regard as indicative of increased ability on her part to accept loss. Earlier in our work, she—identifying deeply with things which are commonly regarded as worthless, and which therefore are ordinarily cast off—always carefully put the butts back into her cigarette package before leaving my office.

Her reference to the patient from many years ago, Ralph Mueller, was very unusual. It has always been a welcome thing for me to hear her mention the name of any fellow patient. Years ago, many months would pass without her ever making any identifiable reference to any of the several other persons who live or work in the same small building where she lives at Chestnut Lodge.

Her suicidal tendencies are something which I have been aware of, and concerned about, for years; but rarely had I found reason to feel as concerned lest she suicide as I had felt at the end of the previous session. This present session left me enormously relieved that the previously imminent threat of suicide had receded, and that she was bringing her feelings of despondency more into our work together. This session added, moreover, some increments of clarification of the determinants of her suicidal tendency.

Writing more generally for a moment, her sharing with me, in a relatively collaborative way, what the introjects in her head are telling her, is a development which had been gradually growing over the previous several years, and marks an enormous advance over the way she functioned during the first dozen or so years of our work, when her daily life, in sessions and apart from them, was very predominantly lived by—governed by—the introjects, holding sway in unpredictable sequence. I used to have to endeavor to cope, largely alone and often in a terrible feeling of unrelatedness, with the introjects, whereas it has now come to be a matter of her working with me concerning them.

The cloth dog is, so far as I know, the first transitional object she has acquired in the course of the therapy. She has had this for some two or three years. The just-detailed session marks the first time she had ever asked me whether she should bring it to the session. I was well aware of her question about this as having a probable significance of a deepening commitment, on her part, to our work together. Therefore, I wanted to encourage her to bring into our work whatever feelings, fantasies, and identity components this cloth dog symbolized, without her actually embarking upon the concrete behavior, inappropriate to adult living, of bringing the actual cloth dog with her to the sessions. Parenthetically, subsequent events seem to me to have validated the wisdom of my decision, here, not to encourage her to bring the actual cloth dog to the sessions for, while retaining this transitional object in her room, she continues to integrate, more and more, into her own ego-functioning the psychological components which she has been projecting into it.

This session clearly indicates that her suicidal urges have been temporarily dealt with partly by projecting them into the cloth dog, which she perceives as having committed suicide. Further, she indicates that it committed suicide by reason of its being a "men" who has been a woman too long, and needs to become a "men." Her confusion, as regards her own sexual identity, had been extreme for years, and this material was not new to me. But I felt that her wish to bring the cloth dog to the sessions was expressive of a wish to bring more fully into the sessions her despondency, her suicidal urges and longings, which were being projected into the cloth dog.

Her amnesia for her suicidal-sounding statement near the end of the previous session—her statement which had so concerned me— was not at all unusual for her. In fact, one of the things which encouraged me about this session was that she became able, during it, to remember as much as she did from the previous session. It required many years of our work together for there to develop the degree of continuity, from one session to another, which is evident in this session.

The probable suicidal depression-engendering impact, upon her, of my having given back to her, in the previous sessions, the several coins she had put on my desk in payment for the session was an important denouement in this session. As she says, decisively, *"our trouble has been that it's too difficult to—to give anything back to anybody."* I have played back that previous session, in preparing these present comments, and have found that she put the coins—two nickels and three pennies—on my desk about ten minutes along in that session. She asked her suicidal-sounding question some thirty-five minutes later, a very few minutes before the end of that session, but prior to my giving back to her these coins with which she had attempted to pay me for the session. But it is probable that my leaving the coins sitting there on the desk, throughout most of that session, without accepting and pocketing them, added to her feelings of worthlessness and unacceptability.

But I do not wish, here, to give undue weight to that incident, important as it may have been. I have seen abundant and incontestable evidence, over the years, that her powerful and tenacious depressive tendency, against which her chronic schizophrenia has been serving as a largely effective defense, is itself multiply determined. My playback of that previous session, for example, shows that she had given, during it, glimpses of several powerful reasons she had for feeling suicidal.

To turn again to the details of this session, it is significant that she says, "they [the university] said that *she* [the baby in the cloth dog] was a *he,* and *that's why* she's so *depressed."* This highlights, again, the sexual-identity confusion aspect of her depression. For many years, she consistently asserted that Joan—who the patient was sure she was not—is a "men."

This session clearly shows that the cloth dog possesses components which Joan is finding, or starting to find, either in me or in herself, or both. She says at one point, for instance, that my left eye looks sicker than the baby in the cloth dog. When this kind of development has progressed sufficiently far, she will no longer need that transitional object. In general, one can say of this session, viewing it in the overall context of her therapy thus far, that she is showing an increasing ability to talk meaningfully with me concerning feelings of depression.

Another determinant of her suicidal urge is expressed in her feeling of having to go back to Chestnut Lodge, a place which she has some feeling of having *outgrown.* This determinant is so closely related to, as essentially to be a part of, the constriction she feels as regards her sexual identity. I have seen, over the years, that her superego-imposed concepts of a "men" on the one hand, and of a woman on the other hand, are enormously constricting. For example, a woman who is at all assertive, or who loves to ride horseback, or whatnot, is, to her, a "men."

To turn somewhat away from the data in the session having to do especially with depression, I found it encouraging that she may be getting, here, a clearer sense of one of the aspects of her enormously severe thought disorder: her head has been "fixed" to turn figurative into concrete concepts.

In this session she shows her large-scale lack—chronically and recurrently shocking to me—of any firm differentiation between human and nonhuman, or animate and inanimate; but I am sure that a close study of the details of this session can reveal clues to the defensive functioning of such dedifferentiation, for at times during the session, this was relatively little in evidence, and at other points it reemerged with jolting schizophrenic concreteness. For years it used to be pretty much the order of the day, during our sessions.

Her experiencing me, at one point, as having left the room and been replaced by another person ("Well, you're another *person!* . . .

Someone went out of the room'') is by no means new; but in this session it is unusual for me to be able to discern a probable relation to an actual change which had occurred in me as I experienced myself: I had shifted my stand, momentarily, regarding her question as to whether she should bring the cloth dog to the session.

The delusional experience which she recalls, from early in her stay at Chestnut Lodge, of being shot with patients, while playing tennis, is a facet, new to me, of her years'-long delusion (a delusion with, as usual, a formidable basis in reality, present and past) of being a "giant doctor"—of carrying, subjectively, an essentially omnipotent-mother responsibility for everyone and everything around and within her.

The brother-Ralph transference material was new to me. The material having to do with the mastoidectomy which she had undergone at the age of eight was unusual and new in some of its details, including her transference to me as being the husband of a surgeon who had figured in her childhood. More generally, concerning this session, I was encouraged by the relatively many realistic bits which I could discern in the content of her delusions—bits, that is, detectably referable to what I experience as the reality of myself and my relationship with her, and the reality of her history as I have come to know that, largely through the evolution of her transference reactions to me, and to a much lesser extent through historical material provided by her family members, and the accumulation of memory fragments verbalized by her to me, over the previous years of our work.

We receive, in this session, some glimpses of murderous feelings and of sexual feelings, both heavily defended against, as usual, by her. Both these realms are known by me, for many years, to be of enormous importance in her life and in her illness.

My narcissism, as perceived by her, has never been so startlingly communicated by her prior to this session—i.e., her seeing me, here, to be *totally* preoccupied with the people in my eyes, and little if at all aware of and interested in her ("Well, you're *more* interested in the *phenomena* of *yourself*"). This perception undoubtedly involves much projection of her own narcissistically-absorbed inner state, but also a degree of probable reality which I find disconcerting. My enormous enthusiasm about, and fascination with, the tapes of our sessions probably contain much more narcissism that I want to believe.

Her being unsure whether one of my eyes is that of Joan indicates that her own real identity, as Joan, is coming more than usual into the relationship between us. It was comparatively rare, at the time of this session, for her to perceive Joan in any part of me. At the time of this session she does not realize yet, at any deeply accepting level, that she is Joan, but for her to perceive Joan in me is a welcome step in that direction. Her communicated perception of me as having been made out of that portion of the mastoid bone which they scraped from her skull during the mastoidectomy was, for all its implications of disease and contempt and whatnot, warmly intimate in feeling-tone, as was her readiness to assume that I could feel it when she touched that area of her head, behind her ear. These were, to me, welcome and encouraging, although not highly unusual, data concerning the symbiosis between us.

I found the relationship, as depicted in this session, between introjects and explosions to be interesting, especially in light of her childhood experience with a mother much given to unpredictable, terrifying explosions of temper.

# POSTSCRIPT
## by Harold F. Searles

I want to explain to my long-time loyal readers, and possibly also to myself, why I have taken part in a project which has involved my accepting the status of junior author to Langs, and my appearing, moreover, in part of the book, as a supervisee of his.

Concerning the background of my experience with him, I served for two or three years, beginning about 1971, as a member of the editorial board of *International Journal of Psychoanalytic Psychotherapy*, of which he is editor-in-chief. He accepted three of my papers for publication in that journal—in 1972, 1973, and the latest one in 1976. For years, then, I have been—and I remain—very grateful, indeed, to him for publishing my work. Although other editors have been receptive to my manuscripts, by no means have all editors been so.

In October 1974, after I had submitted the manuscript of my paper, "The Patient as Therapist to His Analyst," for publication in a volume edited by Peter L. Giovacchini and scheduled for publication by Jason Aronson, I found reason for concern lest, to put it quite simply, Robert Langs had stolen my idea and was about to publish it first, without giving me due credit. To anyone seriously concerned about his contributions to the literature, this is a familiar workaday hazard, and I had never been particularly concerned about this problem. One of my ideas had been published, before I could get it published, by a world-renowned psychiatrist to whom I had told the idea, without his citing me as the source of the idea; but that had never happened before nor has it since, in more than a quarter century of my writing.

But this time, even a more personally secure individual than I would have found reason to feel threatened, by reason of Robert Langs's commanding position in the editorial field, his very close working collaboration with Dr. Jason Aronson, and his prolific authorship of books and papers. It did not allay my anxiety when his letters to me, in the course of our correspondence which clarified and eventually resolved this matter, carried a return address, on the envelopes, of the Jason Aronson publishing house. I felt, in short, a loner up against a publishing combine.

But within a matter of several weeks or a few months, as I recall, I became fully convinced that Robert Langs indeed was, and had been, working in his own right in an area very close to that which I discussed in my manuscript, and that my fear had been groundless. The reader who has come this far in this book has seen how close are Langs's views and my own about the patient as therapist, even though we came to this discovery from rather different directions.

This matter had long since been cleared up, to my thoroughgoing reassurance and restoration of my trust in Robert Langs, when I received, in April 1977, a letter from him inviting me to take part in the dialogues of which this book has become the product. On reading his invitation, I felt honored to be regarded by him as one of a relative handful of living analysts who have contributed significantly to an understanding of the therapeutic interaction; and I promptly expressed my interest in and receptivity to this project.

We met four Saturday mornings at my office, beginning September 10, 1977, and ending December 3, 1977. I found it additionally flattering that he was willing to travel from New York City to my office in the Washington, D.C., area, bringing along heavy sound-recording equipment.

At our first meeting in my office, we had never actually met before, and I felt that we were both rather stiff with one another. I did not doubt that he felt reserved, as did I, about the altercation we had been through a few years before.

I relied largely upon cues from him as to how to proceed in the dialogues, feeling that this was a situation new to me but relatively familiar to him, since he had already had dialogues with each of the other analysts with whom he had planned to converse.

It is understandable to me, in retrospect, that at least in our first meeting, I reacted to this new situation, in which I was encouraged to reminisce about my past, as if it were a quasi-therapeutic one for me; hence the quality of an outpouring on my part. It does not take much urging, in any instance, for me to reminisce, and at our first meeting I sensed that among the impacts which Robert Langs's personality makes upon one is that of a firm container—or as providing, in Winnicott's phrase, a firm holding environment.

Like Langs, in my portion of the editing I have tried to leave intact, insofar as feasible, my remarks, in order to convey the relatively spontaneous and informal atmosphere of the dialogues. I have tried, in editing, to avoid stiltedness, at the cost of preserving ungrammatical usages and a degree of repetitiveness which I hope have not proved too exasperating to the reader.

I have had so little time for writing in recent years that, although this has been my main writing project during the past year, my portion of the editing, begun in November 1978, was not completed until the beginning of August 1979. Over that span of time, sometimes months would pass without my having an opportunity to take up the editorial work again. Each time I did so, I had to overcome misgivings about going ahead with this project, which involved so much of personal revelation. But each time, as I read on, I felt reassured, once again, that the material should, indeed, be published.

I have seen Robert Langs twice in the year and a half since the last of our dialogues in this book, at social functions in New York where we were fellow guests. What I suppose I may be saying is that no one need fear that Bob and I are going to stagger off into the sunset together. But these dialogues have added a great deal to my already high esteem of him, for the many valuable concepts he has developed concerning the therapeutic interaction, as well as, of course, his encyclopedic familiarity with the literature concerning this subject.

In closing, I quote here three letters from my correspondence with Langs, for the interest and possible amusement of the reader who has borne with us this far, with regard to the inclusion of the transcript of my session with Mrs. Douglas, and of Langs's and my discussion of that clinical material.

September 22, 1978

Dear Bob:

The original copy of the transcript of our dialogues arrived yesterday. I intend to start working on it as soon as I get back from Switzerland on October 4th and I surmise that the work will go relatively rapidly.

In reply to your letter of September 8th, I am very sorry, and surprised, that you had assumed that I intended for the recording of my session with my patient, and our discussion of that, to be included in the published material, for that was not my intention.

I had played one or another of the many tapes, from my work with her, to some half-dozen colleagues in the past few years, most of these being persons who have specialized for years in the treatment of psychotic individuals. I had thought simply that you would find the recording to be of interest and, I hoped, edification to you. I must tell you that, in the course of our discussion of the tape, and until the following day, I felt really desperately disappointed and frustrated with your reaction to the recording. I felt that you entirely failed to realize that I am one of the world's leading experts in the psycho-analytic therapy of schizophrenic patients and very possibly *the* world's leading expert. I felt that you reacted to me, for all the world, as though I were one of your second-year, or very possibly third-year, psychiatric residents.

As you can see, I definitely will not have this material included in our book. If it were not for my ability to laugh at myself, I would have remained quite upset about this beyond the following day, but as it was I managed to pretty much laugh it off.

I am quite aware that all your comments to me of a supervisory nature, concerning that tape, may have been very well taken, indeed, and I am certain that at least some of them were. But you must understand that, partly in light of my having the junior authorship of our book, I simply cannot afford to present myself in our book as a student of yours.

All the rest of our dialogues I felt went very well indeed and I continue to believe that the book will go along all right and will meet with an appreciative reception from the reading audience.

Another part of my strong feeling about the matter of the tape from my patient has to do with the fact that, as I well know, you would not be caught dead presenting material from your work with one of your patients.

I plan in the coming few years to do a book concerning my work with this woman, and to include a great deal of detailed material transcribed from the recorded sessions. But the work on that is really quite enormous since the vocal tones and other such nuances are so very important in the work with her.

I shall get in touch with you again when I have been able to make considerable progress in reading the original copy which I received yesterday. Meanwhile, it would be really quite essential for me to have from you, if you please, a copy of your edited version of the dialogues, for I wish to have that in hand as I go along. One of my concerns, and really my main one, is that I do not want all of the daring personal revelations, in the course of our dialogues, to be mine.

With best regards, and I will be writing to you again, probably within a few weeks.

Sincerely,

Harold

\* \* \*

October 7, 1978

Dear Harold:

I have your letter of September 22, and of course, now realize that there was considerable misunderstanding regarding our last meeting and how the material would be used. I can only say this: I attempted to respond to your presentation with both appreciation and the presentation of my own way of listening—which as you know, is most definitely idiosyncratic. I used the same approach with Leo Stone, and he too was somewhat disturbed by it, but included the material for publication once he had done a good deal of editing in which he firmed up his own position in some detail. I mention all of this because if there is any conceivable way that that particular dialogue can be included in our book, I would like to see it happen.

You could freely edit the material, and I would be glad to change the tone of any remarks that seem offensive. I must stress that the issue in no way has anything to do with your expertise in the treatment of schizophrenics, since I fully respect your qualifications and abilities as a therapist. The response has to do with different ways of listening and working, and with giving a reader an opportunity to review contrasting as well as overlapping positions in that regard. We were, I believe, attempting to exchange ideas and insights, and to challenge each other in order to learn and grow—both ourselves and our readers. In any case, if for example the matter depends on who is senior author, or on extensive reediting I would like to try to work something out with you. If not, your decision will most certainly stand as is. Please give it some further thought.

The transcript that I sent to you includes all of the editing that I planned to do. There is no other version of the dialogue, as I kept only a photocopy of the material forwarded to you. In this context, I want to stress that in each of these dialogues I have been serving as a representative of the readership, so to speak, selecting important and creative psychoanalysts and attempting to explore with them their background and their past and present thinking, and to in addition, challenge them with my own distinctive viewpoint. In the main, then, the focus has been on the individual whom I have interviewed, and less so on myself—although I have included candid comments of my own.

I hope that this gives you some further perspective and clarification. I want to reiterate that I am prepared to accept your decision in these matters. I only raised certain questions because I am convinced of the value of the material as it first unfolded, and feel a sense of loss to the field as matters get modified. Still, your personal feelings and sensitivities must come first, and I will therefore wait to hear from you further.

One final matter. I have just completed a paper on the continuous presence of countertransference-based inputs in the therapeutic interaction. There is really no living analyst who has had your experience and insight in this area, and since I expect the paper to be accepted for publication in the *IJPP*, I wondered if you would agree to write a discussion or responsive paper. It would not have to be completed until January or February of next year, and could be of any length you chose. I think that you would find my paper provocative, and that you would respond quite creatively. I very much hope that you will be able to do it.

I hope too that you had a most pleasant and rewarding trip to Switzerland. With warmest regards.

Cordially,

**Bob**

* * *

October 16, 1978

Dear Bob:

This is in reply to your letter of October 7. I also want to keep you informed of my work on the manuscript of our dialogues.

I have read your letter carefully, of course, and have given much thought to it. I must say, at this point, I still remain highly dubious that I will be willing to keep in the recorded material from my interview with the patient.

At this point, I am up to page 45 in the manuscript. I find that I can cover no more than about ten pages per hour, and I have so very heavy a caseload that I can get no more than about two hours a week to devote to this work. That gives you some impression about how rapidly it looks as though I will be able to get this work done. I am devoting every possible hour to this work, for I want to get it over with, along with your wish to do so.

I must say, also, that at this early moment in the reading of the manuscript, I am considerably dubious about the whole venture. I am sure that few if any of the colleagues would be willing for such a personal outpouring to appear in print—such an outpouring as I gave vent to during our first dialogue, at least. But, as you know, I pride myself upon my frankness, and have by no means discarded the venture at this point.

In essence, in another couple of weeks or so I shall have gotten a better sense of what the manuscript as a whole may contain, and you may be sure that it has first priority upon my writing time for the coming two or three months.

It is for this very reason that I find myself unable to accept your kind invitation to discuss your paper, which you mentioned in your letter of October 7. I would very much like to do so, for I am sure the project would be of much interest to me. But I simply must get forward with this book manuscript of ours. Possibly my work on this manuscript may go faster than it has so far gone; but I have no reason to assume that. Moreover, if upon careful reading of the transcript of the patient-interview I should find that I would be willing, after all, for it to be included, I do know that that material would take a quite time-consuming amount of work on my part, for I would have to listen back to the session with great care to describe, in brackets, the vocal tones of both the patient herself and of me, since that is so important in trying to convey what was going on in the interview with the patient.

I shall keep plugging along, and doing whatever I can do, at this juncture, to make our book worthwhile for our reading audience.

With best regards,

Sincerely,

Harold

# REFERENCES

Baranger, M., and Baranger, W. (1966). Insight in the analytic situation. In *Psychoanalysis in the Americas*, ed. R. Litman, pp. 56-72. New York: International Universities Press.

Bion, W. (1959). Attacks on linking. In *Second Thoughts*. New York: Jason Aronson, 1977.

——— (1962). Learning from experience. In *Seven Servants*. New York: Jason Aronson, 1977.

——— (1970). Attention and interpretation. In *Seven Servants*. New York: Jason Aronson, 1977.

——— (1977). *Seven Servants*. New York: Jason Aronson.

Bird, B. (1972). Notes on transference: universal phenomenon and hardest part of analysis. *Journal of the American Psychoanalytic Association* 25:267-301.

Boyer, B. (1961). Provisional evaluation of psychoanalysis: few parameters in the treatment of schizophrenia. *International Journal of Psycho-Analysis* 42:389-403.

Brenner, C. (1969). Some comments on technical precepts in psychoanalysis. *Journal of the American Psychoanalytic Association* 17:333-352.

Chertok, L. (1968). The discovery of the transference: toward an epistemological interpretation. *International Journal of Psycho-Analysis* 49:560-576.

Ferenczi, S. (1909). Introjection and transference. In S. Ferenczi, *Sex in Psychoanalysis*. New York: Brunner, 1950.

Freud, S. (1900). The interpretation of dreams. *Standard Edition* 4 and 5.

——— (1911). Psycho-analytic notes on an antobiographical account of a case of paranoia (dementia paranoides). *Standard Edition* 12:1-82.

——— (1912). Recommendations to physicians practising psycho-analysis. *Standard Edition* 12:111-120.

——— (1914a). On narcissism: an introduction. *Standard Edition* 14:67-102.

——— (1914b). Remembering, repeating, and working-through (further recommendations on the technique of psycho-analysis, II). *Standard Edition* 12:145-156.

——— (1920). Beyond the pleasure principle. *Standard Edition* 18:3-64.

——— (1922). Some neurotic mechanisms in jealousy, paranoia, and homosexuality. *Standard Edition* 18:221-234.

——— (1937). Analysis terminable and interminable. *Standard Edition* 23:209-253.

Fromm, E. (1947). *Man for Himself*. New York: Rinehart.

Fromm-Reichmann, F. (1955). Intuitive processes in the psychotherapy of schizophrenics: introduction. Panel presented at American Psychoanalytic Association, December 1953. *Journal of the American Psycho-analytic Association* 3:5-6.

Giovacchini, P., ed. (1975). *Tactics and Techniques in Psychoanalytic Therapy, Vol. II: Countertransference*. New York: Jason Aronson.

Green, A. (1975). The analyst, symbolization and absense in the analytic setting (on changes in analytic practice and analytic experience). *International Journal of Psycho-Analysis* 56:1-22.

Greenacre, P. (1954). The role of transference. *Journal of the American Psychoanalytic association* 2:671-684.

Greenson, R. (1967). *The Technique and Practice of Psychoanalysis*. Vol. 1. New York: International Universities Press.

——— (1972). Beyond transference and interpretation. *International Journal of Psycho-Analysis* 53:213-217.

Grotstein, J. (1977a). The psychoanalytic concept of schizophrenia: I. The dilemma. *International Journal of Psycho-Analysis* 58:403-426.

——— (1977b). The psychoanalytic concept of schizophrenia: II. The reconciliation. *International Journal of Psycho-Analysis* 58:427-452.

——— (in press). *Projective Identification*. New York: Jason Aronson.

Halpert, E. (1972). The effect of insurance on psychoanalytic treatment. *Journal of the American Psychoanalytic Association* 20:122-133.

Kernberg, O. (1975). *Borderline Conditions and Pathological Narcissism*. New York: Jason Aronson.

Kestenberg, J. (1975). *Children and Parents: Psychoanalytic Studies in Development*. New York: Jason Aronson.

Khan, M. M. R. (1963). The concept of cumulative trauma. In *The Privacy of the Self*. New York: International Universities Press, 1974.

——— (1964). Ego distortion, cumulative trauma, and the role of reconstruction in the analytic situation. In *The Privacy of the Self*. New York: International Universities Press, 1974.

——— (1973). The role of illusion in the analytic space and process. *The Annual of Psychoanalysis* 1:231-246.

Klein, M. (1952). The origins of transference. *International Journal of Psycho-Analysis* 33:433-438.

——— (1957). *Envy and Gratitude. A Study of Unconscious Sources*. New York: Basic Books. Republished in 1975 in England by the Hogarth Press and in the United States by Delacorte Press/Seymour Lawrence, under the title, *Envy and Gratitude and other Works, 1946-1963*.

Kohut, H. (1971). *The Analysis of the Self*. New York: International Universities Press.

——— (1977). *The Restoration of the Self*. New York: International Universities Press.

Langs, R. (1971). Day residues, recall residues, and dreams: reality and the psyche. *Journal of the American Psychoanalytic Association* 19:499-523.

——— (1973). *The Technique of Psychoanalytic Psychotherapy*. Volume I. New York: Jason Aronson.

——— (1974). *The Technique of Psychoanalytic Psychotherapy*. Volume II. New York: Jason Aronson.

——— (1975a) The patient's unconscious perception of the therapist's errors. In *Tactics and Techniques in Psychoanalytic Therapy, Vol II: Countertransference*, ed. P. Giovacchini, pp. 239-250. New York: Jason Aronson.

——— (1975b). Therapeutic misalliances. *International Journal of Psychoanalytic Psychotherapy* 4:77-105.

——— (1975c) The therapeutic relationship and deviations in technique. *International Journal of Psychoanalytic Psychotherapy* 4:106-141.

——— (1976a). *The Bipersonal Field*. New York: Jason Aronson.

——— (1976b). *The Therapeutic Interaction*. New York: Jason Aronson.

——— (1978a). *The Listening Process*. New York: Jason Aronson.

——— (1978b). A model of supervision: the patient as unconscious supervisor. In R. Langs, *Technique in Transition*, pp. 587-625. New York: Jason Aronson.

——— (1978c). *Technique in Transition*. New York: Jason Aronson.

——— (1978-1979). Some communicative properties of the bipersonal field. *International Journal of Psychoanalytic Psychotherapy* 7:87-135.

——— (1979). *The Supervisory Experience*. New York: Jason Aronson.

Langs, R., and Stone, L. (1980). *The Therapeutic Experience and Its Setting: A Clinical Dialogue*. New York: Jason Aronson.

Little, M. (1951). Countertransference and the patient's response to it. *International Journal of Psycho-Analysis* 32:32-40.

——— (1957). "R"—the analyst's total response to his patient's needs. *International Journal of Psycho-Analysis* 38:240-254.

Masterson, J., ed. (1978). *New Perspectives on Psychotherapy of the Borderline Adult.* New York: Brunner-Mazel.

Meissner, W. W., and Wohlauer, P. (1978). Treatment problems of the hospitalized physician. *International Journal of Psychoanalytic Psychotherapy* 7:437-467.

Milner, M. (1952). Aspects of symbolism and comprehension of the not-self. *International Journal of Psycho-Analysis* 33:181-185.

Modell, A. (1976). "The holding environment" and the therapeutic action of psychoanalysis. *Journal of the American Psychoanalytic Association* 24:285-308.

Myerson, P. (1978). Failure and recovery: a mythic approach to treatment issues in hospitalized psychiatric patients. *International Journal of Psychoanalytic Psychotherapy* 7:468-479.

Olinick, S. (1969). On empathy, and regression in the service of the other. *British Journal of Medical Psychology* 42:41-49.

Powdermaker, F., Frank, J., et al. (1953). *Group Psychotherapy: Studies in Methodology of Research and Therapy.* Cambridge, Mass.: Harvard University Press.

Racker, H. (1957). The meaning and uses of countertransference. *Psychoanalytic Quarterly* 26:303-357.

——— (1958). Psychoanalytic technique and the analyst's unconscious masochism. *Psychoanalytic Quarterly* 27:555-562.

Rangell, L. (1975). Psychoanalysis and the process of change. *International Journal of Psycho-Analysis* 56:87-98.

Rosenfeld, H. (1965). *Psychotic States: A Psychoanalytic Approach.* New York: International Universities Press.

Sandler, J. (1976). Countertransference and role-responsiveness. *International Review of Psycho-Analysis* 3:43-47.

Searles, H. F. (1951). Data concerning certain manifestations of incorporation. In H. Searles, *Collected Papers on Schizophrenia and Related Subjects.* New York: International Universities Press, 1965.

——— (1955). The informational value of the supervisor's emotional experiences. *Psychiatry* 18:135-146. Reprinted in Searles 1965.

——— (1958). The schizophrenic's vulnerability to the therapists unconscious processes. *Journal of Nervous and Mental Disease* 127:247-262. Reprinted in Searles, 1965.

——— (1959). Oedipal love in the countertransference. *International Journal of Psycho-Analysis* 40:180-190. Reprinted in Searles, 1965.

——— (1960). *The Nonhuman Environment in Normal Development and in Schizophrenia.* New York: International Universities Press.

——— (1961). Phases of patient-therapist interaction in the psychotherapy of schizophrenia. *British Journal of Medical Psychology* 34:169-193.

——— (1962). Problems of psychoanalytic supervision. In *Collected Papers on Schizophrenia and Related Subjects.* New York: International Universities Press.

——— (1965). *Collected Papers on Schizophrenia and Related Subjects.* New York: International Universities Press.

——— (1966). Feeling of guilt in the psychoanalyst. *Psychiatry* 29:319-323. Reprinted in Searles, 1979a.

——— (1971). Pathologic symbiosis and autism. In *In the Name of Life: Essays in Honor of Erich Fromm,* ed. B. Landis and E. S. Tauber, pp. 69-83. New York: Holt, Rinehart and Winston.

——— (1972). The function of the patient's realistic perceptions of the analyst in delusional transference. *British Journal of Medical Psychology* 45:1-18. Reprinted in Searles, 1979a.

——— (1973a). Concerning therapeutic symbiosis. *Annual of Psychoanalysis* 1:247-262. Reprinted in Searles, 1979a.

——— (1973b). Some aspects of unconscious fantasy. *International Journal of Psychoanalytic Psychotherapy* 2:37-50. Reprinted in Searles, 1979a.

——— (1975). The patient as therapist to his analyst. In *Tactics and Techniques in Psychoanalytic Therapy, Vol. II: Countertransference.,* ed. P. Giovacchini, pp. 95-151. New York: Jason Aronson. Reprinted in Searles, 1979a.

——— (1976). Transitional phenomena and therapeutic symbiosis. *International Journal of Psychoanalytic Psychotherapy* 5:145-204. Reprinted in Searles, 1979a.

——— (1977a). The analyst's participant observation as influenced by the patient's transference. *Contemporary Psychoanalysis* 13:367-371. Reprinted in Searles, 1979a.

——— (1977b). The development of mature hope in the patient-therapist relationship. In *The Human Dimension in Psychoanalytic Practice,* ed. Kenneth L. Frank, pp. 9-27. New York: Grune and Stratton. Reprinted in Searles, 1979a.

——— (1978-1979). Concerning transference and countertransference. *International Journal of Psychoanalytic Psychotherapy* 7:165-188.

——— (1979a). *Countertransference and Related Subjects: Selected Papers.* New York: International Universities Press.

——— (1979b) Jealousy involving an internal object. In *Advances in Psychotherapy of the Borderline Patient,* eds. J. LeBoit and A. Capponi, pp. 347-403. New York: Jason Aronson.

Seitz, P. (1978). Review of *The Bipersonal Field*, by Robert Langs. *Journal of Nervous and Mental Disease* 166:374-375.

Singer, E. (1970). The patient aids the analyst: some clinical and theoretical observations. *In the Name of Life: Essays in Honor of Erich Fromm*, ed. B. Landis and E. Tauber, pp. 56-68. New York: Holt, Rinehart and Winston.

Stone, L. (1961). *The Psychoanalytic Situation*. New York: International Universities Press.

Strachey, J. (1934). The nature of the therapeutic action of psychoanalysis. *International Journal of Psycho-Analysis* 15:127-159.

Szasz, T. S. (1963). The concept of transference. *International Journal of Psycho-Analysis* 44:432-443.

Tudor, G. E. (1952). A sociopsychiatric nursing approach to intervention in a problem of mutual withdrawal on a mental hospital ward. *Psychiatry* 15:193-217.

Uchill, A. (1978-1979). Deviation from confidentiality and the therapeutic holding environment. *International Journal of Psychoanalytic Psychotherapy* 7:208-219.

Wangh, M. (1962). The "evocation of a proxy": a psychological maneuver, its use as a defense, its purpose and genesis. *Psychoanalytic Study of the Child* 17:451-469.

Winnicott, D. W. (1949) Hate in the countertransference. *International Journal of Psycho-Analysis* 30:69-75.

——— (1953). Transitional objects and transitional phenomena. *International Journal of Psycho-Analysis* 34:89-97.

——— (1965). *The Maturational Processes and the Facilitating Environment*. New York: International Universities Press.

# INDEX